UNDER GOD'S SPELL

Workers begin building the Union Congregational Church in Guernsey, Wyoming, at 7:00 A.M., May 3, 1900.

Union Congl Church, Guernsey
12 O'ck. M. May 3rd 1900. Wyb.

By noon the structure is nearly complete.

By day's end the church stands, built in 20 hours by contributed labor.

# Under God's Spell

## FRONTIER EVANGELISTS

## *1772–1915*

## by Cathy Luchetti

Harcourt Brace Jovanovich, Publishers

*San Diego    New York    London*

ENDPAPERS: Simnasho Mission on the Warm Springs Reservation,
Wasco County, Oregon

Permissions and sources for original texts
and photographs can be found on pages 235–243

Library of Congress Cataloging-in-Publication Data
Luchetti, Cathy, 1945–
Under God's spell: frontier evangelists, 1772–1915/Cathy
Luchetti.—1st ed.
p. cm.
Bibliography: p.
ISBN 0-15-192799-5
1. Evangelists—United States.  2. Evangelistic work—United States.  3. Frontier
and pioneer life—United States.  4. United States—Church history. I. Title.
BV3773.L83   1989
269'.2'092273—dc20      89-34540
[B]

Design by Camilla Filancia
Printed in the United States of America

First edition    A B C D E

*Theirs has been the labor
and theirs should be the praise.*

—Annual Report,
Board of National Missions, 1927

Temporary shelter for the Congregational congregation in Shoshoni, Wyoming

# Contents

x
◄§

*Contents*

Early sod-and-timber Episcopal church, Wichita, Kansas

A Wyoming cowboy preacher and his horse, "None Such," as photographed by Reverend W. B. D. Gray

# Preface

A work of history ultimately becomes a dialogue between past and present, between the object of research and the researcher; the questions posed and the answers discovered often lead in unexpected directions. For me, compiling this book has been a remarkable dialogue, partly because of a discovery I made about my own pioneer ancestors along the way.

It began with the family Bible: Weathered, gilt-edged, and weighing more than twenty pounds, the King James had made its way across the plains from Indiana to Oregon in 1845, accompanying family members west to their new home. All that remained of this hardy group were the faded names and the record of births, deaths, and marriages lightly traced in the book's first few pages. But they were only names. How had they traveled? What were their lives like?

Then, in the course of my work on this book, I came upon a recent reprint of a journal written in 1920 by a frontier itinerant, A. J. McNemee. There I found the name of my great-great-great grandfather—and the information that the Reverend Mr. McNemee was my great-great-great uncle, and that the reverend's father had hunted with Daniel Boone. Further, I read that during the arduous

crossing, McNemee's sister and many more had died, and when the guide, Steve Meek, led them to a dead end called Stinkey Hollow, the settlers threatened Meek's death. McNemee's father—my great-great-great-great uncle—postponed the lynching at riflepoint for three days, long enough for the disoriented guide to escape and leave the party to find its own way to Oregon.

None of this rich intelligence had been a part of family lore. But now, thanks to the Reverend Mr. McNemee's memoirs, a vanished link with the past had reappeared. One more piece of the family past had gently dropped into place.

It is my hope that this book fill in other gaps of understanding; that the Christian couriers who traveled, ministered, starved, exulted—and sometimes suffered utter defeat, only to resume their course and try again—be seen afresh through the medium of their own words, and touch other lives as they have touched mine.

To praise or judge is not the motive of this book. Nor is it to analyze America's religious history—as Martin Marty did so well in *Pilgrims in Their Own Land.* Instead, this book springs from a desire to discover America's Christian roots through personal experience, in as dramatic and in-

Camp meeting at Post Oak Mission, Oklahoma

timate a fashion as possible. It is concerned, too, with the "after effects" of Christian commitment; the years lived after receiving "the call," after settlement in the West.

In *Escape from Evil* Ernest Becker cites the modern loss of "an ideal of heroic sainthood." It is the goal of this book to recoup that loss, not with the stories of stereotypical figures devoid of immediacy, but with stories of lifelike men and women who, despite illness, family losses, prejudice, rivalries, and financial cares, persevered in the Holy Word and came forever to be . . . under God's spell.

A Wyoming frontier family gathers by the stove at night to hear scriptures read.

# A Note on the Texts

Many evangelists were unschooled, but those who kept journals were generally literate authors of sermons and tracts. Indeed, some were theological scholars, able to pen educated prose with a philosophical flourish or round off a thought with poetry stanzas.

The text selections in this book embrace a wide range, literarily and historiographically. Some stories are novelistic, written with an eye to eventual publication; some seem impossibly ornate. Many, though, are simple and matter-of-fact, the narrative voice restrained by hardship or modesty to a bare chronology of events. Because of the generally high level of education, few grammatical falterings exist. Most flaws have been smoothed away by previous editorial intervention. All the works have been abridged, since most journals were book length and simply too long for complete inclusion. Paragraphs have been imposed only for emphasis, or to curb a meandering text. Most original spelling has been retained. Some punctuation has been silently added; editorial additions to clarify a subject have been placed in brackets. Throughout, I have made every effort to respect the writer's original style and intent.

Sister Mary Alenie's manuscript was compiled from handwritten daybooks, in which her impressions flow nonstop from one page to the next. As an aid to the reader, some sentences have been broken into shorter ones and paragraphs have been imposed. Her thoughts were beautifully traced in a flowing hand—easy to decipher, a pleasure to read, and representative of her sensitive nature.

David McClure's account of Indian evangelization in pre-Revolutionary Ohio contains an abundance of rich description. McClure attentively recorded Indian conversations verbatim, listed numerous Native American words— with translation—and vividly recalled each change of scenery. Indians were his primary concern; here much interaction with other missionaries, local churches, and wayside travelers has been edited. Early English spelling, along with the frequently used ampersand, remains untouched.

Lorenzo Dow is referred to as "Crazy Dow" by other ministers of the early nineteenth century. His voluminous outpourings do, indeed, reveal a highly opinionated, idiosyncratic personality; they are filled with harsh criticisms and character defamations. But throughout runs a thread of genuine Christian zeal. I have tried to maintain this zeal, bypassing many of the epithets that earned him the name "Crazy."

James Leander Scott, anticipating future publication, included many descriptions of flora, fauna, routes, terrain, and inhabitants for use by future travelers, along with passages of his own poetry. His grandiloquent Victorian prose reflects both his own personality and the prevailing literary style of the time. His story has been trimmed of its travelogue material, leaving the narrative thread intact.

Bishop Charles McIlvaine's letters to family members were published posthumously. The open, warm style reflects his candor with family members; he wrote with no end in mind but communication. The letters have been edited for length only, with no more than brief and occasional editorial explanations.

Elkanah Walker, writing in a slightly waspish and cantankerous vein, uses daily journal entries to describe the hardships of missionary life in Oregon. The major portion of his entries has been edited, both for economy—Walker wrote hundreds of pages during his lifetime—and to narrow the focus toward his evangelism, rather than the domestic details of his life. Frequent nineteenth-century spellings, such as "headake" or "thot," have been left unchanged.

Benjamin Brown and Bert Foster both wrote in retrospect, thus providing an evenness and flow to both accounts that lend a timeless quality. Select chapters from each life story have been edited for use. Brown was an exceedingly devout emissary of the Church of Jesus Christ of Latter-Day Saints, eventually becoming one of its high priests. His detailed descriptions of church theology and of the miraculous aspects of his faith have been edited out, leaving a more balanced narrative. Foster was a remark-

Catherine Mumford Booth, wife of Salvation Army founder William Booth, and a powerful speaker and writer

ably humorous and anecdotal writer, making editing the pleasant task of selecting favorite stories from his ten-year missionary experience in Utah, Idaho, and Wyoming. Spelling and punctuation of both accounts are generally untouched.

Mary Collins's account of her life as a missionary to the Standing Rock Sioux in 1885 is only a small segment of her many writings, which include a published autobiography and numerous religious tracts and pamphlets. Editorial brackets, punctuation, and most explanations have been added by editor and researcher Richmond Clow for an earlier publication. My own addition has been an occasional paragraphing for emphasis.

Annie Bidwell's memoirs, part of a voluminous collection of Bidwell papers at the Bancroft Library, were edited only for length.

A. J. McNemee's life story first appeared in a published autobiography in 1924, and was later edited by Harlan D. Jones under the auspices of the United Methodist Church. The original spelling of the 1924 work has been maintained, although new paragraphs have been created to thread excerpted parts of the story together. Brother Mack's lively and humorous perspective remains unaltered, the narrative's even flow and pacing the result of the writer's skill and the fact that the autobiography was a single creative effort, rather than a day-to-day recording of events.

William Robinson's story is in some ways the most exceptional, since he began life as a Southern slave, completely without education, and eventually traveled internationally, earned a degree, and became a teacher and minister. Robinson dictated his life's story, line by line, to his secretary, Miss Florence Mitchell, which perhaps accounts for the somewhat oratorical style. The text has been edited to eliminate lengthy, unchecked theological musings, with some punctuation inserted and spellings corrected.

These selections are only a sampling of available Christian documents, articles, memoirs, manuscripts, sermons, treatises, and broadside manifestos housed in church archives and elsewhere throughout the country. Many were written by ordained ministers and describe in poignant detail the trials of conversion, recruitment, travel, apathy, illness, and trailside danger. Though many accounts were excellent, I looked for stories that represented not only the individual, but also generalities of time and place. They were chosen to show the time span from 1772 to the early 1900s; to include Catholicism—even though priests and nuns are less commonly thought of as evangelists—and the main Protestant denominations; and to represent geographically the ever-shifting frontiers of the nation. (As circuit riders, ministers, missionaries, and lay religious spanned westward, their horizons expanded from the first frontier of the Alleghenies, through the Old Northwest, the Trans-Mississippi West, and the Southwest to the Far West—a geographical sweep comparable only to the companion changes within politics, sociology, culture, and religion itself.) "Celebrity evangelists" of the twentieth century, such as famed tent orators Billy Sunday, Dwight Moody, and Aimee Semple McPhereson, have not been included, in part because their stories are well known, in part because, as urban preachers working after the last waves of overland migration had passed, they are not really "pioneer" as this book uses the term.

When viewed from today's perspective, the solitary dedication of the pioneer evangelist seems epic. Idealized by the passage of time and by excessive "mything," pioneer evangelists seem men and women larger than life, more gifted or ambitious or more fruitful by far than Christians today. Thus distanced, they become not simply people of the Word but museum saints. Yet a clearer, more intimate look at their lives through the medium of their own words allows these men and women to reclaim their own personalities. I believe that each journal here reveals, in a simple yet heartfelt way, how daily life was—and is—a test of faith.

*A*
*Note*
*on*
*the*
*Texts*

# A Note on the Photographs

Extensive photo research has uncovered images that evoke, in countless ways, the spiritual and territorial progress of westward-bound Americans. Many images are nostalgic, keepsakes of a time and place. Others are timeless evocations of work, play, devotion, celebration, faith, birth, and, finally, death. Some are silver gelatin prints, miraculously preserved through the passage of an entire century; others are crisp and beautifully defined prints made from glass lantern slides, occasionally hand-colored in the popular style of the day. Some bear nicks and streaks, scratches and scars that, to my mind, only enhance the dignity retained after countless years in wagons, albums, basements, attics, and, finally, in libraries, museums, and historical societies. Like the negatives of the Reverend Andrew L. Dahl, abandoned in his brother's tobacco barn for more than half a century, many were victims of dust, heat, cold, and damp—not to mention unstable chemicals and improper fixing.

But by chance and good fortune, hundreds of frontier images do remain to document the passage of westward-bound Christians across the continent. Nearly every group occasion bore religious overtones, and nearly every pursuit, from wool-dyeing to barn raising, was an evangelical opportunity. Many images are congregational portraits, taken with great pride as church members in their Sunday best posed formally, each member standing expressionless on the steps, in straight rows. Other, more haunting, images are Christian only by inference: a bowed head at table, or a woman sitting in repose, sunlight etched across the book—a Bible—in her hand.

It must be mentioned that less fortunate images also abound, such as those of Native Americans, huddled on mission steps, awaiting handouts or weekly rations from the missionaries in charge. Their tragic position in American history reflects the unconscious ethnocentrism of Western Christians, and brings uncomfortably to mind the overblown vision of Manifest Destiny. Other minorities are also documented, usually in relation to local missionaries, school directors, or benevolent-society representatives.

This book seeks to capture the spirit of frontier Christian life as lived by ministers, missionaries, pious women, and circuit riders. To maintain immediacy, formal portraits have generally been avoided in favor of more spontaneous events, unrehearsed and vibrant with detail. Evangelism's path stands evident in the mission school

Reverend Perry and Deacon Phillips conduct an outdoor baptism at Cache Creek, Oklahoma, ca. 1913.

grammar class as well as with the members of the Sunday choir.

Some photographs correlate with the actual evangelists in the book, but many do not. Whenever possible I have included the writer's portrait but, lacking that, have used other photographs to illustrate some aspect of the individual's story.

Since many journals were written before the advent of photography in the 1840s, some license has been taken in "creating a mood" through photographs that postdate the actual writing but still effectively suggest the author's time and place.

Photographs have been assembled from over thirty archives in fifteen states. Each is intended to capture, through light, shadow, and image, part of a life long passed. Taken together, they contemplate America's Christian past through the many works and many faces of the pioneer evangelist.

ह०

*A*
*Note*
*on*
*the*
*Photographs*

Episcopal priests hold services on Mount of the Holy Cross in Colorado.

Catholic priests with Father Machebeuf (third from left)

UNDER GOD'S SPELL

Evangelist Pete Johnson exhorting passers-by at Ferguson Alley in Los Angeles's Chinatown

# Introduction

America from the first was a celebration of God's promises: she was history and prophesy combined, a "new nation" foretold by scripture (Psalm 18) and won by an ocean crossing that seemed to the Puritans like a spiritual rebirth. From Columbus, Cortés, and Junipero Serra, to the founding settlers at Plymouth Rock, Christian men and women commingled destiny with ministry, finding in discovery and conquest untold gospel opportunities. As the frontier expanded westward, evangelists planted the seeds of Christian growth in scattered enclaves from the Mississippi to the Pacific coast. Worship and wanderlust, twin touchstones of the gospel pioneer, beckoned thousands of evangelists across the American continent. By dugout and horseback, by stagecoach and on foot, they were drawn in ever-increasing numbers to unleash Divine Providence among Indian tribes, backwoods dwellers, and the rowdy unchurched of the American frontier.

Some missioners were selected by presbytery or bishopric to "locate" west; others staked everything and left on their own, eager to embark on a spiritual quest. "The door of inspiration was opened," wrote Shaker leader Mother Anna Lee, and out came a legion of Christian activists, an army of men and women representing denominations as varied as their own talents, humor, identities, and backgrounds. Evidence of their industry remains today, in manuscript and journal, in record and news account, in tales, folklore, and myth. Their passage, too, is tracked through villages christened Faith, Havilah, or Holy Cross, and across such sites as Mount Calvary or Piety Hill.

Once as common as tin peddlers on the byways of young America, pioneer evangelists seem today to be near-mythical figures, a legion grown faceless through the passage of time. They are remembered, if at all, only by their heroes and heroines: men such as George Whitefield, Francis Asbury, Peter Cartwright, and James McGready, or women like Phoebe Palmer and Frances Willard.

Little is known of the individual lives of the men and women who traveled, preached, baptized, and blessed on the frontier between 1700 and 1900. Were they puritanical do-gooders? Misfits? Adventurers? Men and women embarked on a godly mission to which they had been peremptorily summoned?

Some walked in perfect faith; others wrestled with timidity and doubt. Many had families; others were single. Misfits numbered high in the gospel ranks—individuals so blasphemous or quixotic they would never win approval

A Seventh-Day Baptist sod schoolhouse in Farnam, Nebraska, 1894

by a local congregation, finding instead power and anonymity in the ever-changing rounds of a circuit preacher. Others were genteel folk of status and education who took to the trails and the Overland Route and often proved surprisingly plucky when faced with the ordeal of frontier life. Some were entirely church-supported; others wielded hoe and axe as homesteaders, laborers, miners, or ranchers. Whatever their talents, whatever their trades, the western-bound evangelists differed from those who stayed behind by the specific lineament of what Catholics termed vocation and Protestants named "the call." For both, it was a lifelong commitment to forgo financial gain, worldly comfort, and even respect, often along with church protection and family ties, to further the social good of mankind and fulfill an inward duty that was, to the evangelist, clearly mandated from above.

Early evangelists served an important function in America's history. As emissaries of religious thought in a country that routinely viewed business, politics, social practices, and religion in the same light, evangelists often found their function greatly expanded beyond the pulpit. They furthered westward exploration and settlement through their constant soul-seeking, while influencing politics, social legislation, Indian policies, and social welfare. They sponsored public education by founding colleges and universities, Indian missions, schools, and orphanages. The early Catholic mission system girdled the country with religious, cultural, and agricultural centers, and the Methodist extension system of circuit riders served as one of the most active agencies for expansion in the West. Even Protestantism's Second Great Awakening of 1801 coincided with the first stirrings of the Great Westward Emigration. Americans were "going forth from the Garden of Eden to subdue the earth," while Overlanders were compared to Moses and Aaron leading the Children of Israel through the wilderness, toward a promised land.

Politically, Protestant evangelists endorsed American democracy as the work of the Almighty, touting Reformation theology as the inspiration of the Declaration of Independence and promoting temperance legislation, Sunday "Blue Laws" prohibiting commerce, and emancipation of blacks. The churches they established, often on free land donated by the railroads to encourage responsible settlement, were community centers, predating granges, co-ops, and farmers' associations.

Religion encouraged collective responsibility; yet it also embodied a spirit of self-reliance and independence, an ethic that some credit as a root of capitalism. Competition among independent-minded evangelists created schisms, sects, and dissension, with evangelists often changing public sentiment for or against a creed or denomination. The resulting diversity helped foster a spirit of religious toleration. Another legacy of the pioneer evangelist was the camp meeting, with its modern secular counterpart, the political rally.

It is also fair to surmise that without the remarkable activity of frontier evangelists—and left simply to politicians, the military, and land-seeking immigrants—the American zeal to reform, to build, and to expand would hardly have been as great.

# Catholics

In America, Protestantism nervously coexisted alongside the Church of Rome. Both were locked in a struggle for ascendancy. Protestants preached "new birth," Catholics

Father de Smet, Jesuit missionary to the Flathead tribe of Oregon, with chiefs at the close of the Indian Wars, ca. 1850

Franciscan friars grouped in the walkway of a mission

their historic catechism, but each proved zealous to the point of death in establishing its creed and baptizing native "gentiles" into church ranks. Catholic explorers and accompanying priests pushed into the New World, beginning with Ponce de León's fantastic quest for the Fountain of Youth in 1513 and followed by a steady influx of Franciscans and Jesuit "blackrobes" whose efforts were so successful that by 1650 the church had gained nearly twenty-six thousand Indian converts.[1]

The Spanish, envisioning an imperial empire on American shores, sent Fray Junipero Serra and two hundred foot soldiers a distance of nine hundred miles from Mexico to Upper California, where they arrived, weary and footsore, at San Diego in 1769. Mingling avarice with altruism, they briefly upheld the banner of Christianity, lowering it quickly to satisfy demands for gold, land, and the tangible rewards of native industry. Though Serra foresaw a future of Indian saints happily ensconced behind the adobe walls of his missions, and had even baptized six thousand neophytes by the year 1784,[2] achievement fell short of ambition, and he died without seeing his chain of twenty-one missions completed.

Nor, ultimately, was the Catholic church able to realize its dream of unity: a holy state reaching from Canadian New France west to Louisiana, wherein French, Spanish, and Portuguese Catholics would transcend nationalistic differences to join the New World in a centralized Catholic domain. Instead, Catholic dominance gave way as Protestants who settled on the Atlantic coast began to move west. Less than a century after Serra, however, the same Catholic dream of unity flickered briefly as European immigration swelled the ranks of the church from thirty-five thousand in 1790 to over a million and a half in 1850.[3] Almost without warning, the Roman minority was the largest single body of churchgoers in a resolutely Protestant nation. Why was Rome flourishing in a Puritan domain?

The answer lay in part in the steady stream of European Jesuits, Franciscans, Ursulines, Sisters of Charity, Sisters of Loretto, Sisters of Notre Dame, Sisters of Providence, and more, who eagerly thronged to western shores. These religious felt a deep moral obligation to civilize and convert the native population and, in later years, to sustain the spiritual well-being of Catholic European immigrants. Catholic missionaries raised up schools, colleges, orphanages, hospitals, and Indian missions, while Catholic nuns brought social services to the frontier as early as 1639, ministering to Canadian Indian children.[4]

Nuns served as ideal civilizers because their moral guardianship and obedience went unquestioned. These young women—usually well-bred young students from comfortable homes, trained in music, sketching, and domestic skills—would seem highly unsuited to the rigors of frontier life. Few had faced major hardships, save occasional family opposition to the convent rather than a propitious marriage. One Flemish family was so distraught over a young member's vocation that the aspirant was forced to step over the prone form of her favorite nephew, placed in the doorsill by her brother-in-law to prevent her exit for the convent. "Walk over this darling, if you have the courage!" he challenged, and with great determination she did.

For many sisters, vocation and holy vows were commitment enough, providing lifelong satisfaction behind convent walls. But for others—a unique breed called into foreign service in the New World—Holy Orders was just the beginning. Choosing the Creator over "creature" comforts, faced with the grim realities of lice and dysentery on the frontier, they quickly learned to battle adversity through prayer. The missions they eagerly sought called for high courage and a spirit of self-sacrifice, along with the practical abilities and excellent health deemed useful at a frontier outpost. "It is stimulating to meet emergencies," Sister Blandina wrote in her journal. "I do not know what fatigue feels like."

Abilities aside, there were still cultural misunderstandings that took the nuns by surprise. Some, such as Sister Aloysia, had to steer carefully through Protestant society, remembering to refuse wine at dinner parties, as drinking, for a woman, "was not in good taste." Others, such as Sister Catherine Mallon, would experience "rude and unkind remarks" from heretical Protestants, or the sting of indifference and lack of respect. Sister Mallon worked as a mendicant—in other words, begged—to offset continual parish bankruptcies, walking weary and footsore through the intermountain West, seemingly impervious to pain, cold, and hunger in her efforts to fund the archbishop's new hospital.

Her fortitude in the face of hardship was true evangelical form—a strength that came from an uplifted nature and deep prayer, rather than physical prowess. Like other evangelists, she found adversity spiritually profound and seldom refused a dangerous mission because of fear or inconvenience. Although Sister Renilde of the Oregon Mission "burst into tears" when the first Indian she ever saw appeared from his wigwam in June of 1844, she "soon became accustomed" to Indians and proceeded teaching catechism—and cleanliness—with vigor. An historic predecessor and Jesuit Isaac Jogues, tortured daily as an Iroquois captive in 1643, revealed the same spirit of self-sacrifice, desiring to stay with his tormentors even if there was a chance for escape. Sister Martha of the New Mexico Sisters of Charity responded with "patience and fortitude" when her leg was crushed under a wagon wheel. What better proving ground for a Catholic evangelist than a life of poverty, illness, isolation, and danger in the New World?

In this, pioneer Catholic evangelists could well reflect upon a medieval past richly worked with tales of the martyred saints. "The life of a . . . Missionary is a Long and slow Martyrdom . . . an almost continual practice of patience and of Mortification; [it] is . . . truly penitential and Humiliating . . . especially in the cabins, and on journeys with the Savages," wrote Father François De Crepieul, an "unprofitable servant" at the Montagnaix Mission in Canada, in 1697.

Though familiar with the discipline of the *Rules of Saint Francis,* and the grueling *Spiritual Exercises of Saint Ignatius of Loyola*—and even the use of hair shirts or penitential iron belts—some Catholic religious still despaired of the unremitting hardships and grew weary or heartsick in the strange new setting. Sister Reine of the order of Notre Dame begged to return home even before her Oregon-bound vessel left France, so painfully embarrassed was she by foul shipboard language. Father E. O'Connell, an emissary sent from Ireland in 1850 to raise funds for All Hallows College, was appalled at the "calculating, smoking and bell-ringing Californians" encountered daily, and pleaded weekly to return to Ireland. Young Jesuit Noel Chabanel, a seventeen-year-old sent to live among the Hurons in the Great Lakes area in 1630, found the Indians "irksome" and his linguistic progress "slight"; he came to dread sleeping nightly "on the bare ground . . . in a little hell of smoke," covered in the morning by "snows that drift on all sides into the cabins of the Savages." Poorly nourished, tormented by frustration, and

7

☙

*Introduction*

Chapel at St. Paul's Mission, Proctor, Kentucky, formerly the dining room of McGuire's Tavern, 1904

Choir loft at the Mission in Santa Ynez, California. The curtain forming the arches is made of rawhide painted by local Indians.

deficient in the native tongue, Chabanel despaired to the point of losing his vocation. Even the legendary Father Marquette, lying sick near Fort Kaskaskia in southern Illinois, suffered a loss of faith concerning his Indian converts. Would they still believe in Christ if he were to die? The thought so bothered Marquette that he had himself carried back to Lake Michigan for yet another round of proselytzing—despite his illness.

The wavering in, or loss of, a vocation was an ever-present danger on the frontier. Sister Catherine Mallon hinted that "some of [her] own sisters" might be at risk, and she pointed out to them the advantages of a religious life, no matter how vexing, over that of a "poor woman with five or six children" trying to cook for twenty men. "I thank the Good God for saving me from such a fate," wrote Sister Catherine, marveling at "the inconvenience . . . and abuse" married women endured for love, and thanking God again for calling her to the religious state. Sister Mallon's words can be taken at face value—or read as an attempt to give strength to her sisters in a mission grown almost too difficult to bear.

Early Catholic evangelists were prepared to baptize as many Indians as possible into the church with only the briefest preliminaries. It would be a simple matter to sprinkle the holy water first and then, once the convert was safely in the fold, to pursue deeper catechism study. But priests and nuns quickly discovered that ministering to American Indians demanded all the patience and inspiration that prayer and a firm vocation could provide. Native tongues were often baffling, and tribes were liable to move restlessly back and forth from mountains to valleys to plains, following a yearly food-gathering cycle that made no allowance for leather shoes and the mission school. Deities, taboos, clan affiliations, lore, and bonding practices shifted and changed from one territory to the next, confounding the Catholic prelate whose only means of communication, outside of an interpreter, remained the sign of the cross. But, undaunted, Catholic evangelists continued to preach their "gentle Christianity" in halting jargon, knowing that the Indians drawn to their ceremonies, vestments, candles, and incense also respected their celibacy and ability to overlook unobtrusive heathen customs. California Indians who hung shyly back from Junipero Serra's first joyful Mass of celebration, perhaps stunned at the "continuous salvo" of cannons instead of music and "the smoke of powder" used for incense, were eventually won over by Serra's ebullience, as he "praised the Lord; kissed the ground . . . [and gave] thanks" for finally meeting his long-awaited "gentiles." The miraculous was never far removed from Catholic life, and this was something easily understood by Indians of a like spiritual mind. They easily marveled at such events as the "sea being stilled" when Father Serra tossed bits of the Indians' own sacred grass into the turbulent waters. "I cannot be positive it was a miracle," Serra admitted, but called it nonetheless a "prodigy and a merciful act of God."

Like Serra, many priests were university graduates, often scholars and poets who showed wisdom and sensitivity in dealing with the Indians. In efforts to use tribal authority patterns to best advantage, they always selected the leader for conversion first, confident that the rest would soon follow. Missionary priests recognized, too, the value of pageantry, and never lacked for holy days to celebrate. They were also energetic travelers, going from one encampment to the next as itinerants, determined through continued contact to maintain their converts' interest. Catholic evangels viewed Indian customs with scientific curiosity rather than scorn, and sought to understand the Indian as the first step toward proselytization.

"They have stolen my heart from me!" Junipero Serra exclaimed of the California coastal Indians, voicing an enthusiasm that caused Serra, and many of his later counterparts, to flourish in their western outreach. One such was Archbishop Lamy, the erudite French prelate who tweaked the ambitions of Baptist missionaries in New Mexico by his gentleness and close cultural involvement with both Indians and Spanish; or the legendary Pierre de Smet, a Jesuit who was warned away from American soil by a Protestant Westerner even before he landed in Boston. Though Jesuit-baiting was common sport throughout the country in the 1840s, de Smet proceeded unafraid upon his way, arriving finally at a Ponkah village along the Nebraska Territory's Niobrara River to cries of "The blackgown has come," as over a thousand Indians surrounded him with "holy eagerness and attention." Surprised by this outpouring, he concluded that "the spirit of the Lord breathes where it will," and that the Ponkahs, in their desire to hear the words of the Great Spirit, would be able to adopt freely the sign of the cross, the Pater, the Ave, and the Credo.

Because of an attitude of educated tolerance, Jesuit Paul Le Jeune viewed as harmless the Huron morning prayers to the spirit guides. To him, the prayers' lack of a specific deity ("I would be very glad if this day would continue, if the wind would change. . . . ") left ample room for the God of Abraham. It was a perfect gospel opportunity, rather than a troublesome example of heathenism. Jesuit Father Maurice Gailland also reaped the rewards of patience by gaining the devotion of the Potawatomi Indians of Kansas. He spent years camping side by side with the roving clan, mastering their language and ministering to their needs. No call of theirs was ever ignored, and partic-

ularly not that of an unconverted, dying tribesman near the village of Silver Lake. As Father Gailland hurried to the man's side, he caught a chill from an icy stream, which eventually led to his death. When earlier warned of the dangers of fording the stream, Father Gailland had calmly replied, "If I die, another will take my place."

In this he proved prophetic. Despite the pervasive Protestant presence, by the late nineteenth century the Catholic church had more Indians in its charge than any other denomination, and in 1874, the government founded the Bureau of Catholic Indian Missions to counteract federal prejudice in favor of Protestant mission agencies.[5]

But record numbers aside—and centuries of cultural dominance in the Southwest and Mexico—Catholics still found it difficult to claim a significant position in the ranks of mainstream American Christianity. By 1880 Catholics of increased means and education had made their presence felt financially and politically, and by 1900 the Catholic population had doubled to ten million.[6] Yet the prejudice of the old Atlantic stock, the so-called Protestant God's elect, only deepened with each succeeding wave of Catholic immigrants. (Nor did Catholics approve of Protestants, whose paucity of tradition and ceremonies often seemed heretical at best.) After years of exclusion, social despair, and exposure to Protestant nativism, American Catholicism seemed unable to keep up with revivalistic Protestant religious techniques. Protestant numbers were growing, and to keep pace, occasional priests borrowed liberally from revivalism to sow the seed of spiritual uplift amid their sober immigrant parishes. Such "Americanized" Catholic worship was encouraged by priests such as Father Adolf Bakanowski, a Texas circuit-riding cleric who often staged emotional Catholic "celebrations." During one five-day event "no one did a stroke of work . . .

houses were left wide open," and the transfixed Polish population was given up to "unexpected happiness."

Such cross-influence was nothing new; early Puritan Indian missionaries, among them John Eliot, had evangelized the Indians using Jesuit missionary methods that they hoped the tribes would find familiar. Though isolated instances, these exchanges reflect a denominational liberalism that was often beneficial to Roman Catholic evangelists. With patience and an influx of Catholic European immigrants, the church continued to minister in the face of Protestant dynamism, its evangelists ever busy extending Catholicism's active compassion to the unbaptized, the fallen-away, and the suffering.

# Protestants

Protestants had held sway over secular America since the Pilgrims' arrival in 1620, finding validation for their new holy community in scripture, then proceeding as if sacred history and frontier expansion were one and the same. For two centuries Protestant thought reigned supreme—but with a profound internal bickering that left few denominations with the heart to establish their own peaceful covenant, much less pacify the Catholic population. Protestantism came to dominate the spiritual and geographical landscape through an elaborate system of traveling evangelists, lay preachers, benevolent societies, Sunday schools, and missions. But within its ranks, differences were legion and evangelistic types diverse, and steps toward church membership varied from one denomination to the next.

At times it seemed that the only unifying factor among Protestant evangelists was an individual's calling; an event so serious that, whether actively sought or simply received, it was often remembered to the specific day, hour, and minute of its occurrence. No declaration of faith was taken lightly, and even known community figures were publicly tested and examined, with their claims open to refute. Especially subject to scrutiny were the spiritual unknowns; those who were thought to conceal, perhaps, private histories of prodigious drinking or bad company. All converts were soundly questioned about their seriousness before winning holy immersion, or baptism by water; and those aspiring to the ministry were challenged even further.

The call to active ministry singled out men and women who were often unsuspecting—or unprepared. Journals and diaries discuss at length the keen demands of this inner voice that first summons men and women to the clerical life. Heading west as a pioneer itinerant was yet another mandate. As many writings reveal, ministering to Indians and apathetic settlers was simply too arduous, the obstacles too great, and the personal dangers too imminent to interest anyone less than a zealot. "What less than a Divine Ardour," wondered New Englander Joshua Scottow, "could inflame a People . . . to a work so contrary to Flesh and Blood?" Acceptance of a calling was a serious event—a binding contract not to be taken lightly. "Wo, wo, wo is me if I preach not the gospel," Jacob Bower cried out, pitting his natural reluctance to speak in public against the insistent, single thought that continually rolled across his mind: to voice the Good News.

Instances abound of men and women who could resist neither the call to conversion nor the call to preach. Texas evangelists Henderson Palmer and Daniel Carr held out as long as they dared, finally surrendering to God's call on

Mennonite church group in Hillsboro, Kansas, leaves for a Sunday school picnic.

a rainy day in the winter of 1837 in the privacy of William Kesee's corn crib. Presbyterian revivalist Charles Finney's conversion followed a spell of immobility and prolonged weeping, accompanied by the persistent sound of an "inward voice." Was he in pain? a friend wondered. "No," Finney replied, attempting to describe God's miraculous touch. "Just so happy that I cannot live."

## Saddlebag Itinerants

Those finally launched into the public arena by God's holy promptings became the ranters, broadcasters, and apostles who traveled, like Friar Tuck, through the backwoods and plains, spreading the gospel according to denominational warrant. Often uneducated, usually inspired, the itinerant minister, linen bag slung over his shoulder and a Bible beneath his arm, lent a uniquely American touch to the gospel art. Dressed head to toe in black and wearing a broad-brimmed hat, with lawn stockings and hair cut long at the neck, each clean-shaven young Methodist or Baptist wanderer presented an image both morbid and uplifting, inspiring respect in some, ridicule in others, but leaving in his wake a trail of Christian converts. Restless and idiosyncratic by nature, the itinerants were as footloose as any mountain men, proclaiming in the Missouri lowlands or the Rocky Mountain passes their version of Protestantism's Arminian doctrine: "free will, free grace, and individual responsibility." (Arminius, a Dutch Protestant theologian, denied Calvin's doctrine of predestination and claimed the possibility of salvation for all, dependent, in part, on their free will.)

New England itinerants braved the "smoaky Cottages . . . of wild Indians" in the late 1700s, while peripatetic awakeners of the nineteenth century probed the most remote corners of the trans-Allegheny West, bearing John Wesley's new Methodist tidings. Later itinerants kept pace with the emigrant trains, cutting a swath from coast to coast. Spanning distance and social classes, they rambled through a country that, by the mid-nineteenth century, had become frontier historian Frederick Jackson Turner's "new heaven and a new earth in politics as well as religion"—and a wide-open field for the evangelical labor that lay ahead.

It was not work for the fainthearted. Traveling hundreds of miles weekly, malnourished, exhausted, and sometimes, like Francis Asbury, plagued by boils, skin disease, blurred vision, fever, gastrointestinitis, rheumatism, and ulcers, the preacher worked hard to maintain a vaulting enthusiasm. Adversity was a constant companion, both to seasoned "old drones" and "pert ignorant boy[s]," to quote Asbury. But old or young, untried or weary, the saddlebag apostle found in days of isolation ample time to contemplate eternity, which could loom suddenly near in the event of Indian attack or rampaging outlaws. Each succeeding frontier provided its own unique dangers, and the roving "reasoner" seated atop a bedraggled horse was no less terrified of sudden snowstorm, bear attacks, ambushes, or snakebite than those to whom he ministered.

On the frontier, belief in a personified devil responsible for extraordinary events in nature was deeply rooted. Even those most bereft of religious memories still considered fighting plague, fever, crop loss, or Indian attack synonymous with "battling the Devil." Frontier farmers who nightly would leap out of bed at the slightest sound, "as if the great hour of danger had come," readily turned out at first daylight to hear the comforting gospel word; only a fool was unafraid of dying in a sinful state and going to eternal damnation.

Little wonder that the saddlebag orator had such profound appeal. With his packs overflowing with church newspapers, magazines, hymn books, and religious leaflets, he was something of a cultural emissary to isolated backwoods sites, bearing both the Good News and local news, settling disputes, comforting the sick, encouraging the fearful, and solemnizing marriages along the way. Traveling relentlessly, he shared family meals and helped with chores in exchange for bed and board, often pitching hay at noon and leading the elect in nightly devotions. As pioneer Keturah Belknap noted, few escaped the circuit rider's reach, for no sooner had they moved with their families to a different site along the Overland Trail than the "Methodist itinerate" found them and set up weekly preaching. Part of a dense system of elders presiding over districts, circuits, stations, and finally lay evangelists, the "Methodist itinerate" proved an effective means of growth, with 3,988 circuit riders and 7,730 local preachers swelling the church's ranks from a small "splinter" faction of 3,000 in 1775 to the largest Protestant denomination eighty-eight years later, with over a million and a half members.[7] "I became ambitious to find a family whose cabin had not been entered by a Methodist preacher," complained a Presbyterian in Kentucky. "They seem to have knocked on all doors first."

Nearly every denomination had a traveling itinerancy. United Brethren evangelized the border regions of Kansas and Nebraska; Seventh-Day Adventists pitched gospel tents and traveled from town to town in the Midwest; Disciples of Christ, from their foundation in Kentucky, in 1832 promoted conservative New Testament practices throughout the South and southern Southwest; and Presbyterians began their rounds in 1822, with the appointment of three Virginia clerics. Itinerants were, in most cases, ministers. But most ministers, when faced with the grueling prospect of a fifteen-thousand-mile horseback journey such as that made by early Presbyterian James Dickey, would ruefully admit they could not itinerate. To complete such a circuit was a daunting task, some areas being so vast that no person alone could visit a site more than once. Even moderate-sized circuits of three to four hundred miles took six weeks to cover, during which time the preacher lived like a nomad, unable to "attend parties of pleasure, loaf around stores and shops, or read newspapers and chat." Preacher William McKendree's records for an eleven-month period show only eight days of rest.[8] The Reverend Mr. Evans of Eagle City, Nebraska, covered his three-hundred-mile rounds on foot in 1858, while Peter Cartwright, atop a blind horse with a worn-out saddle, clothes patched "until it was difficult to tell the original," cheerfully stuck to his three-hundred-mile circuit along both banks of the Ohio before finally returning to Kentucky for supplies.[9]

Rugged, unconventional men were best suited to the task. Wrinkled and sunburned from outdoor travel, they would appear suddenly and preach to a crowd of curious bystanders like the prophets of old. Many, according to diary accounts, created a distinct physical "presence," as Presbyterian James McGready did with his "remarkable gravity and small, piercing eyes." With his muscular bearing and shaggy brows, California street preacher William Taylor was a striking figure who silenced even the drunkards at San Francisco's Portsmouth Square when he pounded a whiskey keg and thundered, "Jesus reigns!" A quiet Norwegian colony in Minnesota found their new Lutheran minister, the Reverend Mr. Storm, to be "a big, powerful man, with bushy eyebrows and a heavy mus-

Mennonite Elder Abram Schellenberg baptizes a convert in an artesian well in Escondido, California, ca. 1900.

A baptism takes place by Sharps Creek near Piedmont, Oklahoma, September 13, 1908.

Baptism performed in the Washita River, Kansas, while others wait their turn; denomination unknown

tache," who set the local matrons scurrying to find a suitable bride, though it was "no easy task." Brash assurance helped qualify the preacher as a serious figure of authority—along with the ability to back up discipline with fisticuffs if necessary. This last resort was discovered one night by Colorado preacher John Dyer, when ruffians broke up wooden seats at his prayer meeting and mocked his proceedings by "crowing like a rooster." His fighting words, "My honey, I see you!" rang out before he rolled up his sleeves and pummeled the rowdies to the floor. Nor did Methodist Charles Fenton pause when refused shelter in a Montana sod hut. "We are going in anyway," he declared and, taking up his folding organ, simply pushed in the closed door and began to play.

Eminent stature and assertiveness were secondary to spiritual vitality and oratorical skills. Many evangelists, including Lorenzo Dow, were slight and pale and seemingly unfit for apostolic life—but they could preach. They spoke without text, calling freely from memory both scripture and verse and, like Dow, drove themselves mercilessly in sharing their own unlettered version of the gospel. Often they had eschewed formal education for a rigorous, self-disciplined agenda of Bible study based on scripture alone. For reasoners like the Reverend Samuel Council, who preached in Ohio in 1806, the gospel was no metaphor, but God's literal word. In this he resembled evangelist Peter Cartwright, who refused to hunt up a "college or a biblical institute" and instead began his Methodist ministry with only a "hardy pony," "some traveling apparatus," and the declaration "Behold the lamb of God, that takes away the sins of the world."

The frontier orator expected "scores of people" to fall under his spell. To this end he adopted a revivalistic style both sensitive and thunderous, within which divine spirit and human seemed to merge. Lorenzo Dow could advertise the "latest authentic news from Hell" with passion, conviction, and all the skill of a politician, while itinerant William McGee raised his spirits by going "through the house shouting and exhorting with all possible ecstasy and energy." James McGready, one of the "blazing lights" of the evangelistic trail, possessed a "coarse, tremulous voice" that excited in his listeners the idea of "something unearthly." Herein lay the key to evangelical success. Men and women "who had never heard a gospel sermon in all their lives . . . and knew no Sabbath, only to hunt, and visit, and drink and dance" needed passionate proselytizing to counter a religious inertia that even as late as 1866 allowed no more than 23 percent of the population to accept formal church membership.[10]

The revival evangelist knew well how to keep an assembly lively. Colorful, florid hyperbole marked his discourse, all delivered in a booming voice to crowds either packed into a tiny meeting room or gathered outside under the trees. A preacher witnessing indoors would station himself beside a window, to make sure passersby also heard the message. He reckoned success by a surge of emotional response, as when Francis Asbury "aroused great crowds" to repentance "by the awful peals of his voice." To maintain interest, the Methodist itinerant would often withdraw after a sermon or two, turning the meeting briefly over to a local cleric, or "exhorter," who would vary the program with his own brand of drama, often in contrast to the original speaker. Occasional itinerants were not above using scientific knowledge—such as eclipse dates—to dazzle the gathered believers. Lorenzo Dow once persuaded a small black boy with a tin horn (who was even named Gabriel) to secret himself in a tree outside a meeting and blow a prophetic blast at Dow's

signal. These contrived wonders were no less than what the Almighty could provide, he reasoned. Wasn't it the itinerant's work to give a foretaste of eternity?

Despite excesses and occasional chicanery, highly personalized stump oratory was a valid form of religious expression. Employed by talented orators and exhorters of the Great Revival era (a period in the early 1800s defined by revivals and camp meetings) and born of the open spaces and the loose social structure of the American frontier, stump oratory flourished in the arena of the camp meeting, a form of outdoor worship initiated by John Wesley in England in 1739 and vigorously adapted in the early 1800s in South Carolina, Tennessee, and Kentucky. Set amid shadowed groves of trees, lit by flickering candles, and enjoyed by convivial families who had often traveled for days by buckboard, camp meetings lent an air of festive expectation to the monotony of backwoods life. Few who had "passed through a season of sorrow" on the frontier, facing death, illness, and family separation could resist the "friendly hand shaking" or "the great shout in the Camp," wherein "the forest[s] rang with the sound of victory." Preachers, fond of the open sky and their own sweeping rhetoric, often presided over services so emotional and so lengthy that only the most determined speakers could last until conclusion. "We expected to close . . . this morning," wrote Keturah Penton of a local Oregon revival. "But . . . the meting became so interesting that we protracted it over a nother day."

Here hymns were sung both to summon up the spirit and to memorize Bible passages that unlettered Christians could not read. Rousing gospel songs turned reluctant observers into "shouting" Christians, while attracting many of society's rejects with the democratic promise of salvation to all, whether black or white, destitute or comfortable. Friendly goodwill often extended to the picnic basket, with well-provisioned families sharing their food with those less prepared. Larger camp meetings even furnished food for the crowds; though, according to camp organizer H. C. Bailey, "It was no small job to prepare food and provide sleeping room for from five to eight hundred people and their horses." He worried that two hundred pounds of bread and four hundred pounds of beef might not suffice. Bailey also managed the table committee, the chief cook, cooking assistants, dishwashers, fuel, and provisions. Camp organizers eventually called for simpler fare at the meetings—potatoes or dried beef and bread brought from home—to free women from the cooking ordeal and to leave a less-littered campsite.

Open-air encampments grew into highly formalized tent revivals in the late nineteenth century, replete with common terminology, familiar music, and ever-present evil-routing devices, such as the mourners' bench, mourners' tents, anxious seats, prayer circles, and women's prayer meetings—an innovative and radical form of female participation introduced by evangelist Charles Finney. There were rules to cover every stage of activity, beginning with a blast from the preacher's tin horn and proceeding to a vigorous round of hallelujas, hymns, and as white-hot a sermon as the speaker could muster. Sufficiently keen after the opening exhortation, believers would then come forward to give personal testimony, followed by a crowning, emotional altar call. It was a "sene beyond description" when Oregon Methodist Reverend J. W. Starr found his "whole congregation . . . completely Broke down and in tears." Through him, sinners professed faith and struggled to find forgiveness, often fainting with the exertion and emotional release. What seemed "noise, uproar, and fanaticism" to onlookers brought many a transgressor to the point of crisis—and divine forgiveness. Hundreds embarked on a Christian path after attending these events, with converts drawn from all levels of society. Here at last was a milieu without prejudice, where the egalitarian message of the Bible could apply to all, and the same mourners' bench could be shared by anyone, rich or poor. "The whole human family is one blood," healer and evangelist Maria Woodworth-Etter insisted in Louisville in 1888, as she attempted to seat black and white believers side by side. She proved to be ahead of her time, and finally compromised with an obdurately racist congregation by allowing black members "one corner of the tent, seated alone."

Evangelist outriders were much like the scouts who rode advance for Overland parties. Seldom lingering long enough to be assimilated, always plunging ahead, each knew that in his wake would come the committees, elders, mission boards, building funds, and membership drives of the settled church. This solitary advance often stirred up animosity, prejudice, or distrust—depending upon the degree of religious observance encountered. Sermonists of the 1800s found in the backwoods culture of Kentucky or Ohio an isolated, illiterate population almost devoid of religious memory—a "brutal citizenry of the Basor sort" given to heavy drinking, fighting, and games of chance. But midcentury evangelists in the far western territories often found devout rural congregations already framing churches and schools. Church attendance was high, and to many the ministry was deemed an honored profession. By century's end the crowded cities had become the religious frontier, offering urban evangelists the chance to translate Christian victory into social outreach for huge city populations.

Peculiarities of population and geography defined both

Young girls are taught housekeeping skills at the "Practice Cottage," Methodist Girl's Mission.

Cooking class at St. Philip's School, San Antonio, Texas

needs and characteristics of individual churchmen, with, for example, the more rough-hewn broadcasters of the Cumberland Gap in Kentucky differing in education and approach from Midwestern pastors. Further distinctions could be found between denominations, with the "crying-for-joy" Southern Methodist cutting an entirely different swath from that of the staid Anglican or Congregationalist. Thus "Crazy" Bob Martin, the first Southern Methodist circuit rider ever seen in Colusa County, California, braved initial dislike and cultural distrust to share his message of Christian love with local, non-Methodist ranchers amazed by his ready "singing, praying, and shouting, according to his humor." Hecklers ridiculed Martin's groans of joy and his easy tears. Once, as a joke, Martin was directed into a ten-foot-deep channel of water instead of safely through a bog. Dressed in black broadcloth "slick and shining," wearing a battered stovepipe hat, and mounted on a small mule, Martin stayed submerged so long he was feared dead, but finally floated to the surface, "praising the Lord and praying for the fellow who sent him into the water." Pioneer H. C. Bailey wrote of the community's exasperation with Martin's religion, but admitted that, "strange to say," the more they saw of him, the better they liked him. Before long, they were so impressed with his "zeal and harmlessness" that they began "to take an interest in him," looking forward to his monthly rounds. Martin took "jokes and sly fun kindly . . . even answering gross insults with the promise 'I will pray for you, you can't prevent that!' " Like Oregon Methodist Father McKinney, who traveled his three-hundred-mile circuit with "a big Blue Army Blanket with a Hole in the middle to put his Head through And a wide Rimmed gray hat to keep the water from running down his back" and was greeted like a "Ray of Sunshine" by once un-

friendly homesteaders, he simply wore them down.

It was hardly surprising, with so many evangelists afoot, that competition would arise. The evangelists were, after all, addressing the moral life of a nation deeply in flux, and in seeking converts, they rivaled one another with fervent camp-meeting rhetoric or the reasoned homilies of their own denomination. With each church the lexicon varied; ceremonies were unique, and discord often reigned. Campbellites, Presbyterians, Methodists, and Baptists pursued their popular courses, while splinter groups proliferated: Disciples of Christ (a Campbellite offshoot), United Brethren, Mormons, Utopian dreamers such as the Rappites, Shakers, and Icarians. Even the Russian Orthodox were in evidence in California in 1812. One of its later emissaries was the venerated priest and social activist Agapius Honcherenko, who at a hermit's cave—the "Pechera" outside Hayward, California—offered refuge to earthquake survivors and tuberculosis victims.

"Great equality seems to reign," commented the Frenchman Alexis de Toqueville in 1832, marveling at the curious shifting allegiance of American Protestants from one denomination to the next, as they were drawn back and forth in their affiliation by the competing warmth of the evangelists' appeals. Native Americans also wondered why, with only one Bible, the white man had so many religions. But speculation aside, there was no denying the gospel's egalitarian and relentless surge across the continent. The First Amendment to the Federal Constitution, drawn up in the later 1780s, called for no government support of any church, and legal protection for all. Denominations recruited converts through revival, using the charisma of individual speakers to disseminate well-defined statements of policy and belief. Baptists, more argumentative than most and eager to represent the com-

Young women in a sewing class at the Oglala Boarding School, Pine Ridge, South Dakota

Church laywoman Elizabeth Hazleton Bixby Sherrard with children, probably residents of her South Dakota orphanage

mon man, argued for full bodily immersion in water and claimed New Testament antecedents. Methodists cried, "Free grace," and exulted in their expansive new growth on American soil. Both criticized the inelasticity and intellectual remoteness of Presbyterians, but could not deny that denomination's prestige. Congregationalists, descendants of seventeenth-century Puritanism, preached Calvinism and disliked the individualism of revival. Lutherans, soundly grounded in Bible study, proselytization, and orientation toward social welfare, were faulted for lacking skill in English, and often dickered about such issues as singing Americanized hymns in English. Predictably, primitive preachers—those who sought to revive "primitive" or biblical Christianity—avoided literate, urban settings, while those of "too high a calling" made little headway in a rural domain. Thus African Methodist Episcopal pastor Daniel Payne was shocked to find his duties ended by his congregation in 1850 because he was "too intellectual" and, unfortunately, "had too fine a carpet on the parlor floor." Nor would he let the congregation sing cornfield ditties.

By no means were denominations monolithic. Baptists between 1820 and 1845 preached "heartfelt religion" to a population that was 90 percent agricultural,[11] yet numbered in their ranks intellectuals such as early predecessor Isaac Backus—who admired the social theories of John Locke—as well as the unlettered rural preacher who shod horses or built fences or tilled the soil, spending his days like any other until needed for weddings, baptisms, or funerals. "I have no learning," lamented Jacob Bower. "I cannot speak in public. I am not qualified for the great work. I live on poor land, have a growing family to provide for, and poor clothes to stand up in.—People will laugh at me." But Bower, like many of his counterparts, was judged

not on delivery, social standing, or financial footing, but on his ability to convey with warmth and skill the drama of his own conviction, using song, story, gospel, and exhortation. But those without charisma, walking in faith without the appeal of personality, were representatives of what Isaac Owen, in his San Francisco letters of 1852, delicately referred to as "weak circuits." In private correspondence with his bishop, Owen refused the services of a Brother Ercanbrach, for lacking the necessary talent. "Please send us no one, either for schools, or for the regular work," Owen pleaded, "unless they are *A.No.1.*"

This same quest for perfection often hindered Presbyterian expansion on the frontier. Puritan in origin, democratic in nature, the denomination grew slowly because it sought well-educated evangelists who often ministered only to fellow Presbyterians when on the trail, and, early on, were assigned territories so vast they could preach to a homestead or village only once, briefly, in a year's time. "We are drifting toward an uncertain future," worried C. A. Briggs in 1888, recognizing the drawbacks of such restrained conservatism, upheld by a denomination whose legions of college-trained men were the largest in the West, and who had long been represented by intellectuals such as John Witherspoon, the only clergyman to sign the Declaration of Independence. Yet from the same ranks tumbled unlettered advocates such as James Axley, who tossed half-eaten chicken bones to the dogs during dinner with the governor of Ohio, and James McGready, whose hard-hitting, emotional sermons in Red River, North Carolina, were anything but stereotypically Presbyterian. Likewise, individuals undermined the cliché of the "typical" Anglican itinerant, the "typical" Methodist itinerant, and so on.

Special mention should be made of black evangelists,

who ministered to black Christians in both segregated or reform-minded, mixed congregations, despite stiff prejudice and opposition. Christians had long struggled with the egalitarian effects of revival, which swept aside barriers of class, vocation, and race and posed the bothersome question of Who is a Brother? Many were unable to overcome barriers of prejudice and social distrust, even as blacks, both slave and free, joined the Protestant denominations in ever-increasing numbers. "You must not kneel here," an Episcopal elder at Saint George's Church in Philadelphia cautioned a black parishioner. In 1794, within a year of this affront, the Reverend Richard Allen established the first Protestant denomination solely for blacks: the African Methodist Episcopal Church.

Black evangelists, once banned from preaching by rules passed in 1830 in Virginia, and later in Alabama and Georgia, found their powers expanded as emancipation drew closer. "Thrilling speeches," the earmark of the populist preacher, flourished in black congregations, with skilled orators such as Dempsey Kelley, Charles Ray, John N. Marrs, and Jeremiah B. Sanderson condemning racism from the pulpit. Abolitionist churches and religious bodies throughout the country continued to support black freedom efforts—as long as they were conducted in separate churches. Black Christians struggled to find an acceptable racial climate—even in the newer western territories—but turned increasingly to their own preachers and evangelists for direction and inspiration. Most of these, such as Baptist leader Booker T. Washington, urged, at the very least, conformity to the Protestant ethic. To the firebrand black evangelists were often entrusted community leadership positions of far greater reach and influence than those of their white counterparts. They presided over school boards, town councils, and charities; they formed "Moral, Mental & Religious Improving Associations" and "Intelligent Committees"; they organized church frolics, lectures, reading classes, and socials. Black society recognized that church was its highest institution, and black evangelists its most respected emissaries. Well-meaning white churches and right-minded legislators could only make token headway against prejudice. It was up to black Christians to win the respect of their communities and proceed in living to the full of their legal rights. To this end, black evangelists, well-trained for leadership in the pulpit and on the stump, led their congregations in cultural and religious advocacy to claim American justice in the shadow of the altar.

## Ministers

As the country's mobile population eddied and slowed, forming young townships in rugged terrain, the saddlebag preacher was edged aside by the stationary evangelist—men and women less venturesome than their traveling brethren, but, as Luther envisioned, each "a teacher, a light in the world . . . a true, faithful parson or preacher."

Seldom first to break new ground, these ministers were assigned by boards and committees to frontier sites, often arriving in the territories well after their flock, anxious to begin Sunday schools and Bible classes, refute biblical errancies, and if possible counter the undisciplined effects of "dangerous amusements" and frontier individualism in general. They often found informal devotional meetings already established in log cabins, barns, or the general store—folk congregations self-led in song and praise, often with no more than "an old-style tuning fork . . . to strike the tone" for the hallelujah chorus. No dwelling was too poor

The Tabernacle Church represented a turn-of-the-century shift from outdoor revival tents to stationary, indoor sites.

for fellowship, even in the Dakotas, Wyoming, and throughout the intermountain West, where perpetual winds, absence of water, and terrible heat and cold made gatherings of any kind difficult.

Far from the apathy and "low moral tone" of the trans-Allegheny West, a newly arrived Western preacher might find that "the men, the children, the relatives, the in-laws, and perhaps a tin peddler" he chanced to shelter with in bad weather were already obedient Christians who passed each Sunday in "singing, reading, and eating melons." Or, like teacher Mary Sears, they were believers who often pondered the "vanity of worldly people [and] the sin of pride and extravagance" and seldom dared to risk the eponym "Sabbath-breaker" just to keep abreast of exhausting chores. Frank Hoyt recalled his mother's embarrassment when an uncle came to visit from Nebraska City and noticed the wash boiling on the stove. "Margaret," he asked, "why do you wash on Sunday?" The pot quickly came off the stove, at least until his uncle left.

For want of their own churches, newly arrived ministers often held joint services, preaching to rural congregations largely indifferent to distinctions of denomination. This informal banding together revealed to settlers and pastors alike the surprising joys of ecumenical kinship. When Tommie Clack's fellow Texans stayed for church after Sunday school in the late 1800s, it was "regardless of who had the services, Methodists, Baptists, Presbyterians, or what." Settlers of all denominations shared both hymns and hardships, and the unity of these ragged bands—many denominations together, reciting psalms and offering fervent "amens" against a background of crying infants—gently rebuked the spirit of denominational rivalry that came with the advent of assigned ministers. Lutheran Barbara Levorson recalled the sudden discord

The Salvation Army headquarters in downtown San Francisco, California

Group of children before daily vacation bible school—6 weeks of "games, music and Bible stories" in Oakland, California

Evangelist L. A. Platts with the Seventh-Day Baptist Women's Evangelistic Quartet, ca. 1890

created in her small Minnesota settlement when the denomination's Reverend Mr. Gullickson arrived. Once, the homesteaders had joined in the schoolhouse services of the United Church pastor "regardless of affiliation." But the new pastor seated himself on the schoolhouse doorstep and forbade his congregation to enter the building with a series of "highly unsuitable remarks." His dictatorial style lost him a number of friends among the friendly settlement people, who had "reverence for God's work as well as his servants."

The stabilization of the Christian population after the westward crossing created an opening for evangelists of all classes and all ages—and both genders—to minister to a people equally diverse. Christian gentry now expected orthodoxy as well as hyperbole, which paved the way for evangelists who could spiritually quicken members of the middle class and guide their passage through the storms of modernity. So-called liberal clergy—Congregationalists, Presbyterians, and Unitarians—from the East reintroduced the habit of formal dress, often sporting silk hats, striped trousers, and the latest look in spats. Well-dressed children attended Sunday schools, receiving weekly "premiums" for punctual attendance and good behavior. Hymns regained a measure of propriety and deliberation—depending upon the formality of the denomination. With less emphasis on thunderous delivery and divine manifestation, there was greater acceptance of ministers such as Emma Newman, who was urged to preach despite her "bad voice"; her brother reminded her that the community "might need a minister rather than a speaker." Evangelism of the late nineteenth and early twentieth centuries embraced a wide array of practitioners, from the "nice Gentle sermons" of Oregon circuit rider Father McKinney to the "red hot exhortations" of revival camp preachers such as Methodist Brother Raynor.

Post–Civil War evangelism was the duty of any Christian, ordained or not, and often brought laity to the gospel forefront. German physician Matthias Klaiber would visit malaria-stricken residents of the Vandalia Mission in Illinois, dispense "a concoction," then "[kneel] on the floor and [pray] earnestly" for their spiritual and physical health. California ranch owner and congressman John Bidwell, an ardent Presbyterian, based his work and life on the Bible and was so set against the evils of intemperance that he even uprooted his costly vineyard and smashed the winefilled casks when he found his workers tippling. Fur trader and mountain man Jedediah "Bible-totin' " Smith sought victory over sin through hymns and scripture, broadcast indiscriminately among grizzled fellow trappers, friendly Indians, and overland emigrants. Personal evangelism became the hallmark of "the higher Christian life" aspired to in post–Civil War America, providing a ministry for the matron pushing the baby carriage as well as for the seasoned stump orator. Presbyterian matrons in particular took to heart the late century's prevailing self-confident sense of "perfectionism, moralism, and evangelicalism." Armed only with hatpins and umbrellas, they raided brothels and dens in San Francisco's Chinatown, bringing the slave women to mission homes and, ultimately, to the faith.

As these laywomen demonstrated, the Christian walk was not for the fainthearted. To keep up with their independent congregations, ministers were expected to be role models of strength and zeal; able to keep tight discipline—as did Charles Finney at his tent revivals—while inspiring from the pulpit. Journals and diaries evidence that, far from being secure in their assigned locations, ministers had to be equally "thunderous" and convincing from the pulpit. Like any endeavor, skill reaped its rewards, and the talented orator could usually count on offerings of food or clothing, or an invitation to stay the week. Liberal Presbyterians, who enjoyed a temperate drink or two, often earned kegs of whiskey as payment. The able preacher was "love[d] and reverenced" by all, and his Sunday message was the occasion for a "good time and a chicken dinner."

Yet meek and tremulous orators also made their way west, sustained, like the biblical David facing his giant, by a vision far greater than stature or ability. Journals and diaries evidence the surprise and reluctance many men and women felt when first summoned to preach. They distrusted their abilities, lacked eloquence, and were sadly without stamina; but resisting the call soon seemed to teach them that it was wiser by far to adopt a servant attitude and follow divine bidding—no matter how frightened or tongue-tied they were. "I tried to beg off because of my timidity and lack of education," wrote W. G. Trudgeon, who delivered his first Methodist sermon and "many thereafter" by "pressing his knees against the pulpit" to steady himself and give his body some support. "I would rather have cut wood or carried a hod than to have to preach," wrote Methodist itinerant A. J. McNemee, whose moderate skills led him to conclude that a Methodist preacher who could not preach was "certainly in a hard place." Jacob Bower became "wonderfully alarmed" when Divine Providence nudged him toward the pulpit, and "immediately called into question" the fact that he was "the least Christian in the church, and the most ignorant and unlearned." Bower feared that people would laugh at him, and after finally announcing his first sermon spent an anticipatory week in "fear and trembling."

And well might he have been concerned. To stumble, to lose inspiration, to appear ridiculous in public were only several of many unpleasant obstacles to pastoral success. An evangelical ministry, even under the best of circumstances, frequently plunged its practitioners into a stressful gamut of family difficulties, financial distress, and grave physical danger. Even the most qualified candidates often lost heart when faced with the grim realities of parsonage life. In January 1851 forty Methodists applied for ministries in Oregon and California—yet only five took up the work.[12] Those were no doubt dismayed to find that the "brotherhood of poverty" had scarcely changed since the first years of the early Baptist church, when to expect cash for gospel work was unthinkable—save for a salaried cleric, or "money preacher." Having the "call" and doing God's bidding was reward enough, since placing a dollar value on Divine Mandate might run counter to God's plan in some unlucky way. When official church stipends were finally paid, few could live on the typical Methodist salary of $64 per year before 1800,[13] an amount that rose to $100 annually by 1816, with a "married" allotment of $500 at the century's end.[14] "Every Methodist conference in the Union [is] insolvent," boasted Bishop Francis Asbury, who thanked the Lord daily for keeping "the traveling connection . . . poor." "We were all poor together, preacher and people," wrote W. G. Trudgeon after bedding down in a Dakota shack and sleeping on the floor in temperatures of forty-five degrees below zero, after having "tramped around" outside in the snow as a courtesy to the family he was staying with—allowing them the privacy to prepare for bed. Poverty bound them together, preacher and settler, uniquely close in spirit and hardship in a way that ministers of a finer cloth would seldom comprehend. Poverty meant dependence and vulnerability, conditions in which the spirit of God could freely flow. Yet as the fron-

The Salvation Army distributes food in Denver, Colorado.

tier preacher married and tried to raise a family, poverty's virtues were overshadowed by the preacher's need to pay his bills.

Marriage as bane or blessing—who could decide? "To marry is to locate," Francis Asbury sadly reckoned at a time when Methodism's ministers were male, and one after another of his best itinerants would find a wife and request a fixed location. He could only hope, as did the men themselves, that their wives were women who would succor them through poverty and—in the case of circuit riders—endure the husband's prolonged absence without complaint. The Western evangelical wife, beset by debts, burdened with children, and expected to dispense tea, advice, and good cheer with equanimity, often found herself living in circumstances that defied imagination. Separated from childhood friends and family, squeezed into a shanty or dugout, or boarding with members of the congregation, the preacher's wife had ample opportunity to sorrow over her choice of husband.

Isaac Owen called for "the right sort of woman" to accompany his ministers west, hoping to attract educated and genteel women to act as the church's necessary social arbiters and interlocutors of polite society. Unmentioned in his prospectus was the "squirrel-infested parsonage measuring 12 × 15″" or the bed of "thirteen pounds of pine shavings on the floor" that greeted Mrs. A. S. Gibbons in the mining town of Columbia, California, or the board-and-batten shanty, directly across from a Buffalo Gap saloon, that was home to Maryanne Trudgeon, who nightly dodged bullets randomly shot through the Tudgeons' walls. "O this MISERABLE GODFORSAKEN COUNTRY," cried Baptist wife Harriet Shaw about Santa Fe in 1852, finding this Protestant excursion into Catholic territory a "bitter disappointment." More acceptable—and more expected of the good ministerial wife—was the biblical acceptance with joy, shown by Reverend Matthew's young bride, who spent hours alone in an isolated cabin, often surrounded by howling wolf packs. "Let the wolves come," she told her itinerant husband. "I will never murmur." She admitted that her discomfort and fear were secondary to her husband's greater work, and with God's help she would "stay and care for [the] home" while he was out "caring for souls." Isaac Owen's wife chose to live for months in Sacramento in a tent hand-stitched from "the remains of [their] old wagon covers and a few bed quilts"— to save the missionary society money.

Mary Richardson Walker, living with her husband at an isolated wilderness site in Oregon in the 1830s, at first imagined her husband to be "a special blessing conferred by Heaven," but after months of hard labor and unrequited affection, "began to feel discouraged," even wishing she "had never been married." However, the preacher's wife was, before all, a Christian woman, able to find solace in prayer despite the circumstances. Annie Taylor, wife of California evangelist and later-to-be bishop William Taylor, refused to let despair stand in her way when asked if she would move west. She prayed away her hesitations until her "whole being . . . was filled and thrilled . . . with a desire to go." Like countless other clerical wives—whether Methodist, Presbyterian, Lutheran, Episcopal, or Baptist—she was expected to bear hardships without a tremor, excel at hospitable traditions, and dispense fritters and jam to neighboring families with quiet Christian assurance. Her measure was taken, not in framed pictures or silver tea settings, but in the ability to support her husband's efforts with biblical good sense of her own. While the pastor handled sacraments, meetings, and prayers, his wife was expected to juggle children, do-

Sunday night street meeting in the South led by a Baptist Home Mission Board evangelist, 1912

nation parties, socials, and Sunday school. Calling and counseling duties were shared equally between pastors and their wives, who were often forthright women unashamed to sweep into a sickroom and query: "Are you a sinner?" God's glory took precedence over natural reserve, allowing a once-shy homemaker such as Annie Taylor to sing "The Royal Proclamation" wharfside at the San Francisco harbor, accompanied by her husband mounted on a beer barrel at her side.

Working together, husband and wife learned to live simply, alongside neighbors who were often equally poor. Few escaped the exigencies of need, as the Reverend Thomas Barr discovered while trying to balance his ministry and a family of nine on a salary of $380. He finally gave up in despair. "The circuits [and, by inference, the parsonages] in those days were pretty shy of finances," W. G. Trudgeon gently wrote from What-Cheer, Iowa, hoping that devotions and divine intervention would provide his immediate needs. Like countless other men and women who lived by faith, his solution to poverty was prayer, and judging by frequent miraculous incidents recounted in journals and manuscripts, help often came. With Trudgeon, a minister who often traveled to outlying areas but was without a horse and "greatly depressed in spirit" by that lack, Providence was a "good Methodist brother" who unexpectedly handed him a hundred dollars with which to buy a mount. San Francisco Baptist parson Francis Prevaux discovered a "small grocery store" stocked with delicacies, from ginger to tongue to tapioca, on his doorstep each week, sent by an unnamed benefactor. Evangelist Mary Collins received in the mail one spring "a package containing two sheets, two pillow cases, and two towels"—the exact number of goods she had used

to bandage a wounded Indian the previous winter. "God sent some servant of his a wireless Message and I was supplied," Collins marveled. Just as faith was forged in hardship, such generosity was a gentle reminder that the work of the pioneer minister had found its due recognition.

# Missionaries

None better upheld the evangelistic and expansionary vision of the nineteenth century than the missionary. Drawn from the sheltered confines of seminaries and universities, a host of young men and women flooded the western territories after 1840, intent on reaching the country's unconverted Indians, Chinese, and Japanese. Here was a Christian province calling less for sizzling oratory than sheer persistence.

Missionary efforts began early on the Eastern seaboard. Puritan settler John Eliot, called "The Apostle of the Indians," ordained twenty-four Algonquin Indians in Massachusetts in 1689, and Quaker evangelist William Penn formed historic bonds of friendship with Indians in Pennsylvania. In 1747 David Brainerd, the "best-known missionary of the 18th century," slept on the ground beside his Iroquois friends, relentlessly telling them, over and over, the story of Christ. Gideon Blackburn, the "Daniel Boone" of the pulpit, evangelized East Coast Indians in 1803. (Few imagined that their efforts would later become part of a tangled skein of federal control, tribal removal, treaty breaking, land accessions, destroyed leadership, and cultural erosion that left the original salvation theme increasingly obscured.) Thus Christians of the nineteenth century could lay claim to a history of missionary outreach, even if their own efforts seemed "mired in the dynamics of frontier conquest and settlement."

Nineteenth-century missionaries were generally unable to separate Christianization from Americanization, and by 1846 an impressive cadre of over 17,000 scholars from the American Missionary Association's 166 training schools, established in over 14,500 communities,[15] were unified in their attempts to assimilate American Indians into the prevailing Anglo-European culture. In sixty years of ministry to the Indians, envoys of the Board of Foreign Missions sought cultural conversion as evidence of spiritual right-mindedness, seeing in Western dress, the English language, and individual property ownership the agreeable signs of assimilation. Ephesians 4:11 invites "some to be apostles, some prophets, some evangelists, some pastors and teachers." But those summoned to a western outreach, ministering daily to the Osage, Dakota, Navajo, Choctaw, and countless other western tribes, were called upon to endure hatred, tribal superstition, and calamities nearly biblical in nature. Missionaries struggled to impart classroom skills along with the Good News, when possible persuading tribes to "loan" their children to mission schools for practical training in agriculture, arithmetic, carpentry, and the like. To this end, hundreds of men and women weathered despondency and danger to confound distant tribes with unfamiliar biblical imagery, English literacy, and sacred hymns sung in three-part harmony.

Every manner of Christian walked the missionary trail. Most were eager to bring "God's stepchildren" into the Christian fold—even ready to "dot heathen soil with their lonely graves" to do so—but they were seldom prepared for the resistance encountered. Native Americans, accustomed to freedom and autonomy, were psychologically demoralized by repeated conquest. Christianity, coming in the wake of this humiliation, was often viewed as a white man's tool, used only to accustom Indians to their failure in the new, white man's world. "Indians are much prejudiced against the Christian name," Methodist Benjamin Lakin noted in 1810. Most of these urban evangelists did not have the skills to survive in the dozens of Quaker, Methodist, Baptist, and Presbyterian outposts that dotted the Overland Route from Council Bluffs, Iowa, and Saint Joseph, Missouri, as far west as Oregon. These young and college-trained evangelists, on the vanguard of social reform in the East, imaginations fired by tracts and rousing sermons, discovered quickly the vicissitudes of living without funds, food, or linguistic skills. Well-bred women such as Mary Riggs "had not been accustomed" to washing by hand enormous piles of dirt-stiffened laundry, and, as her husband Stephen wrote from their Dakota mission in 1837, "it came hard to her." (Like most missionaries, the Riggses had married before coming west; missionary boards frowned upon single women in far-flung outposts, and by 1820 the United Foreign Missionary Society had sent only six single women west of the Mississippi. Of those, three married and one lost her sanity due to illness.[16] The Centennial Survey of Foreign Missions listed only 11 single women in 1873, 15 in 1883, and 160 by 1894, rising finally in 1900 to a total of 1,095.[17]) Without regular salaries, and dependent upon charity boxes from the East, missionaries at frontier stations found life rugged enough with or without a spouse. Women, whether they were wives or single teachers, passed tedious days mending and patching used clothes, trying to fashion new garments out of old. Precious belongings mysteriously disappeared.

Stereoscopic view of a church wedding, Wyoming, ca. 1850

Marriage of Wilbur Raymond and Jetti Walker, Pikeville, Kentucky

"Everything that could be was stolen," Mary Riggs lamented, noting that vanished scissors, mirrors, books, and tools could seldom be replaced. Gone were the delicate handicrafts of memory, white grape jelly and marzipan hearts, beeswax candles, fancy workboxes, and silk flowers. Instead, female missioners wrote lessons on old newspapers tacked to the wall, gingerly spooned up dinners of baked polecat or blood boiled with onion, and, just like the men, carried their knives in scabbards.

In the missionary world, efficacy often depended upon vocabulary, and those able to speak an Indian tongue grew, as did Oregon missionary Narcissa Whitman, to have a heart "more and more interested" in their Indian brothers. Presbyterian Cyrus Byington, realizing that the Holy Spirit "could convert not only men . . . but language," learned Choctaw by going from Indian to Indian with pencil and paper, pointing out items and asking, "What is this? What is that?" Others furthered communication by translating the gospel into the various Indian tongues. The outpost evangelist unable to preach in the language of his congregation was hardly able to lead it through the steps to salvation—the knowledge of scriptures, repentance, and acceptance of grace. Not only was the harvest of souls impeded, but simple existence threatened—as the Gormans in New Mexico discovered when trying to barter for food in the local language. They nearly starved in their marketing attempts—finally becoming so desperate they had to "sell their underclothes" to purchase local Indian corn, chilies, meat, and beans that were readily available in the pueblo market.

The faith of missionaries such as the Reverend Bill Williams often waned in the face of Indian resistance. Williams tired of explaining the invisible God of Christianity to those accustomed to more self-evident deities of sun, moon, rain, and thunder, and after a time quit the ministry, married an Osage woman, and lived the life of a guide and trapper.

Each convert was prized, for evangelists knew that often the efforts of an entire missionary force, working for decades, would gather only a scattering of lifetime Christians. Such was the Presbyterian Choctaw outpost in Mississippi, which after twelve years of labor by up to eighty-one men and women,[18] at a total cost of $140,000, produced only 360 converts.

Wearied by the uphill struggle and undermined by a discernible shift in popular church support in the 1850s away from Native Americans to Asians, many evangelists, grown middle-aged in frontier service, packed their bags and left for more settled ministries. Those who stayed, content to run boarding schools or day schools or teach blacksmithing or agriculture, often forged strong bonds of friendship and trust with native residents, whether the Indians had been "buried in baptism" or not. Missionary children, such as those born near the Lac qui Parle Dakota village in Minnesota, were warmly embraced by the local tribe and given Indian names: Snow Bird was the Riggses' firstborn son and Curly Head the daughter. Before her death Narcissa Whitman's daughter Alice was called Cayuse Te-mi, or "Cayuse Girl." Missionaries also served as friendly mediators between Indians and government agents, who often withheld tribal annuities and government-issued provisions of corn, wheat, and meat from the Indians, relinquishing them only after threats or persuasion.

Evangelists ministering to West Coast Chinese during the Gold Rush era and to Japanese after the 1880s faced humanitarian and social demands of a different nature. The evangelists were thrust into America's most bustling economy and into cities where the Chinese were considered "an unmixed evil," denied citizenship, taxed unmercifully, and darkly viewed as slaveholders, opium addicts, and lords in secret societies called "tongs." Lurid tales of the "yellow peril" and slave trafficking stoked a frenzy of anti-Chinese sentiment in the 1870s. Washhouses were burned, Chinese-staffed factories threatened, and many of the 150,000 Orientals who had immigrated to the country by 1875 were robbed, and attacked by angry mobs.[19] Often the unlucky Asians had no advocate but a minister, to whom they turned with increasing frequency. One such spokesman was Presbyterian mission founder William Speer, whose Cantonese linguistic skills made him a logical choice to protest a proposed mining tax increase that would impoverish Orientals. Methodist minister Otis Gibson, also a Cantonese speaker, recognized that spreading the Good News to Asians depended mainly upon the immigrants' facility in English, and persuaded six Methodist churches to found English-language schools. Yet he and other evangelists faced resentment from the business community for their efforts. West Coast clerics were expected to develop loyalty to the local community—which in the late 1870s showed more interest in anti-coolie clubs than social and humanitarian services. The Reverend Mr. Gibson's San Francisco school was stormed by angry crowds, and he received volumes of hate mail. It was, as the Reverend S. V. Blakslee noted to the State Bar Association of Congregational Churches, a time easily compared to the tragic and volatile period of slavery in the South.

Despite having to face desultory waves of racism and misunderstanding, American missionaries—working through tract societies, Bible and colonization societies, and the Sunday-School Union—continued their minority ministries well into the twentieth century, bringing America ever closer to the original Protestant vision of an evangelical empire.

## Women Evangelists

Those who best succeeded in reaping God's harvest during this difficult time were often the dedicated women of the Occidental Board of Home Missions, whose annual reports, beginning with the board's foundation in 1873, describe in novelistic detail the daring rescues of slave girls and young Chinese children by an active contingent of Presbyterian matrons. "If it were not for the Jesus people," said a woman in a Chinatown alley in San Francisco, "Chinamen could not live one hour in this city."

The "Jesus people" did not take their responsibility lightly. Evangelical women, particularly those associated with the Presbyterian Mission Home in San Francisco, were determined to end slave trafficking, illiteracy, and any Chinese customs that hindered the convert's Christian growth. They hired attorneys to fight the slaveholders in court, alerted police before every confrontation, and marched through dens and brothels to find young girls held illegally—knowing that, as virtuous women of San Francisco's better class, none would dare stand in their path. Once rescued, the Chinese girls sheltered at the mission home faced a daily regimen of English lessons, Bible study, and Western housekeeping practices, along with music lessons, prayer meetings, and weekly Sunday school. The 350 harbored there in 1876 learned scriptures, the Lord's Prayer, the Commandments, the Beatitudes, and the Catechism. "In time," noted evangelist and lay worker Mrs. M. S. Carey of San Jose, California, "the Idol worshipers [will] bow down before Him and call Him Father." Like countless other victorious rescue workers, Mrs. Carey's "light to the nations" brightened perceptibly when her charges "kept their houses . . . cleaner than formerly" and in other ways demonstrated a proper degree of acculturation.

The later efforts of the Presbyterian women were part of an evangelical tradition that began with the second Great Awakening, when the awareness of universal sin and free salvation raised the possibility that women, as well as men, could be used publicly in God's grand work. The common man was recognized at last as a brother in grace, and women, who had been excluded from authority in traditional churches, were swept up in the momentum in surprisingly public ways.

Some women in the early 1800s had already taken to the pulpit, others to the trail. Free at last of their symbolic assignment to a "female pew" by church hierarchy, they struck out to minister, proselytize, and convert. Without the aid of map or guide, prey to Indians loyal to the British cause and ruffians without chivalrous respect, women such as Anna Nitschman are legend. As the future wife of Count Zindendorf, the leader of a German sect of Moravians, Anna Nitschman traveled as an itinerant missionary throughout Pennsylvania in the early 1700s, riding horseback for miles, sleeping under the stars in dense forests, often encountering Indians. Her travels were matched by the equally brash Margaretta Grube, a sister Moravian who spent bitter winters in a wigwam in the Blue Mountains, keeping her child alive between the warm flanks of Indian dogs, while she and her husband ministered to the tribes.

But for most nineteenth-century women, church hierarchy was a constant reminder that to minister, exhort, conduct classes, act as a group leader, or, in some cases, even sing hymns, would break the timeworn taboo against women "preaching to men." The gentle gospel encouragement, "She hath done what she could . . . " (Mark 5:26) would differ emphatically, decade by decade, as denominations merged, families moved west, and church politics shifted. Thus the appearance of outspoken "female messiahs," such as Shaker Mother Anna Lee and her successor Lucy Wright, was considered highly unusual, bearing a trace of the miraculous that may have worked, ultimately, in the women's favor. Jemima Wilkinson—known to superstitious colonials in 1787 as "the woman who walked on water"—was unusual in her prominence. Self-elected the "Publick Universal Friend," she was the first American-born head of a religious cult: the Society of Universal Friends. Distinguished by a grim voice and dark clerical costume, Jemima "had the look of a [man] to [those] unaccustomed to the sight of a woman's bare head. When she did wear a covering, it was a beaverskin Quaker hat just like a man's.

By virtue of their sheer numbers, women of the 1800s, especially in the later post–Civil War decades, rose to prominence on the sawdust trail of revivals and tent meetings. "Sometimes I wish I were a man and a minister!" sighed Sarah B. Mayes, speaking not only for herself, but for other evangelical women who sought broader arenas than the Female Praying Society, Female Mite Society, and the Female Harmony Society. Many did take to the pulpit, led by such examples as Winifred Wirts Dague, an

Mrs. Riggs instructs Sioux children in music at Oahe Mission, South Dakota.

Reverend Andrew Dahl photographed this Madison, Wisconsin, family—probably members of his Lutheran congregation—in front of their log home, ca. 1876.

Sisters Finnbar Collins and Agnes Kenniff visit prostitutes in San Francisco, California (figures at bottom left have been erased from the negative).

evangelist finally licensed by the Cleveland Presbytery in 1919, who served faithfully both as minister and revivalist to her Ohio congregation. Edith Livingston Peak was approved for active evangelism in a location too remote for the local male circuit rider to reach. Despite a flurry of regional protest she was named in his place, traveling and preaching extensively along the West Coast in the 1890s, and was eventually praised in a Presbyterian publication as "a public speaker and able expounder of the gospel . . . superior to the average evangelist, man or woman."

Reform-minded women had long thought to challenge male hegemony, but religious and social changes occurring after 1830 gave renewed vigor to their efforts. The second Great Revival era of the 1800s had produced a religion more emotional—more "feminine." The westward crossing, emancipation, and ultimately suffrage in turn produced women that were stronger, more forthright. The wives who presided so predictably over hearth and crib began to seek fresh challenges in the temperance movement, missionary ministries, and benevolent and relief work. With "two-thirds of the church [being] women," many refused to settle for their traditional role as weaker vessels. Critical influence was wielded by leaders such as Ellen White, founder of the Seventh-Day Adventists, Mary Baker Eddy of the Christian Science church, and Phoebe Palmer of the Pillar of Fire church. There were also heroic female evangelists from the Salvation Army: Victoria Booth Demarest (granddaughter of the founder William Booth), who was an itinerant evangelist, minister, singer, and dramatist, and her mother, Evangeline Cory Booth, a vigorous streetside exhorter.

Distinguished by strong voices, steady vision, and a burning desire to correct societal wrongs through personal ministry, women of the nineteenth century, having already established forty-one foreign mission boards in the country between 1861 and 1900,[20] were a force to be reckoned with. The term "evangelist" was no longer limited to those who were ordained, traveled, or staffed foreign missions; evangelism was the medium by which "all the women and children of the world" would come under the "transforming power of the gospel." As such, the ministry laid claim to housewives, homesteaders, shopkeepers, teachers, and female ministers alike. None was immune from encounters with these evangelists: Attendees at rag parties (where old clothes were donated to charity), socials, and lectures were persuaded to put "Christ in their hearts" by middle-class women so ardent that they were dubbed "Protestant nuns." "Have we a religion for men?" mused Congregationalist minister Howard Bridgeman, startled by the feminist bent that religion was taking and how quickly "the home was going forth into the world."

The motivation to build Christ's church was strong; for women prosperous or poor, courageous or timid, Eastern or Western, clerical or lay, the key was in the calling. "By night and by [day] I scarcely think of anything but becoming a missionary. I think I feel more engaged in religion than I have ever before," wrote Mary Richardson in 1836, shortly before marrying and traveling to Oregon with her husband. Speaking up for generations of like-minded Christians, she and others of the same conviction led the Great Migration of God's People across American soil, hoping through prayer and right living to further the Puritan vision of a "new Heaven, and a new Earth, in new Churches and a new Common-wealth"; to be visible saints on a new landscape, and to lead with vigor successive Christian generations in the march of ages.

# Diaries,
# Journals,
# and
# Photographs

Nuns with Indian children outside the Mission in San Diego, California

# Sister Mary Alenie

" . . . I felt perfectly happy, calm, and resigned to the holy will of our heavenly Father. I said to myself, this is indeed God's own work. I did not ask to come here, I dislike the place. I begged of our Dear Mother Constantine to send me to Oregon. So to have the merit of obedience, now I am perfectly satisfied. I am in the hands of the good God, he will take care of me as he has always done."

—Sister Mary Alenie,
upon hearing that her mission
would be in California

Mary Alenie was born January 26, 1826, in Verviers, in the province of Liège, in what is today Belgium. Her father was a wholesale grocery dealer, while her mother's noble lineage led directly to the court of the emperor of Austria.

Catholicism was a strong family persuasion. Many relatives were priests (her godfather was the bishop of Namur), and none thought it odd when Mary Alenie, instead of playing with dolls, led her friends to the cellar amid casks of sauerkraut to perform penance to the crucified Christ by pinioning their arms beneath heavy stones.

She was a delicate child, highly emotional, and given to attacks of nerves. Once the vengeful wife of a laborer tried to frighten her by giving three long, slow raps on her window at night, then presenting the sight of her pale, bloodless face pressed against the glass; three nights of this propelled Mary Alenie into the convent of Notre Dame de Namur for rest, though she was still too young to be a novitiate.

Despite her weak constitution, Mary Alenie hungered to convert souls for Christ, and considered China, then Africa, and finally Oregon as suitable missionary sites. She petitioned her mother superior for an Oregon assignment. At the time, Alenie was becoming noted as a "living saint" by the order; her heart was so compassionate she often made beds for stray dogs and cats whom she feared others had neglected. Perhaps this gentle thoughtfulness qualified her for the mission. In any event, she was selected to sail from Antwerp to New York, then to Panama, then up the coast to California. Though she intended to go on to Oregon to join the small community of nuns of her order in the Willamette Valley, she remained in California at the request of Bishop Alemany. She died at San Jose on September 20, 1896.

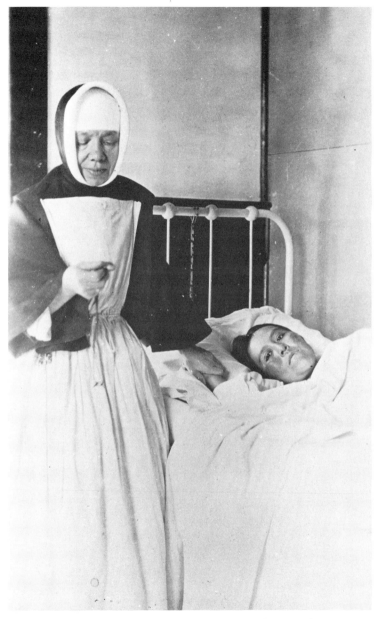

A Sister of Providence nursing a Coeur d'Alene Indian

ON BOARD THE SAILING VESSEL *The Fanny:* We left our dear "Maison Mere" [Mother House at Namur] on July 30th. We are ten Sisters . . . O! What bliss in the blending of souls when a Sisterly union brings such happiness on earth.

As the wind was contrary, we were obliged to wait nearly two weeks, until it changed, which took place on August 13. On the morning of that day, the captain came to inform us that we would sail that evening. During the afternoon Rev. Father Schoff S.J. came to hear our last confession on Belgian soil, soil so dear to our hearts . . . At 4 P.M. the Father gave us an exhortation . . . but not a tear was shed by the missionaries, so privileged to be chosen for America!

We reached the wharf about 6:30 P.M. [They sailed from Antwerp.] The crowd near the vessel was very dense. Sister Superior Stanislas had given a bottle of brandy to S. M. Donatilde to be used in case of sea sickness, and as Sister got out of the carriage, the bottle fell and broke; the strong perfume soon let the bystanders know the contents of the bottle, which made them enjoy a good laugh.

The vessel, "The Fanny," belonged to M. Spilliart of Antwerp. This was to be our home while crossing the Atlantic. Five cabins containing ten berths were assigned to us. We entered them and placed ourselves in the hands of Divine Providence, confident that we would reach the harbor in New York safely.

. . . The Captain and [we] ten Sisters were the only cabin passengers. Notwithstanding, the 10,000 francs from our dear S. Superior Marie de S. Francois had paid for our passage to America, [and] our very dear mother had amply provided us with all kinds of provisions. But heaven seemed to delight in delaying us by sending contrary winds, thus making it impossible for us to advance. Our

Students from the Convent of the Presentation among the ruins in the convent garden after the San Francisco earthquake, 1906

provisions were rapidly being consumed, hence we dreaded starvation on the ocean, and to increase our fears, the Captain told us that on his preceding voyage he had passed through that terrible ordeal. On such occasions, it is customary to cast lots on all on board, even on the Captain, and on whosoever the lot falls, that one must be killed and eaten. On that trip, the lot fell on a sailor boy. As soon as he was informed of his destiny, he asked the Captain, if a vessel were sighted, would he be spared? The poor boy, receiving an affirmative answer, quickly mounted the highest mast and, with the aid of a spy glass, sighted a ship at a great distance. Filled with untold delight, he hastened to give the joyful news to the Captain, who immediately hoisted the flag of distress on the most conspicuous mast . . . The good captain (of the approaching ship) had nothing but rice on board, and this he shared abundantly with the vessel in distress. Our captain gave them the filters belonging to our ship (for water), and failing to provide another, we were at this time deprived of that very useful convenience during a sea voyage.

[We were becalmed] for 24 days, and anchored before Ternense. Our diminishing provisions, fortunately, we were able to increase before launching on the deep. Our colony of 10 sisters with the Captain were the only cabin passengers. In the second [class], a man who had been captain in the army, along with his family, had full sway of that department. The third [class] passengers consisted of emigrants with their families. These, with the sailors, cabin boys, etc., formed the crew of "The Fanny."

On Wednesday, Sept. 4, 1850, the captain made his usual daily visit to Ternense and, on his return, handed us a letter from our beloved Mother Constantine, which ended, "Now sisters, in the name of the Good God, I command you to start!" Scarcely had we finished reading this sentence, when the Captain hastily entered the cabin, saying, "Good news, Sisters, the wind has changed at last, we leave immediately." The anchor was raised and in a very short time we [sailed] onward, no more retracing our course.

But oh! About five o' clock the terrors of sea sickness seized us. While under this feeling, we cared very little what became of us. We felt that nothing save death could relieve such anguish. Impossible to depict the sleepless nights of torture. S. M. Donatilde & M. Icavarius were the only ones spared, but their gentle ministrations could not bring comfort to the poor sufferers.

The following day, between 5 and 6, we were opposite England, and we heard the Captain say, "Sisters, by a special protection of the Good God, we find ourselves almost miraculously on the broad ocean. We are sailing on the Atlantic. I have never made this distance in my life in that length of time, it has always taken 11 or 12 days." We attributed this remarkable gain to the prayers of our venerated Mother Constantine, in whose great heart every one of her children was made to feel she held a place. We did not however expect, or even hope, to be favored during our entire trip, as this remarkable headway had been a great gain. The dangers naturally attending a sea voyage seemed nothing compared to the one in store for us.

One Friday evening after supper, while the Captain was conversing with us in the cabin, the first mate entered, carrying a very large lantern. In this lantern was a man's skull, under which was written in large, conspicuous letters, "Prepare for Death." He stood before every one of us, showed the contents of the lantern, then left the room. We then asked the captain for an explanation of that scene. His reply was that he had until now concealed from us that there was a mutiny on board. The captain in the second cabin wished to kill the Captain and the first class passengers, then take possession of the ship. He had already gained to his side one half of the steerage passengers. The Captain, however, did not seem anxious, as the Azore Islands were in sight, and this disturber could easily be put ashore.

We all begged and implored the Captain not to make the first attack; this he finally promised, but remarked, "I must make precautions for self-defense." As the Captain did not know at what moment the mutineers would break for us, he told us not to appear on deck next day, and to keep our post port holes and blinds closed. That night he loaded 18 pistols, 18 guns, 2 cannons, sharpened 18 swords, 18 knives, 18 daggers, etc. Then during the dead silence of the terrible night of Sept. 18, 1850, he discharged the artillery from the deck. This was done to let the mutineers see that preparations were being made for any emergency.

We, in the meantime, were perfectly resigned to do God's holy work, feeling assured nothing could befall us without His adorable permission. Still, the danger was such as to give us an opportunity of making the sacrifice of our lives to our Heavenly Father. Nothing more took place during that eventful night. The wise measures of the Captain in discharging the artillery opened the eyes of the insurgents, and their wicked scheme was not carried out: still we continued in a state of great anxiety until Oct. 21, when we were able to return grateful thanks to Divine Providence, to our Immaculate Mother, and the whole celestial court.

From September 18th, we had very calm weather, not advancing more than 4, 5, 6, and 7 knots per hour. On Sept. 28, our vessel was surrounded by beautiful dolphins; they seemed to crave protection from our ship. We remarked to the Captain that these dolphins were more beautiful to see, "Oh yes," he replied, "very beautiful to look at, but their harboring around the vessel predicts the approach of a very severe storm." All the sails of the ship were ordered lowered. Scarcely had this been done, when the wind began to rise, and in a few moments, we were tossed by the most terrific tempest. Not an eye was closed during that night, as the storm increased until Sept. 29, feast of St. Michael, when it was at its height. As we had already prepared for death, this new danger did not disturb our peace of soul; we realized that we were in the hands of God after leaving our very dear mother, and the dear mother house, and our own country to go to the New World, to labor for the salvation of souls. Divine Providence would watch over us.

. . . The storm raged until Tuesday, Oct. 1, when the weather became calmer. On Monday the 7th, our captain informed us that we had escaped another great danger, for a water-spout had struck the ship. Fortunately our Captain, who was on watch, perceived it in time to save us. The poor emigrants were the greatest sufferers, as their cabins were all under water. Every person on board, the 10 Sisters excepted, lent a helping hand at the pumps, with God's help this was the means of assuring our safety once more.

After the storm came a calm, which we experienced on the feast of St. Francis Borgia, Oct. 10th. When we were becalmed, our vessel stood perfectly still. The waters of the ocean were so exceptionally clear that we could see a most beautiful variety of colored stones on its bottom. While in this motionless state, a very large whale was perceived spouting around; here again God's protection covered over us by directing the whale in an opposite course, and our poor vessel was spared one more upset. In the evening of the same day, we witnessed the grandest sight of our voyage, a Sunset at sea! How different than on

5 3
≥●

*Sister*
*Mary*
*Alenie*

terra firma. We were really lost in contemplation . . . if St. Theresa was wrapped in contemplation at the sight of a little flower, how sublime would have been her vision at this grand scene . . . We fairly beseiged heaven with fervent prayers for favorable wind that would bring us to the land of our desires. The next day God heard our prayers, and our ship made 6, 7, 8 knots an hour. Our Captain was obliged to deceive his enemy, who was still on the war-path, and would come regularly on deck to see how we were advancing. This he did by writing 10, 11, or 12 knots on the slate, and he (the enemy) imagining we were thus near New York, began his preparations to land, while we were still very far on the broad ocean. We profited by our delay to study the English language. [Her journal is written in perfect English.] Sr. Eusebie, who was quite proficient in that language, kindly gave us lessons.

I think I omitted telling you that our Captain is a very fervent Catholic; he has great devotion to the Blessed Virgin, and daily retires to his cabin where he says his rosary. Are you surprised then, to hear of our numerous miraculous escapes? This good Captain loves St. Anthony, and recites his litany very faithfully on Tuesdays. He is very attentive to our needs . . . and in all our intercourse with him, his demeanor was most respectful. He was accompanied by his wife as far as Ternense, but had no permission to take her further. When we were within 500 miles of New York, another terrific storm came upon us, and this attended by more danger . . . We learned afterwards that a vessel which had braved the terrific storms of mid-ocean was wrecked here. The fog was so dense they could not see the rock which caused their destruction.

On the morning of October 20th, the first rays of the sun revealed to our eager gaze the shores and mountains of the "New World," the land of our sighs and hopes! Oh! How grateful we were. Our eyes fairly feasted on the dense forest covering the grand picturesque mountains [as] we entered an immense basin called the lower Bay at dawn on the feast of St. Ursula, Oct. 21.

. . . We were prepared to pay heavy custom-house duties, having a large number of well-filled boxes, but S. Anthony was our business agent, and a very successful one at that. The Captain invited the custom-house officer [a member of the Freemasons, who were anti-Catholic at the time] to dine with us. We found him exceedingly obliging; our boxes were not opened, [and] they passed free of duty. When the custom-house officer returned to shore, he kindly sent us a basket containing a variety of delicious fruit.

At last we were able to say a fervent DEO GRATIAS as we stood on American soil, so long the object of our burning desires. Would that I could depict the lively emotion of our grateful hearts, but this I must leave to your own imagination. Such emotions could never be portrayed by pen or paper.

As we drove down the streets of New York, we were much surprised to see the car conductors dressed like citizens . . . so different than in Europe.

On October 26 we resumed traveling [to the convent of Notre Dame in Cincinnati] and joined our other sisters on a steamer on the Hudson river, where the captain had already transferred our baggage. After a few hours we reached Albany, took dinner at a hotel, and about 2 P.M. we boarded a train as far as Lake Geneva [New York], where another steamer awaited us: on this steamer we met a young lady somewhat advanced in years, who begged us to receive her as a postulant, but the poor young lady was refused on account of her age.

At 9 P.M. we changed from the steamer to the cars again.

There were about 30 cars, so crowded that we could get no seats, but . . . a kind gentleman, who we sur-named St. Rafael the Archangel, begged to have another car attached to the train; his request was granted and we entered [it] together. Several of the windows were broken, so the snow drifted in freely. This our kind friend stopped by hanging his cloak against the windows, and walked up and down the car all night. On reaching the station, we were to leave the cars, but the drivers of the omnibuses fairly bewildered us by their screaming. It was impossible to decide which one to take. Finally Sister Superior Louis de Gonzagne [who had come to New York from Cincinnati to accompany them] said she would take the one belonging to the hotel nearest to Lake Erie, thus settling the matter. As a storm was raging on the lake, we were obliged to remain four days in Buffalo. During that time, we were happy being able to assist daily at Holy Mass and receive Holy Communion.

We were also very much surprised to see pigs roaming about the streets. In Belgium such animals are not allowed to promenade with the people.

. . . At last, heaven be praised, we were at the station in Cincinnati and, at 9:30 P.M., at the door of our cherished convent on 6th street. Guess who opened the door? Our own beloved Sister Superior Louise. Her first words to us were "Welcome, you arrive here just ten years after us, we in 1840, you in 1850, and at the same hour." Our feelings were beyond expression. We were at last in America! Yet in coming here, I had no intention of remaining in the United States. [Oregon was then outside the United States' dominion.] I thought they were too near Belgium in civilization [so] before entering the carriage in Namur, I had hastily run to put a letter on our dear Mother's desk, begging the favor of being sent to Oregon by the first occasion.

[*Notre chere Mere*, or "our dear Mother," is used when referring to the mother general of the order.] Now, in Cincinnati . . . I heard a knock at the door . . . it was Sister Superior Louise. I was startled by her great humility. She sat near me and, among other questions, asked if I had ever desired to go to Oregon. "Yes!" I replied. "Is the favor granted?" Our dear S. Superior replied, "Yes, notre chere Mere gives her consent. Here is a letter for you."

My joy was intense. I wept for gratitude. From that moment I devoted myself with double zeal to learn English and practice on the piano, which I had not touched since leaving school in 1844.

Immediate preparations were made for our departure on the first steamer that would leave for the Pacific Coast. But for some unaccountable reason we were delayed. Afterward, we looked upon the delay as Divine Providence, when we heard the steamer had sunk before reaching Chagres [Panama].

We were 4 Sisters named for the Oregon mission; S. Julia had been selected, but Heaven willed otherwise and S. Aloysius took her place. S. Mary Donatilde, S. Catherine, and your humble servant formed the Missionary band for Oregon.

Traveling at that time was very dangerous, hence our prudent superiors waited for confident persons who could consider our interests their own, and [these] we found . . .

We left our dear convent in the evening. It was as dark as the night we arrived, so we saw nothing of the city. We went directly to the ladies of the Sacred heart on reaching New York . . . [The nuns did not leave New York until May 13. The final California-bound party consisted of the Reverend Father O'Connell, six sisters (two of the Dominican order and four sisters superior of Notre Dame) and two priests in two cabins on board the steamer *Empire City*.]

First communicants in Monterey, California

Young Catholic girls being blessed by Franciscan James Del Valle (left to right: Isabel Del Valle, Felicidad Abadie, Matilde Rimpau, Josefa Del Valle, Frances Alexander, Alice Bowers, Sofia Rimpau, Rosa Del Valle)

As we neared Chagres, where we were to land, we asked Rev. Father O' Connell if he could hear our confession before we left the steamer. At this time I could not explain myself very distinctly in English, but . . . [managed] to write down what I wished to say. We put black lace veils over our caps, for we were dressed as seculars. The sisters begged me to go first. On entering Father's cabin, I was struck by his great humility. He had spread his cloak on the floor to serve as a carpet. I immediately took it up, shook it, folded it carefully and placed it on the bed . . . after I had opened the way, the other sisters found it easier to follow.

Thursday, May 22, 9 A.M. found us at the entrance of the Chagres river. A canoe rowed by Indians came to meet us, took us to the middle of the river, then left us there and went away. In a few moments a severe tropical rain came near sinking our little canoe. The day passed and still found us in this distressing plight. Before leaving the "Empire City" we had put on calico dresses; hence [if] we had been plunged in the river, we could not have been more completely drenched. When the rain stopped, we saw the shores of the Chagres river crowded with men crying out, "Ladies, go no further, you will be murdered." But what could we do? There we were, stationed in the middle of the river, without oars, unable to stir. Our party consisted of nine persons: Rev. Father O'Connell, Mr. & Mrs. Hefferman, and the 6 sisters. As it grew dark ten naked Indians armed with knives, daggers, and bundles of dried roots came to our canoe. The good God . . . visibly held us in his hands. The moment of our deaths had not yet come. Divine Providence inspired Dr. Rabbe (a Jew) to come to our rescue. He came to us accompanied by other gentlemen, well armed, with pistols. These good gentlemen told the Indians they would kill them if they did not row us at once to the shore. As they were cowards, this frightened them and they did so very quickly. Dr. Rabbe also obliged them to return our money, which they threw on the sandbank. The good Dr. Rabbe conducted us to a hotel near the river. Once there, we were glad to be able to change our dresses and take supper, for we had not [eaten] dinner that memorable day.

The room assigned us contained two beds; a piece of calico was an apology for a door. We had seen a crowd of men in one of the rooms, trying to rest before traveling the next day. Rev. Father O'Connell insisted on our trying to sleep, assuring us that he and Mr. Hefferman would guard the calico, one on each side, with loaded pistols. Sleep was impossible, tired out as we were, for the Indians were roaming around the hotel with their musical instruments which sounded like a hammer striking a tin pan. Of course we did not take off our clothes.

The sun rose brilliantly on the morning of the 23rd. The weather was delightful . . . and we took passage on a small steamer that ran from Chagres to Gorgona. The landlord advised us to take provisions for one day, as Gorgona would be reached by evening. Early in the morning, guided by our visible Angel Dr. Rabbe, we boarded the steamer, considered superb in those days. While on deck admiring the grandeur of the tropical scenery, we heard loud voices saying, "Ladies downstairs!" We obeyed, but Mrs. Hefferman said, "I am not going down, I must know and see what is going on."

A few moments afterward she came to us, saying that the gentlemen had requested us to go down as they wished to save us from the unpleasant sight of two murdered bodies floating on the river. These unfortunate persons proved to be the two Germans who had started in the canoe before us.

. . . At that time the United States was building a railway across the Isthmus of Darien, but the work was carried on very slowly, the men being frequently in a starving condition, as the provisions forwarded them by the government were taken, and the messenger killed. This caused a great delay, as no one was left to tell the tale, and [there was] no means of communication from the workmen.

As the Chagres river was very low, the steamer made little headway [and] the first day we were sand-bound, our provisions giving out. Fortunately, we had with us a box of sea biscuits, which our dear S. Superior Louise sent out to the sisters in Oregon. This we gave to the Captain, and indeed, it was most gratefully accepted. At the end of the third day, the Captain went on shore to look for a means of getting to shore as the steamer could go no farther. During his absence we took a walk on the shore, to admire more closely God's beautiful scenery. How can I describe the mountains, cascades, rivulets, the beautiful shrubbery and gorgeous flowers, wafting their perfume far and near? We could in these enchanting surroundings almost forget our perilous situation. How our hearts were uplifted to the great Creator! This gratification, however, was purchased by a little thorn. I caught a branch of poison oak, and was entangled in it. When we returned to the steamer, our walk made us very thirsty, and a glass of Chagres water was given us. We felt its poisonous effect at once. Good Father O'Connell came near dying. We fabricated a bed with carpet sacks (there was no such luxury as beds on the steamer) and applied such restoratives as were at hand. He revived, thanks be to God, but rather slowly.

The Captain's return was hailed with delight, as he had gotten a large rowboat, which took us to Gorgona that evening, very tired and half-starved. Our accommodations were somewhat better than Chagres, but still, this meant very little. Noise and bustle were the same throughout the long weary night, and it was impossible to sleep. We gladly welcomed the dawn of day, and blessed the Lord for preserving us again that frightful night. After breakfast we were told that our mules were ready . . . I paid $64.00 for 4 mules and the transportation of our baggage as far as Panama. A boy between 12 & 13 was to be the guide of the company. Just as Sister Donatilde mounted, her mule gave a jump which prostrated the poor sister to the ground, to the great amusement of the lookers on. Rev. Father O'Connell had a very slow mule, so had your humble servant. Fortunately for us, the good Sisters of Mercy in New York had provided us with drawers. We were very glad of their forethought, for while crossing the Isthmus, we found them a necessity.

. . . Through the mountain gorges, one mule trots very quickly, another slowly, while the third is very slow. The grandeur of the scenery is a subject of deep meditation, as in some places the passage of mules seems almost miraculous. Our boy guide was only seen in the evening, but happily the mules were drilled to the road . . . To describe the road crossing the Isthmus of Panama [is impossible]. You must go through it to conceive any idea of its dangers. Streams have to be crossed on mules. Frequently the water is so deep that it is impossible not getting the feet wet. Then [would come] dry rugged land, deep into which the poor mule would stumble, or projections from the mountains, which obliged us to bend over on the neck of the mule to avoid being crushed. In passing through a forest, the foliage . . . was so dense that we were grateful to escape with our clothes intact. S. Louis of the Dominican Sisters left her veil entangled in the branches. Again we had to ascend a mountain which seemed to reach to the skies, by a narrow winding path, to the left of which was a deep precipice. We feared to turn our heads, lest we become dizzy and roll to the bottom. We came across mules that had dropped dead under heavy burdens. At one point of this perilous road, I was entirely alone. God knows where the rest of the company were . . . This just happened to be the most rocky place [and] my mule, which until now had traveled very slowly, took fright and began running so quickly that I was thrown off on the sharp rocks. God in his mercy stopped the mule, otherwise my head would have been crushed to atoms, as the foot which had gotten tangled in the poison oak on the banks of the Chagres river had become so swollen that I could not extricate it from the stirrup. I remained some time in this trying position, renewing the sacrifice of that life which He had spared on "The Fanny," and on the Chagres river. I was at that moment perfectly calm and resigned to God's holy will. Grace worked in my soul, and I felt this was one of the happiest moments of my life, though I never had an unhappy one. This [moment] bore the impress of pure joy, as on the day of my first communion, and my cherished vows. Still, God's holy will was to prolong my existence.

. . . Mrs. Hefferman had given me a belt containing $200 when we left the "Empire City," saying that the Indians might suspect she had money and would kill her, but would never touch a religious. The responsibility of the money gave me a very uncomfortable feeling. As we rode along, we saw a man hanging to a tree . . . and went to him quickly, and to our great joy found that he was not dead . . . The Indians had taken the $200 he had for passage to California. He was placed on Mrs. Hefferman's mule, then we four continued our journey. That evening we sighted Panama. Here, the beauty of the surrounding country surpassed anything we had yet seen. The high mountains, covered with luxurious vegetation, the waterfalls glistening under the rays of a gorgeous tropical sunset, wrapped our souls in sweet contemplation. On entering town we were taken to a hotel, where a Spanish supper was prepared for us. This cooking was so different . . . that we could hardly eat it. Our sleeping apartment was a very large room containing berths like on steamers, in place of beds. The heat was so intense we could get but little sleep . . . As S.M. Donatilde was about putting on her bonnet in the morning, an enormous rat jumped out. These disgusting animals had been promenading from berth to berth all night. The next morning, May 25th, being Sunday, we went to Mass . . . The Rev. Fr. O'Connell kindly went in search of a convent. Only one remained, in which there were four very old religious of the Immaculate Conception. We were taken to this place, that once bore the name of convent, but was in such dilapidated condition that it resembled a barn more.

. . . These good religious were so poor that they could not let us have our meals, so the Dominicans and one of our Sisters of Notre Dame went in the town to buy what we needed. On the Rotation days . . . while our sisters were out visiting the churches, one of the old Religious made me drink a small cup of black coffee with brandy in it. I felt great repugnance to take it, but did so through a spirit of obedience and mortification, which the good God seemed to bless, as the dose cured me.

On Ascenscion Thursday, the good Father O'Connell went to ask permission of the Bishop to say Mass, but could not make himself understood in Latin, and not knowing Spanish, was deprived of that happiness. We heard Mass at the end of a large Church, from which a grating separated us. We could see cattle walking through God's holy house. The priest came from the altar to the grating,

Main plaza in front of the Cathedral of San Fernandes, San Antonio, Texas

which was quite a distance, to give holy communion to a few of us. Some of the sisters were too frightened and horrified at their surroundings, and preferred waiting. The Mass lasted about 25 minutes . . . the four Religious of the Immaculate Conception had neither chairs or benches; they sat on their heels with their little dog near them. When Rev. Father O'Connell saw the poverty of these religious, he thought it better for us to return to the hotel, where we could be much more retired, as we would not have to leave the house to procure our meals. As our hotel was near the bay, we could easily walk on its shores, and we gathered a most beautiful collection of pebbles . . .

In the early part of June, the "Sarah Sands," an English steamer, was making her last trip to California before returning to England, and we gladly secured passage on her. She was at the entrance of Panama Bay, and we were conveyed to her by a little tug boat. There are no such conveniences as wharves in Panama, so we were obliged to allow ourselves to be carried by Indians to the tug. However, S. Louis O.S.D. would not consent to this arrangement. She preferred walking upon the marshy beach, but alas! The tide rose suddenly, and the poor sister would certainly have drowned had not the Indians hurried to her rescue and brought her, drenched to the skin but safe, to the tug where we anxiously awaited her.

. . . During our first night on the ocean, a frightful tempest came upon us, followed by an earthquake, which is said to be far more terrible on the ocean than on land. The next day, the weather was delightful, and we realized that we were on the ocean whose calm rippling waters drew from Balboa its significant name Pacific.

A number of emigrants were huddled together in the steerage, while the cabin passengers numbered 45. Among them was a lady whose babe lay at death's door. The poor mother expressed deep regret that there was no protestant minister on board to baptize her darling. On hearing this I carefully watched a favorable moment to open heaven for this precious soul. My earnest desire was granted; the afflicted mother left her little one a few seconds [and] during that time I slipped in, baptized the poor child, then hurried away. The next day it went to heaven and, we hope, obtained graces.

While the vessel anchored at Acapulco to get provisions, we went on shore to visit the church. The heat at this place was intense. We bought a few fresh eggs, and when we returned to the steamer, we amused ourselves by cooking them in the scorching sun that beamed upon the deck . . .

Saturday, June 28, we were making great headway on the Coast of California. On Tuesday, July 1st, the fog was so dense that the Pilot steered towards Oregon, but at midday, perceiving his mistake, he retraced the route to California and we entered the great "Golden Gate" so appropriately named, and so majestic to behold. The magnificence of the scenery, the calm waters of the Bay, so deeply impressed us; yet the sight of the town had quite the contrary effect. There we realized one was the work of the Creator, the other of creatures. When the steamer reached the harbor, a crowd of men boarded her, and the first information given was that of the terrible conflagration during the preceding month. [San Francisco had many damaging fires in addition to those caused by earthquakes.] It had destroyed the greater portion of the city . . . We decided that the very name California was synonymous for the rendezvous of all the criminals of the universe, whose only aim was to get gold by murder and robbery. I remarked to the sisters, "What a blessing we are not to remain in such a country!"

When Right Reverend Bishop Alemany, accompanied

by his vicar Rev. Father Langlois, boarded the vessel, Father O'Connell knelt for his blessing, but his lordship bade him rise quickly, saying, "We cannot do this in this protestant country." Having placed the two Dominican sisters under his vicar's care, he turned to me and remarked, "So, dear sisters . . . you will all remain in California. We have no convents, no schools, you may go where you wish, this new country is at your disposal." Then respectfully we informed his lordship that our Superior General had given us strict orders not to remain in any place they wished to keep us, as our mission was for Oregon.

"Well, then," his lordship replied, "Half may go, the other half remain here."

"Oh no, Lord," I quickly answered.

The good Bishop listened very patiently to me, then, quietly taking a letter from his pocket, said, "Sister, please read this." On opening the letter, I found it to be from Sister Superior Loyola, stating that during her long stay in California waiting for us, Divine Providence had made other arrangements, and it was evidently the holy will of God that the sisters should have a foundation in California. Immediately upon reading this letter, I felt a complete transformation in my sentiments. I felt perfectly happy, calm, and resigned to the holy will of our heavenly Father. I said to myself, this is indeed God's own work. I did not ask to come here, I dislike the place, I begged of our dear Mother Constantine to send me to Oregon, but to have the merit of obedience, now I am perfectly satisfied. I am in the hands of the good God. He will take care of me as He has always done.

63
ﻉ

*Sister*
*Mary*
*Alenie*

Mountain cabin in Virginia, typical of the trans-Allegheny area where itinerant preachers ministered

# David McClure

"I felt . . . that I should not . . . go among the Indians. The idea of wild Indians was an impression on youthful minds at that time of some degree of terror, as [the Indians] had spread desolation among the English settlements. [But] I concluded it to be my duty to accept the invitation & accordingly . . . embarked . . . amidst the tears & affectionate embraces of my Mother & the blessing of my Father."

—David McClure,
leaving for Dr. Wheelock's college

David McClure, although serving only briefly as a traveling missioner, actively evangelized the Delaware nation during America's first great expansion: the push west of the Appalachians before the War of 1812.

McClure was born in Newport, Rhode Island, on November 18, 1748, and spent much of his early life in Boston, tending his father's small grocery store. A religious youth and a scholar, he had read the Bible through many times. When his father's business failed, he was sent at the age of fifteen to Dr. Wheelock's missionary school at Lebanon, Connecticut, to prepare to minister to the Indians.

He entered Yale in 1765, graduated in 1769, and began his Western mission in 1772, after ordination as a Congregationalist minister. His task: to convert the Delaware Indians on the Muskingum River in Ohio. Nothing, however, in McClure's early writings indicates an interest in Indians. In fact he often spoke of his fear regarding "the savages," and he dreaded working among them.

McClure found Ohio highly charged with prerevolutionary tensions and alive with Indians assisting their British allies against the hated colonists. The Delawares at Muskingum were predictably hostile and often murdered settlers. Fellow missionaries were also unfriendly—particularly Presbyterians, who distrusted the more cerebral Congregationalists. They were irritated that McClure and his companion, Frisbie, did not "belong to a presbytery" and viewed them as propagators of rational thought over religious belief.

McClure's mission eventually failed. He was unable to establish a mission among the Indians, although he tried repeatedly. He returned to New Hampshire and married Hannah Pomeroy, the niece of Dr. Wheelock. The remainder of his life was devoted to scholarly study of the Bible and to raising his family. He died at East Windsor, Connecticut, on June 25, 1820.

JULY 7, 1776.—Set out from Lebanon Crank for Onoida in company with Messrs. Kirkland; Aaron Kenne; Teconda, a Seneca chief who came with Mr. Kirkland; & three Indian lads . . . We passed through the fine country of the German flatts, & the upper settlements of the Castle of the Mohawks called Cagnawaga. From the German flatts we had a wilderness of about 40 miles to the place of our destination . . . Night overtook us before we could get through. We groped in the darkness among the trees to find the path. Mr. Kirkland, who had lived a considerable time among the Indians, late in the evening said he believed we were not far from an Indian encampment, as he smelled smoke. He hallowed or yelled in the Indian manner several times & was answered by a corresponding yell forward. We proceeded and soon discovered a light. We came to it, & found an Indian & his squaw & one or two children. The woman & children lay on boughs of trees around the fire, covered with blankets. The man was sitting by the fire, roasting, upon sticks stuck in the ground, a small animal that appeared like a Racoon.

Weary and sleepy, I was about to wrap myself in my great coat & lie down to rest. But Kirkland observed that it was contrary to rules of Indian politeness for strangers to encamp where females slept at the same fire. Taking a burning brand we went some rods distant & kindled a small fire, principally as a defense against swarms of mosquitoes & a very small fly, called a gnat.

I passed the night without very much sleep. A wide branching tree protected us from the dew. After returning thanks to God for his protecting care of us, we looked up our horses & set forward early in the morning & reached an Indian town about 6 miles from the place we had lodged.

This town was called the Old Onoida Castle & con-

tained fifteen or 20 log houses & bark houses. The Indians there had always shewn an aversion to attempts to Christianize them. We entered a house in which we were entertained with hospitality, perhaps from the expectation of receiving presents, which we bestowed at our departure. We carried some small articles of provisions with us . . . I was agreeably surprised to see the squaw of the house pour from a tea pot some tolerable tea for our breakfast.

We let our horses loose, & stung & tormented by the large fly, they ran furiously in all directions. My horse, seeing the door of an Indian house open, to get clear of his bloodthirsty enemies, rushed into it. I immediately followed & caught him & found the women & children within in a great fright. I apologized for the intrusion & they answered in their language, which was as unintelligible to me as mine to them.

The aversion of the human heart to the holy religion of the Saviour has been strikingly evidenced by the Indians of this town, in their rejection of repeated offers of missionaries & School masters. They chose to remain in pagan darkness . . .

JULY 23.—We arrived at the upper castle or village of the Onoidas called Canawahrookhahre. It contained about 40 dwelling houses of bark or logs. The Indians received us with kindness. Mr. K. conversed with them in their language. There was a small church made of hewed logs, in which they met on the Sabbath . . . I began to learn their language, & by Mr. K.'s assistance, we formed a kind of grammar of it.

Wah-wah-tu-vat-hah:  I am going hunting.

Wah-jah-tu-vat-hah:  You are going hunting.

Wah-hat-tu-vat-hah:  He is going hunting, etc.

1767, JUNE.—I returned to join my class at Yale College.

1771.—The winter of '71-2 I passed at College, part of the time attended the School. Theological authors & expositors of the Scriptures also engrossed my time. I preached in sundry towns & settlements near the College . . .

Dr. Wheelock [informed] me that there appeared a prospect of introducing Christianity among the Delawares & other Indians on the River Muskingum. He requested that two missionaries would go to be under the pay & direction of the Board of Correspondents in New Jersey. Mr. Levi Frisbie & myself offered to go.

1772, MAY 20TH.—Myself & Mr. Frisbie were ordained at Dartmouth College to the work of the Gospel Ministry. It was a solemn day . . . "And the Lord said, Who then is that faithful and wise steward, whom his Lord shall make ruler over all his household, to give them their portion of meat in due season?" [Luke 12:42]

. . . To those distant & savage tribes beyond the Ohio, no missionary from New England had ever gone!

JULY 16.—We arrived at the Rev. John Brainard's at Brotherton [about thirty miles southeast of Philadelphia] & tarried with him about a Week . . . The country here is poor pine barren, with here & there some good land. The soil abounds in iron sand Ore . . .

We found that there was no prospect of our having the company of the worthy Mr. Brainard to Muskingum. The reports which he had from Indians from that quarter were very unfavorable. Some murders of Indians by the whites, & of whites by the Indians had taken place near Pittsburgh. The Delawares at Muskingum appeared hostile . . .

67
ॐ

*David McClure*

Daniel Tuttle, Episcopal Bishop of Montana, Utah, and Idaho, established the first Episcopal church in the Montana territory in 1867.

We were at a loss what were the pointings of providence, relative to our duty.

We [then] became acquainted with the minister of the Lutheran Church, Mr. Henry Helmuts. He was a young man, had a wife & one Child . . . Soon after his arrival in Lancastshire, it pleased God to pour out a spirit of awakening among the people, particularly the large congregation of the Lutherans. It was a new and strange thing, among a people seemingly altogether absorbed in worldly pursuits & pleasures. They daily resorted to him, inquiring what they should do to be saved.

The work spread, & was deep and genuine. The principal men of his Congregation came to him, & told him that it was the work of the Devil, & he must suppress it. He told them that it was the work of God, & he must encourage and promote it. Their rage was incensed against him, & they threatened to dismiss him. He was constant in his attention to souls under conviction, in preaching, prayer, & conversion.

The opposition grew more violent as the work of God increased in the town . . . He mentioned that in [his] troubles he used to go to God in prayer for light & fortitude, & found it at times hard to say, "Thy will be done."

Mr. Helmuts proposed to the gentlemen in opposition that they should meet & confer on the important subject. Accordingly, they met at the school house. The leaders were filled with rage against him. With Christian meekness, he said that they needed divine light & direction from heaven . . . & that [he] would address the throne of grace. Wonderful was the effect!

The spirit of God came down upon them, & they who had nashed upon him with their teeth, when prayer was ended, with tears cried out, "Sir, what must we do to be saved?"

I heard him preach on Sunday . . . His manner was pathetic, affectionate & impressive. The music was solemn. The minister's salaries in this place are collected by contribution. This mode of collecting was new to me. At the close of public worship, about 6 men, each with a small black velvet bag fastened to the end of a long staff presented the bag, which had a small bell suspended at the bottom, to each person in the long pews. The tinkling of the bell gave warning of the approach of the little purse. The contribution was speedily finished.

AUGUST 3.—We left Lancaster & arrived at . . . Donnegall. We left Donnegall, & coming to the Susquehanna could find no boat to cross it, nor house nigh. The River was low, & about half a mile wide. A man passing by told us that we might ford it. I set out & Mr. Frisbie followed. It was a long and dangerous ride, the river rapid & the bottom stony and uneven. My horse often tripped, & the water camp up to the saddle. I fixed my eyes on the opposite bank, & kept a straight course. When I looked on the water, [I] could see the fish swimming around me: through good providence we got through, wet and weary.

AUGUST 12.—We set out . . . & in two hours arrived at the foot of the North mountain, which is the first of the Appalachians . . . The road was dismal. It was a hollow through the mountain about six miles, rough, rocky & narrow. It was a bed of stones & rocks which probably the waters falling from each side had washed bare . . .

The next day we rode across the Valley, & had before us the sublime prospect of the Allegheny mountain, which we soon began to climb . . .

Before we encountered this largest Mountain, we purchased, at the house of a hunter, a quantity of excellent dried Venison, at the cheap price of 3d. per cwt. This mountain is 11 Miles over. In some parts so steep, that we [had] to hold by the tails of our horses & let them haul us up. This mode . . . was not so safe as climbing, as we were wounded by the stones which their feet threw back upon us.

[Finally] ascending, we encountered & slew two Rattlesnakes. One had 11 and the other 8 rattles. They were not disposed to be hostile, until we attacked them. We descended, & at the setting of the sun came to the house of a Mr. Millar, 25 miles from Bedford, where we lodged. The growth of the mountain [is] different kinds of Oak, Chestnut, Walnut or Hickory, Wild Cherry, Sassafras, Honey Locusts & some Maple. Before our arrival at Millar's, met 15 horses carrying cannon balls from Pittsburgh to Philadelphia.

AUGUST 18.—Crossed the Laurel Hanning, a pleasant stream . . . Here we found Kiahshutah, Chief of the Senecas, on his way to Philadelphia . . . He was dressed in a scarlet cloth turned up with lace, & a high gold laced hat, & made a martial appearance. He had a very sensible countenance & dignity of manners. His interpreter informed him . . . where we were going. I asked his opinion of it. He paused a few moments, & replied that he was afraid it would not succeed: for, said he, "the Indians are a roving people, & they will not attend to your instructions." He also mentioned that there was a minister at Kuskuskoong, on Beaver Creek, & that one half of the Indians were offended with the other for hearkening to him.

. . . We [continued] travelling, [and] arrived a little before the setting of the sun at [Mr. Irwin's] house, but found it empty. The next house was 11 miles distant, & the road was through a wilderness. We proceeded on and were overtaked by darkness & rain, our horses frequently wandering from the path. About 11 O'Clock we passed through a cleared field, near to which Col. Bouquet fought the Indians in a bloody battle of 1764.

Wandering on, we came to the house of a Dutchman . . . but he refused to let us in. We proceeded on & crossed Bushy Run. The banks were mud & mire, the stream up to the horses' bellies, & such was the darkness that we could scarcely see the water.

By good providence we soon arrived at another Dutchman's, one Tegart. We knocked on the door & awoke one, who held a conversation with us while the rain was pouring down. At first he declined letting us in, alleging that the house was full of Indian traders from Pittsburgh. At last we wrought a little upon his humanity, & he unbared the door . . . Around the dirty room of the Log house lay asleep and snoaring a number of men. No bed or bedding was to be had. We persuaded the fellow who let us in to make up a fire. We were obliged, however, to bring in the wood, & we partly dried our clothes. He also brought us two dirty blankets, & spread them on the muddy floor, before the fire, and we lay down, supperless, to try to sleep. But such swarms of fleas from the blankets attacked us that sleep refused [to come] . . . We [finally] quitted our uneasy couch at dawn & got our horses. Mr. Frisbie's horse tiring, we walked most of the way to Pittsburgh, 7 miles. AUGUST 19.—Arrived at this place [Pittsburgh] about sun set. The first object of our attention was a number of poor drunken Indians, staggering & yelling through the Village. It is the headquarters of Indian traders, & the resort of Indians of different & distant tribes, who come to exchange their peltry & furs for rum, blankets & ammunition etc. . . .

The Fort is a handsome & strong fortification . . . The

Village is about ¼ Mile distant, & consists of about 40 dwellings made of hewed logs & stands on the bank of the Monongehala: opposite, on the south side of the river, is a hill of several miles in length, running parallel, which appears to be a body of stone coal [anthracite]. A smoak issued, in one place, from the top. It took fire accidentally a year past & has formed a small bason by the caving of the earth. The coal is used by the inhabitants.

AUG. 23.—Preached at the request of Major Hamilton, in the Fort, to a garrison [of] about 200 . . . A great part of the people here make the Sabbath a day of recreation, drinking & profanity . . .

Providentially, near Pittsburgh, we found a Christian Indian, who became our Interpreter. His name was Joseph Pepee, of the Delaware nation, and he was an aged man.

AUGUST 30.—Sunday I preached two sermons to a serious & attentive audience. Some of the settlers had not heard a sermon for 14 years. There was no settled minister or church organized in all the country westward of the Appalachian Mountains. The people are generally Presbyterians. A few illiterate preachers of the baptist persuasion have preached about, zealous to make proselytes.

SEPT. 1.—Mr. Frisbie remains unwell. It is the opinion of the Dr. that Mr. Frisbie [should not] attempt going into the Indian Country. It was indeed disagreeable to go without him, & to encounter the hardships of the wilderness alone, & without a companion with whom I could hold friendly & Christian conversation.

SEPT. 3 & 4.—Preparing for my journey to Muskingum. Engaged Robert McClellan to go with me as a waiter . . .

tarried at Mr. Gibson's over Sabbath . . . Monday, my interpreter not arriving, I set out with Robert to find him. Mr. Gibson was kind enough to ride with me to a small town of Mingo Indians, on the N. bank of the Ohio, & to send his servant a few miles further to show us the path.

The roads through this Indian country are no more than a single horsepath, among the trees. For a wilderness the travelling was pleasant, as there was no underbrush & the trees do not grow very closely together. We travelled diligently all day. I was apprehensive that we had missed the path. Robert was a great smoaker of tobacco, & frequently lighted his pipe, by striking fire, as he sat on his horse. Often in the course of the day he exclaimed in his jargon, "Ding me, but this path will take us somewhere."

At sun setting we arrived at Kuskuskoong, & found my interpreter Joseph there. He had been detained by the sickness and death of a grandchild.

SEPTEMBER 15, 1772—Set out . . . and crossed the Allegheny River. Came to Indian ground.

SEPTEMBER 16TH.—Came to the Mingovilage on Beaver Creek. On the green lay an old Indian, who, they said, had been a hard drinker. His limbs were contracted by fits. He told me his disorder was brought on him by witchcraft, that he had employed conjurers to cure him, but in vain. I called his attention to dependence on God, on death & Judgement, but he gave little heed. In answer he told my Interpreter to bring a pint of rum each time he came, and that he would be glad to see him every day. Awful stupidity!

[After] about one mile we came to a pleasant stream of water, where we encamped. My Interpreter kindled a fire & prepared a trammel supported by stakes drove in the ground, on which our kettle was suspended to boil, & assisted me to pitch the Tent . . . I spread a bear skin & blanket for a bed, & my portmanteau was the pillow. We supped very comfortably on chocolate & roast venison, & committing ourselves in prayer to the protecting care of heaven, we lay down to rest.

The Indian chose to sleep in the open air, the Englishman in the tent. I slept but little this night, being kept awake by the howling of Wolves. It was the first time I had ever heard their nightly dolorous yells. They came near the encampment, but the sight of the fire kept them off. Our horses we let go, each having a bell suspended to his neck. The feed in the woods was good and plenty.

SATURDAY 19.—Our path led us along the North bank of the pleasant river Ohio, almost the whole way from Pittsburgh . . . The sweetest red plums grow in this country, & grapes grow spontaneously & wind around the trees . . .

It would add unspeakably to the pleasantness of this solitary wilderness had I the company & Christian conversation of my friend Frisbie. My Indian Interpreter Joseph Pepee appears to be a sincere Christian, but the poor man is ignorant, his ideas contracted, & his english broken.

[David McClure continued along the Ohio River until he reached his destination, the settlement of Kekalemah-pehoong. He approached the Indian king and his counselors and requested the right to preach to them about Jesus Christ. The Indians were polite, but countered his request with an old letter they had received from Quaker missionaries in Philadelphia in 1771. The letter stated that when "true teachers" would come among the tribe, they would bear a letter from the Great Onas ("quill," or "pen")—the Indian name for William Penn, whom the Indians venerated.

They promised to think over McClure's request, but claimed they needed time. Meanwhile, several squaws came back from the trading centers with eighteen barrels of rum. Though the tribe had officially outlawed drink, the leaders were unable to contain it once it appeared. Violent drunkenness ensued, and one brave tried to kill McClure.]

OCT. 4.—SECOND SABBATH. This day they seem more disposed to noise & merriment, and to ramble about, than usual. With taking pains I got about 40 to assemble in the afternoon, and spake with freedom and great plainness on some of the most important truths of the gospel, particularly on a new heart, repentence, faith, and a life of religion, as necessary to happiness after death.

Some were affected and wept. In my discourse yesterday, I mentioned the necessity of receiving the word of God. After I had done preaching today, the Speaker, who appears to be a very sensible and thoughtful person, said to me:

"You have told us that we must receive what is in the book [the Bible].

We believe there is one Almighty, Monetho, who made all things.

He is the father of the Indians and of the White people.

He loves one as well as the other.

He has not sent the book to us.

If he intended it for us, he would have let us know it, at the same time that he let you know it.

We don't deny that the book is good, and intended for you . . .

But the Great Monetho has given us knowledge here (pointing to his forehead), and when we are at a loss what to do, we must think."

*David
McClure*

The king was present, and all seemed waiting for an answer. It was a deistical objection [based on belief in a personal God who is the creator, yet beyond the range of human experience], founded in the pride of erring reason, yet more than I expected from an uncultivated heathen. I spoke to him of the sovereignty of God in his gifts to nations, and to individuals . . . that the will of God revealed in the Bible, teaching men their duty and the way to endless happiness, was a favor that none could claim: but in his great mercy, to lost sinners, he had been pleased to communicate it to one nation in former ages, and commanded them to make it known to others . . . And [that] God commanded us to convey to them the knowledge of it.

To this he made no reply, but immediately started another objection:

"If we take your religion, we must leave off war and become as women, and then we shall be easily subdued by our enemies."

I answered: "We who embraced this religion were not subdued by our enemies, but were free and powerful. And that by embracing & practicing the duties of the Bible, they would be the same &c."

He again objected. "The white people . . . are more wicked than we. We think it better to be such as we are than such as they are."

Said Pepee [McClure's Indian guide]: "The white people with whom you are acquainted [trappers and fur traders] are not Christians. They do not know or do what God has told them in the Bible. Christians will not receive them into their society. If you want to see Christians you must go to Philadelphia . . . "

OCT. 6, MONDAY.—After breakfast [I] was about to ride a few miles to an Indian family [when] I perceived that my movements were watched, and that it was their intention that I should not visit other Indians.

Today, the King sent for me to his house, to deliver this answer:

"My brother, I am glad you have come among us, from such a great distance. Brother, you will now return home & when you get there, give my love to them that sent you. I have done speaking."

The prospect of helping these poor & perishing heathens was no more . . . I asked them what reasons I should give . . . for their rejection. One of them, with great anger, said they did not like that white people should settle upon the Ohio. They destroyed the hunting.

I mentioned that it was our intention to have procured a schoolmaster to instruct their children, and also to furnish them some utensils for husbandry, and a grist mill (as our worthy patron Dr. Wheelock had authorized us to do, and had given us blanks, for bills of exchange, on the school's funds in Scotland).

An aged Councillor & warrior . . . was present, and appeared to scoff at these proposals. [So] I thanked them for their civilities . . . rose, and bid them farewell.

Captain Killbuck [an American officer assigned to the area] came out with me . . . He, and the others, appeared a little surprised at the offer of implements of husbandry. He said, "Perhaps the Council will change their minds."

For the hostile appearance of things, I had, for several days, [feared] for my personal safety. The following circumstances were the ground of my apprehensions:

1. That a War Belt had been sent to them and neighboring Indians, informing them that the English colonists refused to obey the Great King of England, and that the Indians were invited to join in chastizing them.

2. While [I was] at Muskingum, news arrived that the

View of the side altar and confessional at the Mission in Santa Ynez, California, 1904

Wigwam altar decorated for a Catholic Corpus Christi celebration on a Chippewa reservation, in Wisconsin, June 1906

*David McClure*

Episcopal Chapel of the Messiah at Prairie Island, Minnesota, where Bishop Edsall gathers with his congregation

Baptist chapel at unnamed California site, possibly in a mining region

British troops were dismantling Fort Pitt . . . The warriors could not conceal their joy at this event. The fort had been a bridle upon them hitherto, in restraining their murders & depredations on the frontiers.

3. Some of the warriors had told me of their extreme resentment at the encroachments of the white people on their hunting ground. I asked one of them, "Have not the white people bought the land and paid you?" "Yes." "Well then, they have a right to use it." "No, not so," he replied, "for when you white men buy a farm, you buy only the land. You don't buy the horses and cows & sheep. The Elks are our horses, and the Buffaloes are our cows, the Deer are our sheep, & the whites shan't have them."

1772. FRIDAY, OCTOBER 9.—Set out . . . to return to Pittsburgh. We had fine weather, and killed plenty of wild game, particularly Turkies, with which the woods abounded.

On my arrival at Pittsburgh, found Mr. Frisbie in comfortable health. In my absence he had frequently preached to the people there, and in neighboring settlements.

Driven from the present prospect of usefulness among the Indians . . . we concluded to spend some months among the vacant & new settlements in those parts, where the numbers are daily increasing . . . I engaged to preach in rotation to five settlements between Ligonier and the Yohiogeny River. Another motive for continuing there was the hope—though distant—that the hearts of the Indians might be inclined to our return to them.

OCTOBER 28, 29.—Saw an Indian submit to the barbarous operation of having his hair pulled out of his head . . . and likewise his ears cut. An Indian dipped his fingers in ashes, and violently jerked out the roots, one lock after another, until his hair around the scalp was bald. He then laid his patient on his back, and placing a piece of wood under his ear, he cut, with his jack knife, the rim of each ear . . . On the bow made of the rim he fixed pieces of thin lead . . . to stretch it. [The Indian] bore the operation with wonderful fortitude. Now and then he shouted HOCKI, that is, I am a great man.

This is said to be preparation necessary for a warrior.

NOV. II.—LAST SABBATH . . . baptized 2 children of Mr. McKee, and one of Mr. Joseph Erwine. Some rigid Presbyterians in this settlement objected to me because I did not belong to a presbytery, but was a N. England Congregational minister. [American Presbyterianism, like the American government, was built from the bottom up. Its missionaries often distrusted the more intellectual Congregationalists and their offspring, the rational Universalists.] To remove this objection . . . I soon after [wrote] to the presbytery of Donnegal, & requested to be admitted, myself & Mr. Frisbie, which they accordingly did.

DEC. 17.—Attended a marriage, where the guests were all Virginians. It was a scene of wild and confused merriment. The log house which was large, was filled. They were dancing to the music of a fiddle. They took little or no notice of me . . .

After setting a while at the fire, I arose and desired the music and dancing to cease, & requested the Bride and Bridegroom to come forward. They came snickering and very merry. I desired the company, who still appeared to be mirthful & noisy, to attend with becoming seriousness, the solemnity.

As soon as the ceremony was over, the music struck up, and the dancing was renewed. While I sat wondering at their wild merriment, a lady sent her husband to me with her compliments, requesting me to dance a minuit with her. [My refusal] was scarcely accepted. He still politely urged, until I totally refused. After supper, I rode about 3 miles to the house of a friend.

The manners of the people of Virginia, who have removed into these parts, are different from those of the Presbyterians and Germans. They are much addicted to drinking parties, gambling, horse race & fighting. They are hospitable & prodigal. Several of them, having run through their property in the old settlements, have sought asylum in this wilderness.

DEC. 19TH.—Preached in the open air, by the side of a fallen tree, to a considerable numerous congregation, on evangelical humility, & was favored with a comfortable degree of freedom.

Rode a few miles to the house of a Mr. Thompson, an honest and pious Scotchman, who had been prejudiced against me, on account of my not being, as he supposed, a true Presbyterian. Of the denomination of Congregationalists, the people here seem to have no knowledge. In their esteem, all sects of Christians are erroneous who do not bear the name of Presbyterian.

1773. JAN'Y I, WEDNESDAY.—Rode 7 miles to Mr. Stevenson's & preached. The hearers mostly Virginians. Preached in the open air. Several present appeared almost intoxicated. Christmas and New Year holidays are seasons of wild mirth and disorder here.

APRIL 6. TUESDAY.—Received a present of a location of land on Connemoh (about 300 acres) of my good friend Mr. McCune. (This right was however lost to me by the war, & my absence.)

On leaving Ligonier, we began to ascend the formidable mountains. In descending the eastern side of the Laural Hill, we came suddenly on a gang of Wolves. They were near the path, leaping down the Mountains. They were of different sizes and 7 in number. Two of the largest were each about the bigness of one large mastiff. They came & stood by the path, a few rods before us, and we had a fair view of them longer than we wished. They seemed fearless of danger, & we had neither pistol, nor any weapon of defense. They boldly stood, & filled the path before us, & we found no way to get by them . . . the sun shone bright on their winking eyes . . . Their bodies tapered off, from a deep chest to the hinder parts. Their eyes were small, & their ears were short and erect.

As those ferocious animals are unused to a human voice, I proposed to Mr. F[risbie] that we should hallow, & make the most frightful noises we could. This had the desired effect, and at the same time we rode slowly forward, they gradually withdrew from the path. It is said that when pinched with hunger, they will sometimes attack the horse & rider . . .

APRIL 7.—Crossed the Allegheny mountain. Saw a herd of Deer, who more timid than the wolves, ran from us & with surprising agility bounded over the side hill.

8 APRIL, THURSDAY.—Preached in Bedford, a settlement of about 20 families. The inhabitants west of the Appalachian mountains are chiefly Scotch Irish Presbyterians, [and] generally well indoctrinated in the principles of the Christian religion. The young people are taught by their parents and school masters, the Larger and Shorter Cate-

Laying the cornerstone of the Orabi Mennonite Missionary Chapel, Orabi, Arizona, 1901

David
McClure

A tornado levels the church in Herman, Nebraska.

chisms . . . Mr. Eurie lives in a small neighborhood of German Quakers, with whom he can have little or no religious society, as the most of them are very ignorant & bigoted.

FRIDAY.—Crossed Sideling Hill . . . passed a few log huts to-day. When in the valley in the evening, we had a sublime and awful prospect of the mountains on each side of the valley on fire. Either by accident or design, fire [had burst] from the dry leaves . . . on the sides of the valley, and was running up the sides of the lofty mountains to their summits, to an elevation of about 40 degrees. It had the appearance of the heavens in flames. The fire ran through the valley to the north of us, & in some places came within a few rods of the path. As we rode along the margin of the fiery element, & saw ourselves as it were, hemmed in between the flaming mountains, the scene impressed our minds with the majesty of God . . .

SATURDAY, 24.—Reached Ligonier. In this journey we overtook several families removing from the old settlements in the State . . . to the western country. Their patience and perseverance in poverty and fatigue were wonderful. They were not only patient, but cheerful and pleased with the hope of seeing happy days beyond the mountains.

I noticed one family of about 12 in number. The man carried an ax and gun on his shoulders—the Wife, the rim of a spinning wheel in one hand, and a loaf of bread in the other. Several little boys and girls, each [carried] a bundle according to their size. [They had] two poor horses, each heavily loaded . . . on the top of one was an infant rocked to sleep in a kind of wicker cage, lashed securely to the horse. A cow formed one of the company, a bed cord wound around her horns and a bag of meal on her back.

MAY 21.—Yesterday, descended the Chestnut ridge . . . and caught a young [bear] cub. The adventure was perhaps imprudent, & not without hazard, as I was alone and unarmed. After riding about . . . I pursued the little black animal into a thicket of young trees. He ran up one of them, and found no way to get down. I climbed the saplin, but not before looking about for the She bear. He ascended the highest part of the tree: the weight of both brought it down within a few feet of the ground. He fell, & I slipt down, & seizing my whip, pursued him up the bank of a river that ran through the valley. After repeated blows with the but of my whip, he was stunned and fell. With haste, and some fear . . . I dragged him to my horse, & here I was fearful I should loose him, as the horse appeared very reluctant to receive him on his back.

With much difficulty, having lodged him on a low limb of a tree, I got the horse so nigh as to haul him on, & place him before me. He fastened the nails of his fore paws in the horse's mane, & with one hand I held him up, & with the other guided my horse. I forded the river with my little savage companion, & rode about half a mile to the first house, in which a Dutchman lived, who was standing at his door.

Before I arrived, [the cub] had recovered from the effects of the blows, and was very cross and furious, & made several attempts to bite. I called to the man to take him as a present, & letting him drop, the Dutchman received him thankfully, & said he would make good pork of him . . . On reflection, I disapproved of [my action], & should not again have undertaken an adventure of the kind in the same circumstances.

JUNE 1.—Spent my time preaching to the people in the settlements on the Pennsylvania Road . . .

Yesterday arrived at my friend Eneas McKay Esq., at Pittsburgh. Very pleasant weather. Today, 11th, dined on green peas . . . Esq. McKay and his lady are well disposed people and friendly, at least to the form of religion. He keeps 4 or 5 negroes, some of them give him much trouble. One of them . . . came into the house to evening and morning prayer, with a large iron chain on him on account of his stealing and attempting to run away with a negro woman of the place. The poor wretch expressed to me his sorrow, and promised to do better. I interceded for him, and went with him and his Master to the Blacksmith, who filed the iron collar asunder and took off the chain.

In this family I have lived agreeably several weeks . . . for which they refused any compensation.

Being about to return to New England, the two last weeks, I visited the settlements in which I had spent about 7 months, & preached to them for the last time. I found many more friends than I expected, & the parting scene was solemn and affecting. They invited me to return, and gave me the promise of a decent salary & lands.

But we found no prospect of putting into execution the principal object of our mission, to carry the Gospel among the heathen; and now thought it our duty to return, to give account to our honorable employers. While we continued at Pittsburgh, we found that Indian affairs assumed a more hostile appearance, and that we could have no access to them, with any prospect of success, or EVEN PERSONAL SAFETY.

79
&

*David*
*McClure*

A baptism in Walnut Creek, near Mansfield, Texas, 1909

# Lorenzo Dow

"Many think that ministers have no trials. I am confident this is a mistake; there is no life more trying, yet none on earth more happy . . . "
—Lorenzo Dow,
*Exemplified Experience, or Lorenzo's Journal*, 1804

Lorenzo Dow—known as "Crazy Dow" throughout the backwoods of Kentucky and Georgia, in the valley of the Mississippi, and in his native New England—was a thin, sallow, and consumptive young preacher born in 1777. He often traveled without coat or shoes as he preached his Methodist "heart religion" from Canada to Mississippi, taking time from his American labors to visit the unconverted around the world. "In a few weeks I expect to start . . . WEST again," he wrote in 1817, "but where . . . is very uncertain with me, whether [west] England . . . West Indies—or ETERNITY!"

He proclaimed Methodism, yet proved too headstrong to submit to prescribed church discipline. Calling on families door-to-door, often accusing them of vice or indolence, he never left a village without arousing souls for God, or intense local ire. He was chased by Indians and assaulted at camp meetings by local toughs. The further Dow strayed from conservative expectations, the greater was his impact. According to his journal, thousands attended his camp meetings. He would schedule each nearly a year in advance, then turn up, to everyone's surprise, at exactly the moment foretold. He always sought a "melting and precious" response—yet threatened with the fires of hell in order to achieve it.

Dow had the ability to self-publicize, and his writings are unrestrained. Whether sued for libel by the descendants of a minister Dow had called a drunk, or sued by landholders downstream of his self-built dam, Dow spared not a colorful detail in his extensive memoirs. Although successfully sued in both cases, he entertained himself by viewing the jurists as "grasshoppers." Bemoaning his need to tear down his dam and free its waters to those below, he cried, "I CANNOT HELP MYSELF!—Farewell sweet freedom! My property I cannot call MY OWN! BROTHER GATE TENDERS, LOOK OUT!!!!"

He married Peggy Holcomb on September 3, 1804, on the condition that she would never interfere with his travels. Following this, he immediately left to preach in the South; he journeyed to England in 1805, and again in 1818. Dow died at the age of fifty-seven, in 1834.

I was born October 16, 1777, in Conventry (Tolland County), State of Connecticut, North America . . .

When I was between three and four years old, one day . . . I suddenly fell into a muse about God . . . so that I forgot my play, which my companion observing, desired to know the cause; I asked him if he ever said his prayers . . . to which he replied, no. Then said I, "You are wicked and I will not play with you." So, I quit his company and went in the house . . .

When past the age of thirteen years . . . I broke off from my old companions and evil practices, which some call innocent mirth . . . and betook to the Bible, KNEELING in private, which example I had never seen. Soon I became like a speckled bird among the birds of the forest, in the eyes of my friends . . .

About this time, there was much talk about the people called METHODISTS, who were lately come into the western part of New England . . . Some [said] they were the deceivers that were come in the last times . . . that it was dangerous to hear them preach, lest they should lead people out of the good old way . . .

Shortly afterward, several persons in the neighborhood professed to have found the pardoning love of God, among whom was my brother-in-law FISH.

Sorrows arose in my mind to think that they were heavenward, whilst I, a guilty one, was in the downward road. I endeavored to double and treble my diligence in prayer, but found no comfort to my soul . . .

One evening there being (by my desire) a prayer meeting . . . I set out to go; and on my way by the side of a wood, I kneeled down and made a solemn promise to God: if he would pardon my sins . . . I would forsake all [former] things, and lead a religious life devoted to him . . . One day, being alone in a solitary place, whilst kneeling before God,

these words were suddenly impressed on my mind: "Go ye into all the world and preach the gospel to every creature."

. . . I dared not believe that God had called me to preach for fear of being deceived; and durst not disbelieve it, for fear of grieving the spirit of God; thus I halted between two opinions . . .

MARCH 14. About this time, my uncle made me the offer of a horse, to wait a year for the payment, provided I would get bondsmen: four of the [Methodist] society willingly offered. O! from what an unexpected quarter was this door opened! . . . Not having as yet attempted to preach from a text, but only exercised my gifts in the way of exhortation, I obtained a letter of RECOMMENDATION concerning my MORAL conduct; this was all the credentials I had . . .

SUNDAY APRIL 3D. This day, for the first time, I gave out a text before a Methodist preacher, and I being young both in years and ministry, the expectations of many were raised, who . . . judged me very hard, and would not consent that I should preach there any more for some time . . . I met T. C. [Methodist minister Thomas Coope] who said, if I was so minded, I might return home; which I declining, he said, "I do not believe God has called you to preach." I asked him, "Why?" He replied, "1st, your health—2nd, your gifts—3rd, your grace—4th, your learning—5th sobriety—in these you are not equivalent to the task." I replied, "Enough!" Lord! what am I but a poor worm of the dust, struggling for life and happiness . . .

JULY 3D. This evening, our quarterly meeting being over, from the representatives . . . I received a dismission from the circuit, with orders to go home, which was as follows:

We have had brother LORENZO DOW . . . these three months past. In several places he was liked by a great many people; at other places, he was not liked so well, and at a few places they were not willing he should preach at all; we have therefore thought it necessary to advise him to return home for a season, until a further recommendation can be obtained from the society and preachers of that circuit.

—Jesse Lee, Elder
John Vanniman
Thomas Coope.

The time has been when I could easier have met death than this discharge. Two or three handkerchiefs were soon wet through with my tears; my heart was broke; I expostulated with them and besought him for farther employment—but apparently in vain. The next morning, as we were about parting, he said, "If you are minded, you may [come] to me [at the] Greenwich quarterly meeting next Sunday, on your way home . . . "

From thence to South Kingston, I set out to my native town . . . My parents asked me whether I was not convinced that I did wrong in going. I told them no; [but] others began to mock, and cry out, "This man began to build and was not able to finish."

After a few days I set out . . . to meet C. Spry, who gave me a written license, with orders to come to the ensueing quarterly meeting at Enfield, where he would give me a credential for the conference; and if I was so minded . . . I might travel the Tolland circuit until that time . . .

SEPT. 20TH. Conference came on in the town of Thompson, and I passed the examination by the BISHOP before them, [but] after some conversation . . . T. Coope, J. Lee and N. Snetheren bore hard upon me after I had been sent out of the room . . . so I was rejected and sent home, they assigning as the reason, the want of a written credential,

8 3
ह०

*Lorenzo
Dow*

"Father" Shepherd, the Hermit, possibly a cleric, and an old resident of Colorado, near Telluride

though the greatest part of them were personally acquainted with me.

This so affected me that I could take no food for thirty-six hours.

After my return home, still feeling it my duty to travel, I ... resolved to set off the next Monday: but PHILIP WAGAR, who was appointed for Orange circuit ... sent for me. After he had criticized and examined my credentials, he [took] me on his circuit.

Some weeks ago ... being troubled with the asthmatical disorder, I was necessitated to sit up some nights for the want of breath; but at length lying down on the carpet, I found that I could sleep and breathe easy ...

But September 27th, being on my way with P. Wagar, he said the people would despise me for my lodging, and it would hurt my usefulness: and he insisted upon my lying in bed with him, he thinking it was a boyish notion that made me lie on the floor. To convince him ... I went to bed, but was soon much distressed for want of breath, and constrained to arise and sit up all night. After which, I would be persuaded to try the bed no more.

NOVEMBER IST. I preached in Ringe, and a powerful work of God broke out shortly after, though some opposition attended it; but it was very solemn ...

Whilst I am preaching I feel happy, but as soon as I have done, I feel such horror (without guilt) by the buffetings of Satan, that I am ready to sink like a drowning man, sometimes to that degree that I have to hold my tongue between my teeth to keep from uttering blasphemous expressions, and can get rid of these horrible feelings only by retirement in earnest prayer and exertion of faith in God ...

AUGUST 6TH. After preaching in Conway, I went to Buck-

land; and when the people saw my youth, and were disappointed of the preacher they expected, they despised me in their hearts. However, God made bare his arm, and I have reason to believe that about thirty persons were stirred up to seek God from this day ... In several other places, there was a good revival likewise. At the QUARTERLY MEETING, I obtained a CERTIFICATE, concerning my USEFULNESS and CONDUCT here. [But] J. Lee and several others, of whom some were strangers to my person, took up hard against me, from say and hearsay; and only one at first espoused my cause ... The debate was sharp and lasted about three hours ... at length, it being put to the vote whether I should travel or not, about two-thirds of the conference were in my favor. All that saved me ... from an expulsion was the blessing which had attended my labors.

... I concluded I should be SENT HOME again. [Dow was sent home from the circuit a total of four times in his early career.] ... My trials were great; I was afraid I should become insane; and seeing no chance for my life, I publicly gave up the NAME of Methodist, and assigned the reason why, viz: because the preachers would not receive me as a brother to travel with them ...

But now arose a difficulty from another quarter: I had lost my GREAT COAT on the road whilst traveling, and my COAT was so worn out that I was forced to BORROW one; my shoes were unfit for further service, and I had not a FARTHING of money to help myself with, and no particular FRIENDS to look to for assistance. Thus one day whilst riding alone, facing a hard, cold northeast storm, very much chilled, I came to a wood; and alighting from my horse and falling upon my knees on the wet grass, I lifted up my voice and wept, and besought God either to release me from traveling and preaching, or else to raise me up friends. My soul was refreshed; my confidence was strengthened, and I did believe that God would do one or the other. And true it was; people a few days after this, of their own accord, supplied all my necessities and gave me a few shillings to bear my expenses . . .

After which, I traveled several days in company with S. Hutchinson, who was going to take me to the Cambridge circuit. And on the way said he, "The conference have had a great deal of talk and trouble concerning you, and now you are under my care, and you shall LIVE or DIE at the end of three months: if you are faithful and your labors blest so that you can obtain a recommendation from the circuit, all shall be well; but if not, you shall die."

After reaching the circuit . . . I was convinced that nothing but a revival could SAVE my life; I was therefore resolved to . . . get a revival or else get the circuit broke up. So I went visiting the people [for] house prayer.

Pittstown was the first place I thus tried on this circuit, and preached at night. Thus I did here, for several days successively, and it caused a great deal of talk. Some said I was CRAZY; others that I was possessed of the devil; some said one thing and some thought another. Many it brought out to hear the strange man, and would go away cursing and swearing, saying that I was saucy and deserved knocking down, and the uproar was so great among the people that the HALF-HEARTED and LUKEWARM Methodists were TRIED to the quick, and became my warm opposers, complaining of me to my traveling companion Timothy Dewey, whose mind at first was prejudiced! However, it was not long before I had the satisfaction to see some of the fruits of my labor there . . . Thus round the circuits I went, visiting from house to house, getting into as many new neighborhoods as I could, and sparing no character in my public declarations. Many were offended at my plainness both of DRESS, EXPRESSIONS, and way of ADDRESS in conversa-

tions about heart religion, so that the country seemed to be in an uproar; scarcely was there one to take up my cause, and I was mostly known by the name of CRAZY DOW . . .

After preaching at Fort Edward . . . I went to East-town. Here the youth, under plain dealing, would frequently leave the house [during preaching]. Accordingly, after procuring a schoolhouse, I invited all the youth to come and I would preach to them, and the house was filled from end to end; and then placing my back against the door (to prevent their running away), [I] gave out the text and did not spare, and was soon confirmed that God was about to visit the place . . . I besought them not to be afraid of each other, but to continue seeking the Lord . . .

One evening when T. DEWEY was exhorting, a flash of forked lightning pierced the air and rolling thunder seemed to shake the house. Some screeched out for mercy; some jumped out at the windows, and others ran out at the door. From this night the stir became visible, and thirteen of the youth that night resolved together to pursue religion, let their companions do as they would. A young man by the name of GIDEON DRAPER said, "If I can stand the CRAZY man, I will venture all the Methodist preachers to convert me." And when [I] heard of his expression, faith sprang up in my soul, and I felt a desire to talk to him. He objected, "I am too young," but here God brought him down, and he is now an itinerant preacher . . .

During these last three months, I had six hundred miles to travel in four weeks, besides meeting in class upwards of six hundred members and spectators, and preaching seventy or seventy-five times, and some visiting . . .

SEPTEMBER 10TH, having traveled about ninety miles on foot the preceding week, and preached nearly twice a day, I

85
ह

*Lorenzo*
*Dow*

thought that something broke or gave way in my breast . . . Whilst speaking in the chapel, my strength failed and I gave over, and brother Lodbel concluded the meeting. I went to his house, but was soon confined to the floor with a strong fever. [I was] destitute of money [and] bound in body. [There was] but one room in the house, and several children in the family; and the walking across the floor . . . caused a springing which gave me much pain—as I had but a blanket under me. A wicked physician was employed without my consent, whose prescriptions I did not feel freedom to follow . . . Being in this situation, I began to meditate what course to take, knowing that unless I could get help soon I must die . . . I was so weak that I could not bear the noise and shaking, and the extremes of heat and cold [from a] fire [that was] sometimes large and sometimes nearly out.

The man of the house . . . had now gone to conference. I, hearing of another family of Methodists who were rich, persuaded a young man without religion to make a BIER and sew a coverlet upon it, with which (the neighbors being called in) they carried me up and down hills (like a corpse) several miles to the rich man's house, where I expected the best attendance. But alas! I was much disappointed, for they seemed unwilling to assist me with nursing or necessaries; neither could I send to where I had friends, by reason of the distance. Here I despaired of life, and some who were friends to my manner of conduct reported that I was dead, from which it appeared they wished it were the case . . .

The first relief that I got during this illness was from a QUAKER who had accidentally heard me preach. On hearing I was sick he came ten miles to see me. I hinted to him concerning my situation; he went away and the next day came again and brought a quart of wine, a pint of brandy,

a pound of raisins, and half a pound of loaf sugar. These articles seemed to give me new strength, but were soon out. My nurse, who was a spiritual child of mine, offered to get me what I had need of at her own cost; but she having herself and two children to maintain, being forsaken by her husband, my heart was so tender that I could not accept her kind offer. Then she prevailed upon the man of the house, with much difficulty, to get me a bottle of wine. The reason (I suppose) they were so unwilling to supply me with what I stood in need of, was because they expected no recompense . . .

A man who had heard of me came fifteen miles to know my state and gave me a dollar. Soon after, two men who had heard I was dead, and then alive, and dead again, came thirty miles to find out the truth concerning me. I was glad to see them, and would take no denial until they promised to come with a wagon and take me away . . . The wagon came, and a message from a young woman that if I would come to her father's house, the best of care should be taken of me . . . I waited thirty-six hours for the rain to abate, but seeing it did not, I persuaded them to wrap me in a coverlet, and with straw under and over me we set out—and over rugged hills and mountains, [they] carried me twenty-seven miles in eight hours . . . At this time I was so weak that I was obliged to be carried . . .

The young woman made good her promise . . . and spared no pains for my comfort . . . One evening a thought came to my mind:

"Why is not God as able now to raise me to health as in primitive days?"

Something answered, "He is."

"Why is he not as willing?"

Something replied, "He is."

Another thought arose: "Why don't he do it?"

The answer was, "Because you lack faith."

It stuck in my mind, "Is faith the gift of God? Or is it the creature's act?" The reply was, "The power to believe is the gift of God; but the act of faith is the creature's." I instantly strove to see if I could act faith; and I did believe, if the young people in the room would intercede with God faithfully during that week, that God would, in answer to many prayers, restore me to health . . . Within fifteen hours I perceptibly began to amend; and by the goodness of God, after about ten weeks' confinement . . . I was able to ride alone.

JANUARY IST, 1799. I again renewed my covenant to be more faithful to God and man than I had been. I proceeded to Stockbridge and met my friend Hubberd, who was to go where I had come from, and I to supply his place on Pittsfield circuit. This circuit was in a very low situation, and the most despised of any, as they had frequently sent complaints to conference against their preachers. I at first refused to go to it, lest I should be injured by false brethren . . . But upon conditions that Dewey and Sawyer [fellow itinerants] would stand by me . . . I consented to go . . .

6TH. I preached in Pittsfield: the members were high in profession but low in heart; their prejudice being great, they did not invite me to their houses, but were sorry I came on the circuit . . . Went to Troy, where there was some revival in the class. Thence to Greenbush, where a glorious work of God began.

The second time I went to this place the people flocked out by the hundreds to hear the strange man preach up his principles. I told the people that God had promised me two souls to be converted from that day, and if my labors were not acknowledged, they might brand me in the forehead with the mark of liar, and on the back with the mark of hypocrite.

They watched my words. However, two who were in the assembly thought, Oh! that I might be one of these two; and shortly after both found pardon.

At Canaan-gore, a number of backsliders and sinners were brought to a sense of themselves and joined in a class, one of whom invited me to preach in Green River meeting house, as we had a right to it two days in the year.

As I entered the meeting house, having an old borrowed great coat on and two hats, the people were alarmed and thought it singular that I did not bow to every pew as I went towards the pulpit, which was the custom there. Some laughed and some blushed, and the attention of all was excited. I spoke for about two hours, giving the inside and outside of Methodism. Many, I believe, for that day, will be thankful; though I was strongly opposed by a reprobationist in the afternoon. My hat being taken from me without my consent and two others forced upon me, I was carrying one to give a young man.

In New Concord, religion being low . . . I besought God in public that something awful might happen in the neighborhood, if nothing else would do to alarm the people. For this prayer many said I ought to be punished.

One of a company of young people going to a tavern said . . . "I will ride the way Christ rode into Jerusalem." Instantly his horse started, ran a distance, and threw himself against a log. He spoke no more until he died, which was the next morning. In the neighborhood, the young people assembled again to a gingerbread lottery; and I preached . . . They were so struck that the fiddler who they employed had nothing to do.

At length a revival appeared visible . . . and numbers were added to class.

On my way to Spencertown, at a distance, I discovered a place in a hilly country where I thought God would immediately revive his work . . . I began immediately to visit the neighborhood from house to house. The people thought [it] strange (I being a stranger) and came to see where it would end.

Here too it was soon reported I was crazy, which brought many out to the different meetings, amongst whom was an old man who came to hear for himself and told the congregation that I was crazy, and advised them to hear me no more . . .

In Alford, I preached Methodism inside and outside. Many came to hear; one woman thought I aimed at her dress. The next day she ornamented far more, in order that I might speak to her. But I in my discourse took no notice of dress, and she went away disgraced and ashamed.

The brethren here treated me very coldly at first, so I necessitated to pay for my horse keeping for five weeks; and being confined a few days with the ague and fever, the man of the house not being a Methodist, I paid him for my accommodation. I had said in public that God would bless my labors there, which made the people watch me for evil and not for good. I visited the whole neighborhood from house to house, which made a great uproar among the people. However the fire kindled [and] the society got enlivened . . .

29TH. I rode thirty miles, preaching twice on the road . . . When I first came on this circuit, I felt like one forsaken, as they all appeared sorry to see me, and almost unwilling to feed me or my horse. For all my toil here, I received ten dollars, when my extra expenses were upwards of six pounds; so that when leaving it, I was sixteen pounds worse in circumstances than when coming. Yet it

afforded me comfort that I could leave them in peace and have a joyful hope of enjoying some of them as stars in my crown of glory, which I expected soon to obtain . . .

OCTOBER 28TH, 1803. After an absence of about seven months, I arrived back in Georgia, having traveled upwards of 4,000 miles . . . When I left this state I was handsomely equipped for traveling by some friends whom God had raised up . . . but now on my return, I had not the same valuable horse; and my watch I parted with for pecuniary aid to bear my expenses. My pantaloons were worn out; my riding chevals were worn through in several places.

I had no stockings, shoes nor moccasons for the last seven hundred miles [and] no outer garment, having sold my cloak in West Florida. My coat and vest were worn through to my shirt [and] my hat case and umbrella were spoiled by prongs of trees whilst riding in the woods . . . It is true I had many pounds and handsome presents offered me in my journey, but I could not feel freedom to receive them. It was with seriousness and consideration that I undertook these journeys, from conviction of duty that God required it at my hands. And (knowing that imposters are fond of money) I was convinced that Satan would not be found wanting, to whisper in the minds of the people that my motives were sinister or impure . . .

NOVEMBER 20TH. I arrived at [the] camp meeting at Rehoboth. I took Master "I AM" for my text [and] . . . about fifty souls were born to God. There were 44 tents, 88 wooden huts, [and] 48 covered wagons, beside carriages, &c., of various sorts . . .

NOVEMBER 23. I spoke in Louisville to as many as could conveniently get into the state-house . . . Whilst I was preaching . . . I perceived the chair on which I stood on the writing table to move twice or thrice, the cause of which I could not then ascertain; but [I] set down to prevent my falling. After the meeting a young German observed that a Baptist preacher put his foot under my chair twice or thrice, apparently with a design to tilt me over and set the house in a laughter. [The young man] went and shook his fist in his face, intimating that (if he had him out of doors) he would pay him for his insult . . .

I held a few meetings in Newbern and proceeded to Washington, where I was chilled in crossing by ferry. But after getting somewhat warmed and refreshed with a cup of tea, I proceeded to [the] meeting, where God made it up to me . . . I visited several places around, and took my departure for Tennessee, having a cloak and shirt given to me. My money is now almost out; my expenses have been so enormous, in consequence of unusual floods, &c.

FEBRUARY 14TH . . . I rode across the dismal Allegheny mountains . . . crossed the river French in a canoe, and set out for my appointment; but fearing I should be behind the time, I hired a man (whom I met on the road with two horses) to carry me five miles in haste for three shillings, which left me but one-sixteenth of a dollar. In our speed he observed there was a nigh way, by which I could clamber the rocks and cut off some miles; so we parted, he having not gone two-thirds of the way, yet insist[ing] on the full sum.

I took to my feet the nigh way as fast as I could pull on, as intricate as it was, and came to a horrid ledge of rocks on the bank of the river, where there was no such thing as going round; and to clamber over would be at the risk of my life, as there was danger of slipping into the river. However, being unwilling to disappoint the people, I pulled off my shoes and, with my handkerchief, fastened them around my neck. Creeping upon my hands and feet with my fingers and toes in the cracks of the rocks, with difficulty I got safe over; and in about four miles I came to a house and hired a woman to take me over the river in a canoe for my remaining money and a pair of scissors, the latter of which was the chief object with her. So our extremities are others' opportunities. Thus with difficulty I got to my appointment in Newport in time.

I had heard about a singularity called the JERKS or JERKING EXERCISE which appeared first near Knoxville in August last, to the great alarm of the people; which reports at first I considered as vague and false. But at length, like the Queen of Sheba, I set out to go and see for myself . . .

When I arrived in sight of this town, I saw hundreds of people collected in little bodies; and observing no place appointed for a meeting, before I spoke to any, I got on a log and gave out a hymn, which caused them to assemble round in solemn attentive silence. I observed several involuntary motions in the course of the meeting, which I considered as a specimen of the jerks. I rode seven miles behind a man across streams of water, and held [a] meeting in the evening, being ten miles on my way.

In the night I grew uneasy, being twenty-five miles from my appointment for the next morning at eleven o'clock. I prevailed on a young man to carry me with horses until day, which he thought was impractible, considering the darkness of the night and the thickness of the trees. Solitary shrieks were heard in these woods, which he told me were said to be the cries of murdered persons; at day we parted, being still seventeen miles from the spot, and the ground covered with a white frost. I had not proceeded far before I came to a stream of water from the

The Congregational Missionary Tour breaks camp, with Dr. W. B. D. Gray at the carriage, ca. 1905.

Summer camp in Johnson County, Wyoming, part of Dr. and Mrs. W. B. D. Gray's Congregational Missionary Tour, ca. 1905

Missionary fording a Wyoming river by carriage

Congregational missionaries in camp, Dakota Territory, ca. 1887

springs of the mountain, which made it dreadful cold; in my heated state I had to wade this stream five times in the course of about an hour, which . . . so affected my body that my strength began to fail. Fears began to arise that I must disappoint the people, till I observed some fresh tracks of horses which caused me to exert every nerve to overtake them in hopes of aid on my journey . . . I shouted for them to stop . . . and thus I got on to [the] meeting. After taking a cup of tea gratis, I began to speak to a vast audience, and I observed about thirty to have the JERKS; though they strove to keep still as they could, these emotions were involuntary and irresistable . . .

Hence to Marysville, where I spoke to about one thousand five hundred; and many appeared to feel the word, but about fifty felt the jerks. At night I lodged with one of the Nicholites, a kind of Quakers who do not feel free to wear colored clothes: I spoke to a number of people at his house that night. Whilst at tea I observed his daughter (who sat opposite to me at the table) to have the jerks, and [she] dropped the teacup from her hand in the violent agitation.

I said to her, "Young woman, what is the matter?"

She replied, "I have got the jerks."

I asked her how long she had had it.

She observed, "A few days," and that it had been the means of the awakening and conversion of her soul, by stirring her up to serious consideration about her careless state, &c.

SUNDAY, FEBRUARY 19TH. I spoke in Knoxville to hundreds more than could get into the court-house, the Governor being present. About one hundred and fifty appeared to have jerking exercise, among whom was a circuit preacher (Johnson) who had opposed them a little before, but he now had them powerfully; and I believe he would have fallen over three times had not the auditory [auditorium] been so crowded that he could not, unless he fell perpendicularly.

After [the] meeting I rode eighteen miles to hold [another] meeting at night. The people of this settlement were mostly Quakers, and they had said, "The Methodists and Presbyterians have the JERKS because they SING and PRAY so much, but we are a still, peaceable people, wherefore we do not have them." However, about twenty of them came to [the] meeting to hear [me]. As was said, [they were] somewhat in a Quaker line, but their usual stillness and silence was interrupted, for about a dozen of them had the jerks as keen and as powerful as any I had seen, so as to have occasioned a kind of grunt or groan when they would jerk. It appears that many have undervalued the great revival, and attempted to account for it altogether on natural principles; therefore it seems to me that God hath seen proper to take this method to convince people that he will work in a way to show his power; and sent the JERKS as a sign of the times, partly in judgement for the people's unbelief, and yet as a mercy to convict people of divine realities.

I have seen Presbyterians, Methodists, Quakers, Baptists, Church of England and Independents exercised with the JERKS . . . I believe that those who are most pious and given up to God are rarely touched with it . . . but the lukewarm, lazy, half-hearted, indolent professor is subject to it, and many of them . . . when it came upon them, would be alarmed and stirred up to redouble diligence with God. And after, they would get happy and thankful it ever came upon them. Again, the wicked are more afraid of it than smallpox . . . and they sometimes have cursed, and swore, and damned it, whilst jerking . . .

20TH. I passed by a meeting house where I observed the undergrowth had been cut up for a camp meeting... From fifty to one hundred saplings [had been] left breast high, which to me appeared so slovenish that I could not but ask my guide the cause, who observed they were topped so high and left for the people to jerk by. This so excited my attention that I went over the ground to view it, and found where the people had laid hold of them and jerked so powerfully that they had kicked up the earth as a horse stamping flies ...

I called at a gentleman's house to get some breakfast, and enquired the road. The gentleman, observing my tin case in my pocket (containing my credentials), took it out and examined the contents without asking my consent; when he had got half way through, he looked at me, [and] I observed he appeared pale: he gave me what I wanted and treated me as a king.

I had not been gone long from the house before a runner on foot overtook me, and another servant on horseback, with a request that I should go back and preach: I did (to many of the neighbors who were called in), [but] the mistress deserted during the meeting, which to me she denied, until the servants affirmed she was in the negro house.

I observed ... that her absence was a slight ... and desired to know the cause. She replied, she was afraid of the jerks more than of the smallpox or yellow fever.

[Dow continued to preach throughout Ohio, Kentucky, and Georgia, holding enormous camp meetings along the way.]

FRIDAY, JUNE 8TH. Camp-meeting came on at Charity-chapel. The Lord was precious: but the wicked strove to trouble us.

SUNDAY, IOTH. About five or six thousand were on the ground. The work went on, and the opposition increased. Twenty-five combined together to give me a flogging. They ransacked the camp to find me whilst I was taking some repose. This was the first discovery of their project: as I went out of the tent, one was seen to cock a pistol towards me, whilst a voice was heard, "There he is, there he is!" My friends forced me into the tent. Next day I had one of the young men arrested, and two others fled before they could be taken. The young man acknowledged his error and promised never to do the like again: so we let him go.

The law was read from that stage, and after that we had peace ...

[A Methodist friend] came to a big meeting in the woods, and heard that CRAZY DOW was there, and after some time sought and found me. He accompanied me to my appointments ... He kept what some call a METHODIST TAVERN, i.e. a house for preachers. One of my appointments being near his house, he invited me to tarry all night, observing his daughter would be glad to see me. I asked if he had any children! He replied, "A young woman I brought up I call my daughter." I staid all night, but so it happened that not a word passed between her and me, though there were but three in the family. I went to my appointment where we had a precious time; but whilst preaching, I felt uncommon exercise (known only to myself and my God) to run through my mind, which caused me to pause for some time. In going to my evening appointment, I had to return by the house ... I asked [my friend] if he would object if I should talk to his daughter concerning matrimony. He replied, "I have nothing to say, only I have requested her, if she had any regard for me, not to marry so as to leave my house."

When I got to the door, [his wife said] PEGGY was resolved never to marry unless it were to a preacher, and one who would continue traveling. This resolution being similar to my own, as she then stepped into the room, caused me to ask if it were so. She answered in the affirmative, on the back of which I replied, "Do you think you could accept such an object as me?"

She made no answer, but retired from the room: this was the first time of my speaking to her. I took dinner, asked her one question more, and went to my meetings, which occupied some days; but [returning] I staid all night, and in the morning, when going away, I observed to her and her sister . . . that I was going to the warm countries, where I had never spent a season, and it was probable I should die, as the warm climate destroys most of those who go from a cold country. But (said I) if I am preserved about a year and a half from now, I am in hopes of seeing this northern country again, and if during this time you live and remain single, and find no one that you like better than you do me, and would be willing to give me up twelve months out of thirteen, or three years out of four to travel . . . (and never say, Do not go to your appointments; for if you should stand in my way, I should pray God to remove you, which I believe he would answer) and if I find no one that I like better than I do you, perhaps something further may be said on the subject.

And finding her character to stand fair, I took my departure.

In my travels I went to Nachez county, where I found religion low . . . but [she] lay on my mind . . . But now I find she was still single, and they all willing to comply with my request . . . so our bargain was drawn to a close . . .

[Of their union, Peggy Dow writes in her journal: " . . . My brother-in-law . . . met Lorenzo Dow and invited him home . . . to preach at our preaching house . . . And as he was a SINGULAR character, we were very ANXIOUS to see and hear him. The day arrived, and we had a good time! I was very much afraid of him, as I had heard such STRANGE THINGS about him! He was invited to my brother-in-law's . . . and at last he came. The next morning he was to preach five or six miles from our house, and little did I think that he had any thoughts of MARRYING—in particular that he should make any proposition of the kind to ME; but so it was . . . He returned the next evening, and spoke to me on the subject again, when he told me that he would marry, provided he could find one that would consent to his traveling and preaching the Gospel; and if I thought I could be willing to marry him and give him up to go and do his duty, and not see him, perhaps, or have his company more than one month out of thirteen, he should feel free to give his hand to me. But if I could not be willing to labor in the vineyard of his God, he dared not make a contract of the kind; for he could not enjoy peace of mind . . . He was then on his way to Canada, and from thence to the Mississippi Territory, and did not expect to return in much less than two years. Then, if Providence spared, and the way should open for union . . . WHEN he returned, we would be married . . . ]

# James Leander Scott

"We Baptists began at the Jordan River, and have had a continuous existence ever since!"

—unnamed Landmark Baptist*

*James Leander Scott was born in 1814. He was appointed a Baptist missionary to the western territories in 1842, at a time when Baptist activity in the country was on the rise. The denomination, still recalling its early years of persecution by the Catholic church, was bent on counteracting any Catholic influence introduced by European immigrants. The Baptist church therefore rallied its strongest missionaries to travel through settlements, passing out tracts, collecting offerings from the "friends of Zion," and establishing churches wherever possible.*

*Scott, a resident of Richburg, New York, brought his wife and six-year-old son in an open carriage, in freezing midwinter conditions, on the seven-and-one-half-month journey west through Pennsylvania, Ohio, Indiana, Illinois, Iowa, Wisconsin, Kansas, and Missouri. They sought*

out temperance houses for food and lodging, but often ended up in bawdy grog shops for want of better shelter. Little is said about Mrs. Scott in Scott's journal, but an opening statement—"Feelings were not to be substituted for duty"—indicates that both she and her husband were disconcerted by the assignment.*

*Despite the pervasive moral indifference of many frontier settlers, Scott repeatedly touched off religious "wildfire" during his travels. Although Scott, an educated man, seemed aloof in his judgment of unrefined settlers, he responded with warmth at the first sign of sincerity. He found that "the shouts of the redeemed and groans of the convicted" were "thrilling in the extreme."*

*In the democratic tradition of the early libertarians Roger Williams and Isaac Backus, Scott also promoted temperance and abolition along his route—despite the unpopularity of both issues. These matters found ample reflection in his journal. Scott also faithfully recorded river crossings, daily temperatures, terrain, soil type, local Indian tribes, archaeological finds, and the like. His journal thus became both testimony and travelogue.*

*A long-time lung condition worsened during the grueling circuit, and the Scotts decided to return to New York*

---

*Landmarkism: a doctrine that claimed the historical continuity of Baptist churches from biblical times

*in 1843. Later Scott continued to write and lead revivals. It is believed he died in 1889.*

I entered the Gospel Ministry with a resolution to [minister] . . . in the valley of the Mississippi.

Long had I wept and prayed over the destitute condition of that wild scattered waste. Notwithstanding my feeble health [an unspecified lung condition which worsened during his missionary tenure], when I received the appointment from the Executive of the Missionary Society, I was ready to comply. Not knowing how long [I would be] in the valley, I resolved on having my family [Mrs. Scott and a six-year-old son] accompany me.

On the sixth of January, 1842, we took leave of the Church, and our friends.

[JANUARY] 12TH. In North East, Erie County, Pa., called at Br. Abel Babcock's, who had for long . . . lived without any knowledge of . . . prosperity . . .

15TH. Being Sabbath, spoke to an audience whose number amounted to six, two of them first day people . . . Our Brother Tod is trying to publish salvation in this place— preaches each Sabbath to three persons, except on accidental occasions. He also preaches in the country around.

14TH . . . Part of the time we plodded on through mud knee deep, and so frosty that all the turbid soil adhering to the carriage wheels congealed. Sometimes we were hobbling over the hubs, at others trundling the crazy log and rail bridges. Through swamps and lonely deserts much of our pathway lay. Twice we broke our carriage, costing much time and money to get it repaired again . . . Thus we urged our way on, although [making] little progress. But we felt it our duty to pursue the journey.

JAN. 18. We called at Harrisville, where from appearances I thought [the townspeople] were sometimes visited by the ague and fever; but when I enquired about it, the innkeeper declared emphatically THAT IT WAS NOT THE CASE. Shortly after, a gentleman came in, and drawing up to the stove, said, "I guess, Landlord, my fit is coming on again." After he had shaken for sometime, I enquired if that man was a resident of that town. My host answered, "He is, sir." "Has he been absent recently?" "No, sir." "Well," I replied, "he must have the disease from his own climate."

I mention this as a specimen of the struggling spirit of the inhabitants in the unhealthy countries [generally the lowlands of Ohio and Missouri].

. . . At Ashland, Richland Co., for some cause I was thought to be a friend to the slave, and a club of coxcombs pounced upon me . . . saying they would "egg" [me]. [It was common in pre-emancipation days for "border ruffians" or pro-slavers from Missouri and Georgia to terrorize "free state" settlers traveling through the perimeters of the Kansas Territory and Ohio.] I immediately began to defend the slave when a battle of words ensued; I was unflinching in behalf of the slave, [but] they did not execute their threatened vengeance.

23RD. At night we were caught in the wilderness, far from any house, following an underbrushed road as it wound its way around the large trees. But we were favored with the light of the pale moon, as its borrowed rays found their way through the thick woven bowery above. Thus we crept along over the frozen ground, stumps, and roots at a very slow rate, until late in the evening. And how far from the settlement we could not imagine, for when we entered the forest we were told it was "but a little bit" through. This term I afterwards learned was applied to any distance, however indefinite.

Late in the evening we passed a log hut, which being well lighted within, very much resembled a pole lantern. After passing . . . we found a large tree across the path. Our carriage capsized, falling down a steep bank. In my effort to save my family I was caught under the wagon, with my face so muffled that I could not speak, and it was sometime before I could extricate myself with the aid of my family. This was a gloomy scene, and the more so to my family, as it was sometime before they knew whether I was dead or alive . . . We were then four hundred miles from home, and had been for hours penetrating this lonely desert . . . After unloading the carriage we righted it, reloaded and pursued the journey. By this time I found that my face and head were much bruised. After hobbling along sometime, we came to a log house where we sought [shelter] but to no purpose. I begged for the remainder of the night, but all my entreaties were in vain. We were directed on.

[At] the next house we met the same treatment, [despite] our condition . . . [Finally,] appealing to their sympathy with all eloquence, we [were] admitted, and were kindly entertained.

Thus we were preserved by a kind Providence, and again reminded of our Heavenly Father's care.

26TH. Leaving those kindhearted people, we entered the forest on the way to Belle Fontaine. For many miles it was one continued Causey, or "railroad," which is made by throwing trunks of trees into a marsh and leaving them to settle there. This material is used where the swamps are extremely bad. The jolts, as the carriage fell from log to log, were uncomfortable in the extreme. If in high water any of the logs get washed out of their place, the team first plunge into the mire up to their mid-side, and then flounce for the logway again, when the carriage is drawn into the marsh, well nigh burying the forward wheels. As the team advances, the wheels come in contact with the remaining timbers, and all are FETCHED UP, and there we are a dead set again. Out we must get, and wading through the mud, raise the wheels until they will roll on the logs again, and then we trudge on.

. . . We soon, however, found ourselves in a humble cottage, fitted for [a] gathering multitude. The people came in flocks from all parts; they shot forth from the thickets in every direction, until the house was literally jammed. Anxiety and ambition [was on] every countenance. These people would cheerfully go, aided by their torches, from two to five miles through the woods to worship God . . .

We believe the Lord met with us to bless [them].

The silvery moon came up . . . to aid the returning groups back to their dwellings. The forest echoed with their songs of praise as they returned.

SABBATH. The meeting house in Jefferson was filled to overflowing. And what surprised us most was that some young ladies came on foot six and seven miles through mist and mud. They said they were "well paid" and willing to wear themselves out in the cause of their Master.

We repaired to the bank of the Miami River, which flows gently by this town. This was as beautiful and interesting a scene as we ever witnessed. The people skirted the river up and down. The bank was so formed that the gathering [faithful] ranged in lines, one above another, so that all could with ease behold the scene. The lofty sycamores stood in all their grandeur along the shore. Our souls were filled.

We baptized thirteen, whose ages were from ten to forty-five. They appeared very happy, and crowded to the water's edge, anxiously waiting their turn.

MARCH 8. Left for Bloomfield, Pickaway Co., and passed through Springfield. [Here] we hailed the macadamized road with much joy. The toll on the road is very high, but clergymen are free.

The rain soon began to fall, and by morning much of the low land was inundated. We had not the red sea before us . . . but streams whose depth and fury . . . forbade our fording them. And on the right, the direction we were to go, was rapidly rolling the maddened waters of the Scioto.

We started, and ploughing through the mud, soon stood upon the bank of the foaming river. Here we were brought to a stand. No bridge or boat was there, nor was it possible to ford the river. After searching, we found a man willing to [cross] the river in a skiff, through the broken fragments and floating forest trees. Just below where we were to cross was a towering dam, over which the flood-trash was plunging headlong with the roaring waters . . .

On starting, I left my purse with my family, and the gloomy effect produced repented me of what I had done, for by the act I had betrayed my doubts of success. However we started, and were soon in the river dodging the floating flood-trash. The family stood upon the bank, watching the movements of every oar, until we were safely landed on the opposite shore. I waved my hand as a token of safety, and was soon lost in the forest . . .

Mrs. Scott, as her mind was in perpetual suspense . . . wandered up and down the river, inspecting every moving object until one was seen in the river below the dam, and [she] fancied she saw a man [James Scott] strangling—sinking—gone. The sight was heart-rending to [her]. She was, she supposed, suddenly bereft of a friend and left alone with strangers, six hundred miles from home. But the good Lord had otherwise ordered, for about then we appeared above the dam, ready to try our skill in recrossing the river.

We succeeded in getting the family across, then with much difficulty swam the horses. A few days after, we took the carriage over in a skiff.

We then learned how to sympathize with those who had labored in that country as missionaries; and yet we did not regret our [work], but rejoiced and hailed it as a privilege . . . In that place we found a number of families who were like sheep without a shepherd. Some still maintained the cause of Christ, and had [tried] to brave the storm. Others had neglected to pay their vows, and had grown cold in religion. Some few had wholly abandoned the cause of their Savior; also, a goodly number who had settled with them from the East never did profess religion. Tak[ing] them as a body, they were (religiously) in a distracted condition.

Notwithstanding . . . I was happy to be there.

On our arrival in the neighborhood, a man, who was afterwards converted, said I had better establish a dancing school. The next morning a company of wicked men invited me to join them in a hunting excursion, which I accepted. They evidently hoped to defeat the object of the Mission. In the forest we found a man making rails, and when informed of the Sabbath meeting, he replied, "If the priest will preach this log into rails, I will hear him

On the way to a Seventh-Day Baptist tent meeting in Salem, West Virginia, 1890

preach." (This man was soon after converted to God.) He joined the hunt.

We had not gone far when they began their sport and glee. I well knew this day would decide for or against my usefulness in that vicinity, as the main opposers to religion there composed the party.

I sought the aid of the Holy Spirit which I believe was granted, and joined them in every thing consistent . . . A change for the better was soon apparent. They proceeded to an embankment upon the brink of the river . . . built to guard the bottom land below from the bursting flood in high water. We came to an ancient mound there, in which were human skeletons, very closely compact, and standing erect. The mound was some sixty feet in diameter, of ordinary height. In it was also found flowered earthenware, of modern style.

The river, in washing away its banks, had exposed many skeletons which had been buried about four feet beneath the surface. They lay horizontally with head[s] eastward. They were of a Giant size, and the skull very round and extremely thick. The company, although boisterous in the morning, was now softened. With this vision of bones, they were willing to listen to remarks about the resurrection of the dead. After this day's exercise, they resolved to attend the meetings, and were all, I believe, converted . . . I had the inestimable privilege of baptizing them before leaving the place. After they were converted they often referred to the excursion in the forest, in which they professed to have realized the contrast between religion and irreligion.

Here I was, surrounded by many . . . opposed to the crucified Redeemer. If ever I saw the need of holy devotion, it was this occasion. Their guilty, lost condition—my accountability—the judgement-day, all clustered around my vision, and well nigh overwhelmed my depressed soul. I visited the forest and poured out my soul to God in prayer. In deep agony I implored immediate aid. For it was a morally wild, uncultivated field, and I had but a few days to stay with them. What was done must be done quickly.

SABBATH; many came out this day to hear the stranger. Some of the original settlers acted as though one of the seven wonders of the world had developed itself; and they would gaze upon a Seventh-day Baptist preacher as though he were some awful prodigy in nature, or at least some supernatural production, and would say: "I'll go and hear what he says about Saturday for Sunday." [Like the Adventists and Orthodox Jews, James Scott and his denomination could find no biblical evidence of God having changed the Sabbath from Saturday to Sunday.]

But God was there. His spirit melted the congregation, and the majority pledged themselves in obedience. And with the number were most of my hunting companions. Oh what a change! Deep groans and sighs and prayers were bursting from them on every hand. Hope revived in the heart of the old professors, and there that soul-converting work began. That evening some young men urged a dance, but to no purpose. One young gentleman professed to have his pockets full of religion, and offered to peddle it out. But his wickedness was ineffectual. In fact, this youth was the first to give his hand in the ordinance of baptism.

After services [we] repaired to the Scioto river, a distance of about two miles, and baptized ten happy converts.

27. A larger congregation still. The good spirit fell like rain upon the people, and five more were baptized. The last time we visited the river [for] baptism, the forest trees had

begun to put forth foliage, forming a delightful bowery overhead.

[Suddenly] we were reminded of the passage "When the sons of God came to present themselves before the Lord, Satan came also among them."

A middle aged man ascended a sloping sycamore, and baboon-like, was exerting himself to raise a shout in the congregation. I looked at him again and again, until his attention and that of the congregation were arrested, then said: "If you are a man, exhibit his character, that we may decide what you are." He slid down amid the sarcastic sneers of the crowd, and sneaked off. Profound silence followed, and nothing more transpired to annoy except a mimic baptism on the opposite shore, where some young men were acting the part of [converts] and appeared to improve the opportunity to commit to memory the ceremony.

May God pity such deluded sinners.

[I] constituted a church [here] of nine original members, and received ten candidates. Many more will doubtless join soon. With regard to their location: they are in a rich fertile country, and as healthy as any we have seen in the State of Ohio, [being situated] but eighteen miles south of Columbus, and two miles west of South Bloomfield, the Scioto river and canal. There is not about thirteen hundred acres of wild land in the immediate vicinity, which can be purchased from four to six dollars per acre. The Post office address is South Bloomfield, Pickaway Co, O.

Here is a field of labor for some young man or for any one of God's ministers. And the brightest prospect for usefulness.

The harvest is ripe. Who will go to them? Who will reject God's holy spirit and refuse the call?

. . . At length the day of our departure arrived: the friends gathered, but to bid them adieu, and especially the young converts, was heart-rending indeed . . . They implored us to stay with them, but duty forbade . . .

APRIL 4. We left in search of more of the scattered sheep . . . From Butlerville to Cincinnati we travelled through the most splendid country . . . the forests were loaded with foliage, the . . . fields laden with the rich productions of nature. About noon we struck the beautiful banks of the Ohio river, near five miles above Cincinnati . . . Opposite the city lies Kentucky . . . its towns, banks, hills, dales and mountains would present a pleasing aspect but for the thought that it is a land of slavery . . . [In] many places [slavery] finds a hearty welcome even in the bosom of the church. [The tortured slave] finds no pity from many who wear a Christian's garb. And—most horrid thought—[he] is often sold and his price added to the heathen Missionary fund!

While travelling on the bank of the Ohio, we called at a Tavern to discover the distance to the next house of entertainment [tavern]. The landlord replied, "If you are travellers, this is the place for you; for they commit robberies at the next house." It was too late for us to proceed farther. During the evening we were entertained with robbing anecdotes relative to his neighbors, and particularly [stories about] North Bent [the only tavern where the Scotts felt endangered].

About this time a huge-looking [man] came [to the tavern] for entertainment. On his head was a large piece of a Deer's skin, with the ears standing erect. Over his shoulders was thrown a portion of an old tattered plaid blanket which hung about half way to the ground, and ACROSS his shoulder lay a spruce cudgel, from four to six feet in length, and two inches in diameter, with the knots left

Tent meeting service held at Seventh-Day Baptist conference, 1898

Seventh-Day Baptist student evangelists at Morgan Park, 1892

Seventh-Day Baptist "Little Prairie" Church in Booty (Nady), Arkansas

Gathering of Seventh-Day Baptist evangelists in Milton, Wisconsin, 1898

about an inch long and brought to a point. His entire appearance was huge and savage. The house was swarming with intoxicated Irishmen. We thought THEY had the materials for plundering, and a heart but little too good. We afterwards learned the public was somewhat suspicious of [the innkeepers]. We SPENT or wore away the night as best as possible, and when the [sun] appeared, we hailed [it] with delight . . .

South of Ohio and Indiana . . . many live in shattered, leaky log huts, or shanties . . . We often slept in rooms where the snow, rain, and sleet would sift through the crevices and give us, as they say, a "smart sprinkle" . . . Tidiness is a stranger to many . . . I have often been obliged to walk about the yard while meals were preparing, and then, while receiving my repast, labor to see nothing but what was on my plate, and sometimes shut my eyes while conveying the food to my mouth. "Corn dodgers" is a sort of Indian bread. "Corn and common doings" are common fare. "Wheat bread and chicken fixin's" . . . comprise the extra repasts . . .

How far into ignorance people may fall, and not be "heathen" is not for me to judge, but one thing I DO know, that such society demands the sympathies of the enlightened, religious portion of [the] community. In THAT society what is there to hinder Romanism from having its designed effect? If the Protestant Churches do not send teachers to those destitute regions . . . they must be in a measure responsible for . . . the Papal yoke fasten[ing] upon [them] . . .

We arrived at a town called Paris, just as the sun was sinking in the [west]. On entering the village, we found the black measles had made great ravages with the people. My family had never had the disease, and we were driven from house to house, [finding] . . . no place to lay our weary heads. We at last . . . met a man [who] took us and entertained us for the night. [He lived] ten miles from Paris, [in] two flat-roofed cottages. Nearby stands a straw-covered hovel for a barn. An old shattered bureau on which lay Scott's Bible, as I entered, met my view.

I enquired if they loved and obeyed God.

To which the old man said, "Sometimes a little."

On leaving he said he wanted three cents for the pail of water. This family had thus stayed twelve years, ten miles from any inhabitants, and I was afterwards informed that he always charged for water . . .

At about two P.M. we came to a small cluster of houses, in a little grove, where we called for dinner. On first seeing the inhabitants I wondered how so many dirty, disgusting creatures, inclining to human, could have got together.

But I conducted Mrs. Scott into the "sitting room," which was about twelve feet square, and had in it two beds. It was also the bar-room and druggist shop. As it was about twenty miles across to the next grove, we had expected to tarry for the night. But what a place . . . to abide! The company in the sitting room was about half a dozen half-drunken fellows, and a tipsy quack doctor . . . not very genteel. I made my way to the barn and fed my team, and then those "horse jockeys" eagerly flocked [in] to see them . . . They bantered for an exchange, saying they would give me for my horses another span worth fifty dollars more. I told them I was not after their charity. But nothing would do—TRADE I MUST. I wish all horse traders could have seen this chattering group as they flocked around me; and each patting me on the shoulder was, to appearance, the best friend I ever had. After they found I would not exchange, they said with emphasis, "YOUR HORSES SIR, WE WILL HAVE AT ALL EVENTS." I replied that they appeared as though they could steal a horse, but I had hardly thought they would tell a man of it beforehand.

We then prepared to leave the place . . . which I considered . . . a den of thieves . . . When we were about to start, they appeared somewhat surprised, saying we could not reach the other grove, for the most of the way the prairie was inundated, and in some places . . . the water was four feet deep.

[I] inquired if the roads were more wet than those I had just been traveling. They replied, "FAR MORE DIFFICULT" and more, that strangers would need a pilot. It being very early in the season I feared there might be something in it, as before the water runs off in the spring many of these prairies are not capable of being traversed by a team . . .

We kept to the main road toward Springfield, and stopped the next night at a widow's, where I was compelled to hitch my team under an open shed with a herd of smoking swine. [The widow] was very anxious that I should converse and pray with her unconverted, uncultivated family, which I always rejoice to do . . . She kept us until nine in the morning, then said she would help the cause by taking a very small bill, after which she charged me more than they would at the best Hotel in Springfield.

I notice this to show that all that is called religion does not exhibit its principles of benevolence . . .

[In] . . . this portion of Illinois . . . religion is not a welcome guest. If a man introduces it, he is considered obtrusive. But profanity is . . . always in time, and always in place. Christians must keep religion out of sight and hearing, but the wicked may be as open and obtrusive as they please . . . Gambling is practised to a very great extent.

MAY 24 . . . On leaving the prairies and approaching the Mississippi, we met a man whose mind was all absorbed with the surrounding scenery. I hailed him several times before his attention was arrested. He at length stopped, gazed into my carriage, then, turning and looking all around upon the prairie, said, "I am thirty years of age—I have lived so long in the world, and NEVER, until today, saw a prairie!" Insensible to what I might say farther, he started on . . . It was evident he was lost to every thing around but what was spread out by nature's own hands before him . . .

After passing the wood lands of Flint creek we entered a prairie which was more undulating than any we had yet seen. As we bent our course direct for Fredonia, the road led us through one almost uninterrupted prairie. We could now and then see a clump of timber, and once or twice during the day, our path was through a beautiful grove. We also passed some newly commenced settlements, but none in time for refreshments until we came to Fredonia, a distance of forty-four miles . . . As we entered the forest that skirts the Iowa river, we were puzzled to select our path out of the [many] that crossed each other, leading in every direction. We several times took the wrong road, and run it to an end, until we thought it a heavy tax upon our patience and, more intolerable still, upon our weary steeds. We however happened to get the right road at last, which soon led us down to the bank of the beautiful Iowa river . . . Twilight had already [fallen] . . . we were weary, not having left our carriage since morning; but our hearty reception . . . relieved our burdened mind . . .

MAY 22. At 11 o'clock the people began to flock to Fredonia, and we listened to a discourse from a Methodist brother. At 2 P.M. I addressed the congregation, and commenced a series of meetings which were kept up . . . until my health completely failed, and I was obliged to leave a weeping, anxious people.

JUNE 2. I found my health was fast declining, and felt more than ever the necessity of a fellow laborer. Many were seeking religious instruction, and while they were flocking around, eager to be taught the will of Heaven, I felt the necessity of [another minister] . . . The meetings continued until the eighth, when I was obliged to close in the midst of a sermon. I however baptized one lady who was the first person baptized in that region. [Scott ministered, along with Elder Rolen McReynolds of the "regular Baptist" church, in villages along the Iowa River, returning to Fredonia each night. It is not mentioned how the two resolved their doctrinal differences, particularly that of the Sabbath day.]

The fatigues of the journey, constant preaching, visiting from house to house, answering objections, contending with Infidels and exposure to stormy blasts, & etc., had almost worn me out.

And during these exercises I often felt that I could not endure any longer. When the appointment drew near, I would make my way to the house and lay my weary frame down to rest, saying to the people that I could not preach. [Then] praying would commence, and as the people congregated [this] would almost irresistibly bring me upon my feet, and to preaching again. Thus I was led until my strength was gone, and [I was] compelled to leave that people in the highest state of religious excitement . . .

[Because of my health] I felt I could be of but little service to that people. I [decided to] leave them, and [never before] felt such anguish of soul on leaving . . . that I did on that solemn morn . . .

After leaving the people in Fredonia, we drove directly to Bloomington . . . While we were travelling this day upon the bank of the Mississippi, the roaring of the distant thunderpeals warned us of the gathering of one of those thunder tempests which traverse the plains with their astounding grandeur. I called at the first mansion and sought protection through the storm, which was rushing on with all its astonishing fury. But when I informed the lady that my son was very ill with the whooping cough, she positively forbade my entrance: and though there were different apartments, I could not prevail upon her . . . I left [and] soon found it was vain to seek shelter with any family. When I asked for admittance they would flatly deny [it] and then exhort me not to stop [even] in the town. After I had given up . . . and took a seat in my carriage to take the worst of it, I was hailed by a gentleman who was on horseback. He, after learning of my success, said, "When you get to that distant house, call, it is mine; say not a word about your sick boy, for protection justly belongs to you in this land of strangers." [Yet] his dwelling was far from us still, and the torrent of falling rain was loudly roaring behind us . . . Our child's health demanded better shelter than our carriage afforded. But we felt that "God is ours." Why should we be alarmed?

And as the rain, mingled with hail, began to beat upon us, we were as composed as if we were in [a] palace. But about this time the winds divided the cloud, and the clear sky appeared overhead, and the storm raged before and behind us for a long time. While the lightning [flashed] we were unmolested, except the slippery path . . . was somewhat annoying to our team. Though this division of the cloud might have been only the effect of the contending elements, never [had] I felt more forcibly the watchfulness of [God] . . . I could only adore, and with my [wife] sing praise to God for his wonderful kindness. I [knew] that the object of my mission was the glory of God. But why should he pour so many of his special blessings upon us? . . .

I [then] called on my brother in Palestine Grove, Lee County . . . After spending a few days at my brother's we left for Wiskonsin . . .

23. We left the river and went about twelve miles east, through beautiful prairie and woodland, to Deacon Wm. P. Stillman's . . .

24. In company with Elder S. Coon, visited a gravel mound which is in a forest . . .

25. SABBATH. The people . . . filled the . . . large barn. When I arrived, I could hardly believe my own senses. The horses and carriages were scattered through the grove, and seeing the multitude that had gathered, I could but marvel . . . When the people were "seated" I surveyed them, and searched for [signs] of ill health, but they were not to be found. All was health, vigor and activity . . . Though we were in a barn, the people . . . would have done honor to any chapel in the world. Eastern tastes, customs and order were there retained. Nothing was lost in the migration, but very much gained . . . Wiskonsin is settled principally from the Eastern and Middle States. Hence the society is untainted by the southern atmosphere . . . religion is flourishing . . . and the ministry is not as deficient there as in the north of Illinois, as in Iowa . . . and the interior of Ohio . . . The people do not lounge away their "spare time" as in other parts, by "shooting matches," "throwing the sledge," "pitching quates," "ball and card playing," &c . . .

27. We bade those friends . . . adieu, and left for New York State. I considered my Mission accomplished . . . my appointed time had . . . expired, and I thought best to bend my course as direct as possible towards Berlin, the place where our Conference was to hold its Session in September.

28. Arrived again at my brother in Palestine Grove, where we stayed until July 4, to refresh ourselves and team before leaving for home . . .

12. Passed through Centerville, in St. Joseph's Co., and about seven miles from there, we found Eld. Job Taylor. For a specimen of the water, they gave [our boy] to drink water that had stood all day in a barrel for domestic purposes. This vomited him, nor did he recover until the next day after we left . . . After leaving . . . we passed through the . . . Maumee, or Black Swamp, much noted for its den of counterfeiters. The road [through the swamp] is macadamized, and very good . . . While on this road . . . my horses were much frightened by the approach of a caravan, headed by a huge elephant . . . [No further note is taken of this phenomenon. In fact, an elephant in the backwoods of Ohio would have been an almost unheard-of event in 1842.]

21. Left Pawcatuck for Berlin, and stopped for the night with the brethren at Mystic. About ten o'clock in the evening, a messenger arrived from the First Day Baptist's Church in Westerly, requesting me to return and hold a series of meetings there . . . It was against my previous calculations and will, but I dared not refuse . . . At first I was at a loss to ascertain my duty, but after fasting and praying, became decided.

At length the people became interested, and the holy fire began to burn, saints to weep between the porch and altar . . . then the wheels of salvation rolled on . . .

The shouts of the redeemed, the groans of the convicted, and the agony of the Church, were sometimes thrilling in the extreme . . . The spirit of religion increased until the spirit of opposition rose to such a degree that one man took the anxious seat on a wager, thus defying God and the prayers of his people . . . The result was, God . . . honored his name in converting THAT man to the religion he had so much despised . . .

I was enabled to continue in the meetings about eight weeks, when my health entirely failed, and I was compelled to leave . . .

107
દે

*James Leander Scott*

The Right Reverend Bishop Charles McIlvaine

# Charles McIlvaine

"What a blessing to have been born again!"
—McIlvaine
to his thirteen-year-old daughter
on her confirmation day, Christmas, 1844

*Charles Petit McIlvaine was born in Burlington, New Jersey, on January 18, 1799. He was the grandson of the first governor of Pennsylvania and the son of a U.S. senator. His wife, Emily Coxe, came from a prominent colonial family, and McIlvaine himself held the respected position of Episcopalian chaplain at West Point before ministering to an elite New York parish. Everything in McIlvaine's background—his patrician roots, semi-invalidism due to recurring "head problems," and conservative Anglican evangelical theology—pointed to the reclusive life of a scholarly churchman with his wife and four children.*

*Yet in 1831 he was elected bishop of Ohio, despite his unfamiliarity with—even lack of interest in—the West. Ohio was untamed, unrefined—a backwoods outpost totally foreign to his sensibilities. "My sinful . . . heart rebelled against it," he wrote after receiving the notification, but he went on to serve doggedly for the next forty years, riding in his vestments along the back roads, bap-*

*tizing in out-of-the-way villages and preaching throughout the countryside. He tried to dispell his image as "haughty and proud," but at a time when Americans heartily rejected European formality, he was often unsuccessful.*

*McIlvaine became the most powerful and successful extempore Episcopal preacher of his time. President Lincoln asked him to travel to England as a special envoy during the American Civil War; he received honorary degrees from both Oxford and Cambridge; he was an overseas delegate for the American Bible Society. His correspondence from 1830 to 1873 frequently bears English or Italian or East Coast addresses. Periodic travel provided a "sort of leisure" between the ceaseless "trials of clergy and wants of poor parishes."*

*Bishop McIlvaine died in 1873 in a Florentine hotel during a tour of the Italian countryside. He died without his family, at the age of seventy-four, immediately after sending a message to his wife: TELL HER MY PEACE IS PERFECT.*

I received my education for college at the Burlington Academy, a corporate institution, of which my father was one of the trustees . . . [In] September, 1817 . . . I entered the Theological Seminary of the Presbyterian Church at Princeton, expecting to spend two years there. [But] my health failed, so that I was there only eighteen months . . . In that precious season . . . my religious life began. I had HEARD before: I began then to KNOW . . .

Just before . . . I graduated at college . . . I was at my father's house in Burlington, New Jersey . . . Feeling the need of special seasons of prayer (there being at that time in that town scarcely any intelligent, earnest Christian society to help me), I had a rule of going each evening at the setting of the sun to my chamber for prayer. One afternoon, as that time approached . . . [I] was conscious that as I waited, the disposition to go decreased. I said to myself, I had better go at once: and arose and went. I had no sooner got out of the parlor into the hall, where I was to ascend the staircase, than an indescribable DREAD came over me, as if some mysterious agency of terror were resisting me. I began the ascent by force. As I went up, the dread increased to such a degree that I trembled in every limb, and perspiration broke out at every pore. I took hold of the banister and dragged myself up. By the time I had reached the first landing (my room was on the second story) I was so overpowered with dread, that I stopped, and considered whether I dared to go further.

What it was I did not attempt to examine. ALL I knew was that something, some power, some darkness, some unutterable DREAD was upon me and before me. I considered but a moment, and went on to the head of the stair, the trembling and the dread increasing. There I stood again, and thought whether I dared go on. My room was at the end of the passage: I pushed forward and got hold of the handle of the door. The dread increased. It seemed a HORROR of darkness. I stood for a moment questioning whether I dare open the door. I opened and rushed to the chair at which I was accustomed to kneel at the opposite side of the room. I knelt, and in broken sentences prayed; two or three times looking behind me, as if I expected to see some being there. I could not pray but briefly; I arose, and INSTANTLY the whole dread began to vanish away as a cloud. In a few moments it was all gone: but I was drenched with perspiration, my limbs shook, my nerves were thoroughly shaken, and all the next day the physical effect was upon me. For thirty-six hours my nerves did not recover.

What it was precisely I say not. I was in good spirits when it began. Nothing of the sort had ever come upon me before, and I have had no such experience since.

I believe it was a messenger of Satan. It was an awful encounter. I mentioned it to nobody for years.

One night I was taking tea at the house of John C. Calhoun, Esq., then Secretary of War, with whom I was intimate. To my great surprise he suddenly asked me if I would accept the place of Chaplain and Professor of Ethics at West Point . . . I demurred on account of my youth; for then I had not completed my twenty-fifth year . . .

While considering the question I was kindly warned by military men residing in Washington . . . that I ought to take into account what state of things I should encounter— that I should find not only no religious sympathy or fellowship in the institution, but a widespread infidelity among officers and cadets . . . which my sort of preaching would be likely to arouse into most unpleasant opposition.

I must confess this prospect alarmed me [but] I concluded to say to Mr. Calhoun that I would accept the place . . .

Missionary wife tends Indian children at Fort Apache Reservation, Arizona.

Missionary at Fort Apache Reservation, Arizona, talking with Indian men

I landed at West Point in the spring of 1825 . . . [and] preached my first sermon—THE FEAR OF THE LORD IS THE BEGINNING OF WISDOM . . . At that time, except [for] the Superintendent, there was not an individual connected to the Academy, male or female, whom I knew in the least. I felt very desolate . . .

My reception at the Academy was kind and friendly, such as became gentlemen. No hindrances were designedly thrown in the way of my ministry: but there was a most chilling want of sympathy with the Gospel, except on the part of some three or four ladies—two of them Episcopalians . . . The prevalence of infidelity was as I had been told at Washington. This was especially the case among the junior officers.

By the rules of the Academy my opportunities of intercourse with the cadets were exceedingly limited, even [had they] desired an interview with me . . . Such was the feeling about coming to see me that for a whole year I cannot remember that a single cadet ever visited me, or sought my acquaintance . . . One service on Sunday was all I had with them.

I began my ministry in the dark . . . [but] under God's gracious guidance I was saved from a snare . . .

Thus I began in the spring of 1825, and so continued for a whole year, before anything of the least encouragement appeared, except as evidences of offence . . . meanwhile, CHARACTER came out from time to time, giving me BEARINGS to shape my course by. One Sunday I was walking from church, and some of the junior officers were behind me. I heard them say of my preaching "It is getting hotter and hotter."

[Rev. G. T. Fox, vicar of Saint Nicholas, Durham, narrated the following sequel to Reverend McIlvaine's tenure at West Point: "For a year, Mr. McIlvaine continued to preach the simple gospel to his military audience, without the slightest indication of any response . . . No cadet could come to see him without special permission, except on Saturday . . . At the darkest time, one of the eldest and most high-spirited of the cadets came to him . . . and unburdened a heart smitten with the Word and Spirit of God . . . In a day or two another, a case of conviction, as solitary as the other. Then another, then another, unconnected . . . till they found themselves with others of one mind . . . So it went on . . ."

Charles McIlvaine was offered the presidency of William and Mary College in 1827. He declined, working instead for the next four years in Brooklyn, where his fourth child, Emily, was born. In 1834 he became a bishop in the Diocese of Ohio, where he served faithfully for his remaining years. In the interim, he was overseas delegate for the American Bible Society, and received an honorary doctorate from Oxford. The following letters treat his experiences in the Ohio diocese.]

MARCH 8TH, 1833

I am starving and dying for want of regularity and system in my secret work—my retired seasons, prayer, meditation. I am so encompassed with cares from without, that the care within suffers grievously. How can my soul be in health, if its seasons of taking food are interrupted and hurried and broken up? I need more decision to SHUT THE DOOR . . .

APRIL 14, 1833

This is the last Sabbath . . . with this beloved flock in

Mennonite missionary Heinrich R. Voth with Hopi friend, Qoyawayma

Cheyenne converts—"Native Helpers"—at Mennonite conference, Freeman, South Dakota

*Charles McIlvaine*

Workers and children at the Darlington Mennonite Indian Mission School in Darlington, Indian Territory (later Oklahoma), 1890–1891 (workers, top, left to right: Martha Moser, Marie Suderman, Mrs. J. H. Schmidt, Anna Penner, J. H. Schmidt; bottom, left to right: J. H. Richert, Rev. H. R. Voth and daughter Frieda, Abraham Suderman)

Brooklyn ... My time to work is finished here ... Whatever good has been done, God did it. All the rest was mine.

CINCINNATI
JUNE 1st, 1834
[Written during his first months in Ohio]

I have received a letter of rather an unkind spirit from a presbyter of my diocese whom I love and value, but who mistakes me, mentioning rumours as prevailing in his vicinity that I am haughty and proud in my feelings toward the people of the diocese—that I desire to keep a distance from the unrefined and untutored ...

This communication was certainly unexpected, and not being in a right manner, was the more painful. But still I do hope and pray that it may ... humble my pride.

That I deserve the allegations ... I do not believe; nothing, I think, is more opposite to my nature than haughtiness, and especially towards the poor, and ignorant, and unrefined ...

WAYNESBURGH, OHIO
OCTOBER 8TH, 1839

My Beloved Mother,

I think it would amuse you, could you see me in all my posture[s] and work during a visitation [visit to diocese], especially if you think of me as a MERE BOY OF SOME EIGHTEEN YEARS. [He was forty at the time.] I go from the most refined society of the State, perhaps next to the most uncultivated—now CHARGING the clergy, HORSE AND FOOT, next scolding some parish in the woods for abolition lectures in Church, or for PROTRACTED MEETINGS, or even PERFECTIONISM, the last thing, one would suppose, to be scolded about.

The good people sometimes wonder at the plain taste of the Bishop, when he takes nothing but a bowl of milk and

a piece of apple pie with it. You could explain the mystery. [As a child he had been ill, perhaps calling for a restricted diet.] It is well that I have the GIFT OF TONGUE, for I have to preach FOR THE TIMES, as I find them on arriving, and often [must] judge what NAIL to hit. The course of a long visitation is very fatiguing and wearing, besides the pain of so much separation from my family.

I caused certain matters at the college, which have given me trouble for three years, somewhat of the kind that drove Bishop Chase away (JEALOUS PROFESSORS), to be brought before the Convention and had them well settled by the diocese [to prevent] two or three men from disturbing the peace of their Bishop ... [Emily] has wanted me to bring it to a crisis long ago, for she is not quite so confiding in men's professions as I am, and a little more wise, perhaps, in being sometimes more belligerent. My too strong aversion to hurt feelings and break peace, sometimes too much restrains my ... disposition.

[Yet] ... I become a boy again when I write to you ...
Farewell, Dearest Mother,
Your most devoted Son,
Charles

GAMBIER, MAY 7TH, 1841

My Beloved Mother,

I have just returned from a visitation of a month's duration. While on these excursions, I get a sort of leisure between public services which I have not at home ... At these intervals I escape into the woods, where no ear hears, or man's eye sees ... Recently I have had many such forest interludes. It is told of Dr. Chalmers, that in his earlier ministry, when in a village parish, being fond of botany, he would often get to the church before the people had come, and employ the time in collecting flowers. Once he got absorbed in this pursuit, and suddenly finding that he had overstayed his time, and the congregation had grown impatient, he put his hat on his head full of flowers, and hurried to church. When his hat was doffed at the door, he forgot his flowers, which kept their place on his head-top.

Now, I much query whether my mind and sermons do not sometimes indicate somewhat the like of Dr. Chalmer's head-gear . . .

Your most affectionate,

CHARLES

STEUBENVILLE, OHIO
MARCH 23, 1844
[To his daughter M——, when she was thirteen years old]

Sweetest M——,

What a forgetful man your father is! [but] never mind, I do not forget my sweet children . . .

Tell your precious mother that I want her to tell me WHAT SORT OF A HOUSE I shall buy in or near Cincinnati; whether as big as Bexley Hall, or as Frog Hall [a little log cabin near Kokosing Creek]; also how large a farm, whether as large as the south section, or as big as the barn-yard—she must be PRECISE.

Dear M——, I write in this queer way to make you smile a little and myself too, for this being so much away from home often depresses my spirits very much. When I get by myself, which I love to do, and think of all my precious family, I sometimes feel as if my life were a hard one; but it is for the service of God . . .

If we are now born again of the Spirit, as I fully and thankfully believe you are, my sweet child, then we are in the likeness of God . . . The Lord may come so soon as to find you alive on the earth. Then you will be made perfect in soul and body together. Then you will be SATISFIED . . .

Write to me, my beloved child, and tell me anything about yourself.

Your Most Affectionate Father.

WARREN, OHIO
MAY 23RD, 1854

To Rev. W. Carus,

. . . I left home three weeks ago, but here, at a distant point of my diocese, after preaching twenty-five times in twenty-three days . . . I felt weary this morning in body and mind, and not a little TIRED of the worldliness of the world . . . [The bishop was fifty-seven at the time.]

It struck me a few weeks ago what a spectacle I should have seemed in the eyes of some, who know a bishop only as a man of lawn sleeves and official dignity . . .

A railroad train set me down in a rather wild part of Ohio, seven miles from a little Welsh parish where I had an appointment. I had expected to meet there some conveyance sent to take me from the station. But . . . there was nothing there. I tried in vain to hire a horse—nothing could be got. The few people knew nothing of me, or the parish. They had nothing to be hired. So I shouldered my baggage, which was not light, and overcoat (the day was hot and the road very rough and hilly) and trudged on the SEVEN MILES, occasionally sitting on a log, and taking a book to read, till I had rested my arms from their load; and thus I entered the little Welsh village, to the consternation of the Welsh pastor and his wife. The only ill effect was that I took a severe cold and cough, which have not quite passed away. Such is our dignity sometimes in Ohio!

[The following year Bishop McIlvaine started for Cincinnati on his return from a visit to Louisville. He took a steam ferry. The day was bitterly cold, and the Ohio River

William Eagle Thunder instructing Black Thunder in the ways of Christianity at the St. Francis Mission, Rosebud Sioux Reservation, St. Francis, South Dakota, ca. 1912

Franciscan missionary Reverend Oderic Derenthal with collection of traditional religious objects surrendered by Indian converts as a sign of authentic conversion

Reverend John Jasper Methvin, Methodist missionary to the Kowas and Comanches, shown with group of Kiowa girls and his bicycle, ca. 1894

Kitchen duties practiced at a mission Indian school, Tucson, Arizona, before 1910

St. John's William Welsh Memorial School for girls at the Cheyenne River Indian Agency, ca. 1880

Group of girls in the sewing class at Cut Meat School, Rosebud Sioux Reservation, 1898 (left to right, seated: Gracie Good Bird, Emma Elk Looks Back, Bessie Elk Looks Back; standing, left to right: Maggie Otterman, Rosa Elk Teeth, Nellie Foot, Kittie Turning Eagle)

Interior of a Catholic Boys' home in Idaho

was full of running ice floes swirling downstream toward the falls. The boat lodged against a reef, collected ice in a solid wall against its stern, and began to move slowly toward the falls, placing the lives of the two hundred passengers in great danger.]

CINCINNATI, JAN. 30TH, 1856

. . . When we struck, I believe I stood up immediately, expecting instant death, but said only, "WE HAVE STRUCK." It was after we had passed the falls [that] a little colored boy was found almost frozen. He had no overcoat. The omni-bus man was moving him about to get his blood circulated. I took him under my cloak, which was long and warm, and held him to my body to get its heat; in that situation he became quite comfortable.

The order of the people in the ferry-boat . . . was remarkable. A great many of the men were very profane and wicked river-men, but they did not interfere . . .

After I had prayed with the men, their shrieks brought in a rush of men, who spoke very harshly of the folly of frightening the women. One of them, a steamboat-captain, was foremost. He said the worst thing we could have done was to pray with the women: it was the very thing to frighten them. I turned calmly and kindly, and said: "My friend, there are two ways of looking at that matter. As for me, I believe that God is our only help, and that in such danger nothing [will] soothe [like] prayer." Afterwards, when we had got fastened on the reef, I was standing at the bow of the boat, looking at the ice as it came down with such violence, and in such fields upon us; and that man came to me and apologized for what he had said.

[Meanwhile, according to *The Western Episcopalian,* February 5, 1855: "Each new onset of ice was watched with intense anxiety . . . As the ice struck against the boat, it formed such a mass that it rested on the rock beneath, and formed a breakwater; and the more violent was the onset of the ice, the more strong and massive it did become. The boat lay, as it were, under the lee of this mass of ice . . . In the course of another hour some four or five boats, capable of containing each from four to five persons, came out from either shore . . . all the while, the ice was crushing against the boat, and none knew how soon she would be driven where no boats could reach her."]

. . . The fifth [rescue] boat had now come. When it was supposed the last female had been put in, there was one vacant seat. I was told I must take it. I did so . . . we pushed off; but before we had gone . . . we were hailed back on account of the ice. Meanwhile, as we were pushing off, the captain, a rude and low man, called to me in such a way [as to infer] that I had consulted my own safety too much in taking that seat . . . It made me very uncomfortable. I wished I were out of the skiff. I rejoiced when we were hailed back. And when . . . word was heard that there was one female left, it was a great comfort. It gave me good reason to return. I called immediately to her, and gave her my seat. My mind was thus at ease . . .

How remarkable is the hand of God in causing the ferry-boat to strike the reef just where she did; a little further, and no help could have come to us on account of the current.

The Lord be praised for His unspeakable mercy.

APRIL 24TH, 1857

To Mrs. McIlvaine,

I have had nothing but the most terrible weather all the time since I left home till the past two days . . . Rode twelve miles in an open buggy through awful roads—was almost frozen. Reached Strongville just in time to get a little thawed before I had to go into the church. Preached and confirmed, had only time to get some dinner; then rode seven miles in a driving snowstorm, right in the face, to Columbia. Had five minutes to get warm; preached and confirmed; got tea, rode three miles to the station and got to Cleveland at ten at night. But I have no cold, and my throat is WELL. I have been often very tired, but feel now very fresh.

But what hard work it is. I sometimes ask myself what is my self-denial and self-sacrifice? I answer IN ALL THIS; for whatever it might be to some others who have not such love of home, and quiet, and order, and retirement, and all that they bring with them, it is to me a very great sacrifice. I feel thankful to be permitted so widely to preach Christ; and that—enabled as I am—unwearied in spirit, with a measure of FRESHNESS AND ELASTICITY of mind that often surprises me, considering where I go,—the truth seems always fresh and sweet.

CINCINNATI, JULY 2ND, 1858

To Rev. W. Carus.

My Beloved Friend and Brother,

You will be surprised to know that . . . in two weeks . . . I shall be in England. My health is such that my diocese have urged me to break off entirely from all diocesan cares, and take some months of ABSOLUTE rest. The case is one of an over-worked brain, threatening cerebral disease—apoplexy, or the like. It is my constitutional weakness—that is, a tendency to too much excitement of brain from such duties as mine.

CINCINNATI, JANUARY 1st, 1861

To Rev. W. Carus,

. . . New Year's Day, alas! With what clouds of darkness it dawned upon the land! What confusion, division, strife, conflict, intestine war, suffering, tempests of evil passions may mark its progress . . . Perhaps it is part of the GREAT TRIBULATION . . . the ARK IS HERE, and we, I trust, are shut in. [He is referring to the onset of the Civil War.]

CINCINNATI, MAY 3RD, 1861

To Rev. W. Carus,

. . . I am earnest, and all my family connections, for the Union; but I deeply realize the awfulness of the cause. My spirit grieves over the thought of what separations are to be made. [Yet] it is curious to see how people's hearts are turned to God. The other day the major-General in command of all the forces of Ohio—a fine officer of large attainments—went to his pastor to converse about his soul . . . they prayed together—first the pastor, then HE—keeping together on their knees. The officer arose and said: "I give myself to be a soldier of the Cross, and live and die for Christ" . . . What wonderful times! What is God working!

NEW YORK, JULY 11, 1861

To Rev. W. Carus,

. . . When I last wrote, I said I was going to Washington; I was there about ten days. My old friend, General Scott, gave me every facility to visit the outposts . . . where two Ohio regiments are.

I made them two visits, spent a night with them, preached to them, visited their wounded and sick, as well as other regiments near them . . . I preached at night; the day (Wednesday) was very hot; the men were very tired with guard, picket, and scout duty. After dark, a file of men marched to the General's tent, stacked arms, and thus made four chandeliers in which candles were fixed: the trees of a wood were over us; the men came by hundreds

119

෭

*Charles McIlvaine*

and hundreds, and sat on the ground in the light, and afar off in the dark in voluntary attendance. They sang like a trained choir; a soldier held a candle to my book, while I read a part of our service. I never preached to a more eagerly attended congregation . . . How I did enjoy it!

In the morning, I rode in an ambulance two miles and a half further . . . a picket guard said, "Bishop, suppose you pray with us here." "Gladly indeed." So I went to the desk, and as I began to read a chapter, each of the men of the picket got a Bible from the pews and followed me, and, when I had prayed, each came and asked me to write in his memorandum book my name, the place, [and] the date of the text.

[After the Civil War, Bishop McIlvaine concerned himself with the status of emancipated blacks and worked ceaselessly for their assimilation.]

CINCINNATI, NOV. 17, 1865

To Rev. W. Carus,

. . . Matters are going on WELL beyond all expectation in the country . . . When I was in Philadelphia, at the general Convention, I declined all preaching . . . except to coloured people. One Sunday I preached to the congregation of St. Philip's (coloured). Service excellently read by the rector, a coloured man, educated at Kenyon College. Organ charmingly played by a coloured man. . . . In the afternoon I went to a Sunday School of coloured men and women and addressed them, only I had to avoid certain topics, for fear my feelings would GIVE WAY (nothing melts me so soon as preaching to such people) . . .

[One of the bishop's daughters related an incident provoked by his concern for the newly emancipated blacks. "We stopped at Gambier on our return from abroad in 1859," she wrote. "On arriving, a friend told him that the place was much agitated, because the colored man (Alston), though he was studying at the Divinity School, was not allowed by the chaplain to receive the Holy Communion . . . but instead, was requested to remain until the whole white population of the place had partaken. My father's reply was 'Let no one know that you have spoken of this to me.'

"The next day, refusing to preach in the morning, and purposely leaving his prayer-book behind, he went to the chapel and took his place by the side of Alston, who was not seated with the rest of his fellow-students . . . When the time came [for] the Lord's Supper, my father waited until the clergy of the place had communicated, and then stepping forward, and bidding Alston follow him, advanced and knelt at the chancel, placing the colored man by his side. It is needless to say that with this ended the matter, except in the gratitude of his companion."]

LONDON, JANUARY 18TH, 1873

[To Mrs. McIlvaine]

My Dearest Emily,

I write on my birthday—seventy-four years old! And how well I seem! During the last two months I have increased much in strength.

I sent you a RECORD. It contains an account of the great annual Islington meeting. [A meeting of evangelical ministers from around the world: the bishop had first attended in 1830.] . . . You will see THAT I SPOKE. And this I must explain. Mr. Wilson had written, asking me to take the place of Canon Bardsley, who could not attend. I declined, and went without the least idea of speaking. But I got animated with the speakers; and just when Bardsley's vacancy came, Mr. Wilson URGED ME. I had but five minutes to consider. THE FIRE BURNED, and I could not deny myself. I thought . . . I would try it for once, and I am happy to say I have taken no harm. But I shall not try again . . .

I expect to set out on the 29th with Mr. and Mrs. Carus. The Lord be with you, my dear wife.

Your dearest husband.

ह्ष

*Charles*
*McIlvaine*

Reverend Elkanah Walker

# Elkanah Walker

*We are not going to steal*
*From you people*
*We are not going to tell*
*Lies to you people*
*I am not going to steal*
*From you*
*This is God's Law . . .*

*—Elkanah Walker,*
*The Spokane Primer*

In *Hebrew* Elkanah *means "God is Possessing." Elkanah Walker, a strict Congregationalist and one of six missionaries sent by the American Board of Foreign Missions to Oregon, approached the neighboring Spokane Indians with every intention of possessing them—for God.*

*Walker was born in 1805, the sixth of ten children of a shoemaker from Maine. His early childhood was spent on a farm—a fortunate prelude to later years in Oregon, when his missionary funds were cut off and he was forced to live as a farmer. Walker became a dedicated Christian at the age of twenty-four, and decided upon the ministry*

*at twenty-seven. He was older than most theological students, and further handicapped by a lack of formal education. His wife, Mary Richardson, remembered him as "tall and awkward" at their first meeting, ". . . a rather ordinary, unaspiring man," whom she knew was anxious to marry. Mary wanted to go to Oregon and needed a husband. Elkanah needed a wife. They were quickly engaged, then married. The American Board of Commissioners for Foreign Missions agreed to finance the couple's horseback passage across the Rockies, but once in Oregon they eventually had to live by their own resources.*

*Accompanied by two other missionary couples, the Eells and the Grays, they left on the first leg of their 3,400-mile journey from New York on March 15, 1838. The Walkers settled in Tshimakain, seventy miles north of the Hudson Bay Company at Fort Colville, living there ten years until the infamous Whitman massacre of 1847, when two renegade Cayuse Indians killed Dr. Whitman, his wife Narcissa, and ten fellow missionaries at the nearby Waiilatpu Mission. When the board closed its Oregon operations in 1853, the Walkers turned to full-time farming and wagon trucking to support their eight children. After the Walkers' departure from Tshimakain, lit-*

*tle evangelical progress occurred. The site did not become an active mission again until 1873.*

*Walker died in 1877. He counted among his greatest accomplishments nine years of work among the Flathead Indians and* The Spokane Primer, *a volume of biblical instructions in the local Indian language. He typeset the book by hand and printed it on the mission press at Lapwi in 1842—both endeavors he had never attempted before.*

## 1841

JANUARY: FRIDAY 1ST. Have promised my self to commence a Journal & to continue it. In consequence of my promise, Mrs. W. has made each of us a book for notes and journal. This of course lays me under some obligation.

MONDAY 4. The day set apart by the church universal for fasting and prayer . . . I hope I tried to make a new consecration of myself to God & to humble myself before him . . . Spent a short time this evening at the old Chief's lodge. The Indians had worship by themselves about noon.

TUESDAY 5. Weather cloudy & cold without snow. Made the old Chief a visit & heard a long account from him of their mythology. It is the (height?) of foolishness & immorality. What can be the state of their minds when females will sit & listen to such indecent talk without manifesting [the] least sense of delicacy & even join in the conversation & laughter?

FRIDAY 15. Cold continues. No Indians about the house . . . Read but little or thought much. I am almost ashamed of myself because I make no more advance in the language. Thought tonight that I should be willing to give all my goods, house & all, if I could by it understand the language.

FEBRUARY: FRIDAY 5. Spent most of the day in reading a strange novel of which I did not have a very good opinion . . . I often wished during the day I had started for home, as I want to see my wife & children very much. [Walker had trudged seventy miles to Fort Colville for tobacco, a "filthy habit" he maintained until the age of fifty, much to the distress of Mary and his fellow missionaries.] No man has a wife more deserving of the warmest affection than I have. She is gaining very fast on me. I find I love her more and more daily & hope she will continue to improve as much in her manner as she has of late, & will continue to make the same exertions to please me. If she does, I shall consider myself one of the happiest of men.

WEDNESDAY 17. Quite unwell, did nothing & said but little. I am sensible [that] unless I can be relieved in some way, my health will not endure the task. Rode out with the Chief.

THURSDAY 18. Made a pen for the pig & was so exhausted that I could not keep my eyes open & went to sleep on the floor.

APRIL: FRIDAY 2. Rode out to day & was taken quite unwell with a kind of amazement. Every thing seeming like a dream with an oppressed feeling at the stomach. Felt some better in the evening . . .

SATURDAY 3. Had a pretty good night's rest last night . . . Awakened with quite a pain in my bowels which I attributed to the medicine I had taken through the day.

WEDNESDAY 21. Ordered last night a quantity of grass cut for my bed to make it soft, which was done & retired early to rest & had a good night's rest & found myself free from headake & told the Chief I had grown better. Made a cup of tea & toasted some bread, took a light breakfast, but soon after I had eaten, I began to feel worse . . .

MAY: SATURDAY 22. We all took a ride out for quite a distance. It was too long for comfort & we were all pretty well tired. Mrs. W. had some unpleasant feelings towards me, thinking I did not show as much disposition to accommodate her as I ought. I regret that I did not comply with her wishes.

JUNE: WEDNESDAY 9. We had a short meeting last night [the four couples of the Oregon mission had briefly reunited] & as Mr. Spalding was rather weary from his journey, they called upon me to take the lead of the meeting. I was rather perplexed to know how to get along without calling on the women to pray, but managed to in such a manner as not to come near the women. [Early missionaries Whitman and Spalding believed women should join in social prayer. Walker and Eells did not. When Walker was gone, Mary prayed audibly, but was distressed that her husband might disapprove.]

THURSDAY 10. Took a dose to make me sleep, but it did not produce the desired effect. Was much disturbed by an unpleasant smell occasioned by Mr. E. snuffing the candle in the spit box which contained sawdust. It was a wonder that the house was not burned. I was so excited with the labors of yesterday that I could not sleep. On that account I think that the house was saved.

SATURDAY 12. It was late last night before we retired . . . Most of the day has been spent in conference & I of course was not in much . . . I felt, & so did the rest, that it was impossible for the Mission to ever come together in such a manner as to move harmoniously together. Nothing can, so it seems, bring peace but the removing of some of its members. What is to be the end of these things, I know not. I sometimes think if we despair of doing it ourselves, God may do it for us. This is my last & only hope . . . [Spalding's unforgiving nature and constant criticisms, coupled with his flamboyant personality, caused dissension among mission members—who finally pleaded with the board to remove him. Later, as Spalding's behavior improved, Dr. Marcus Whitman rode to Washington to persuade the board to ignore the missionaries' earlier complaint.]

WEDNESDAY 7 . . . The flies very thick & troublesome.

THURSDAY 8. Nothing special, except I washed my feet in cold water this evening.

JULY: FRIDAY 9. Awoke & found I had considerable of a sore throat which I ascribed to my washing my feet in cold water. I was expecting Mr. Eells yesterday but he did not come & I was told before I was up that Mr. E's horses had come in. I was well satisfied that they had given him the slip & started after him . . .

TUESDAY 27. News came in this morning that Mrs. Eells had a pretty fair prospect of being confined right away . . . I concluded to [return] & did encamp at a small stream about two thirds of the way to Colville.

WEDNESDAY 28. Reached the fort about noon and found that my things were left at [Fort Okanogan].

FRIDAY 30 . . . Did not make a very early start & reached home in the afternoon & to my joy found all well & Mrs. Eells delivered of a boy the same evening I left home. Was nearly beat out when I got home.

SATURDAY 31. Was quite lame last night from a kick I received when near home yesterday . . .

SEPTEMBER: TUESDAY 7. The most important event that took place to day was the unexpected arrival of Mr. Spalding & family. We had rather an interesting time & I hope a profitable one. They appear disposed to make friends & be at peace.

SUNDAY 12. Had quite a number to worship to day. Had worship with them three times & was quite exhausted by night . . . Feel quite lonely. I hope I shall have some company soon. We need some good helpers here to take charge of our secular affairs. I think I want to know something more about the language.

NOVEMBER: SUNDAY 7. Was much fatigued last night & of course felt quite dull to day. Talked to the Indians at noon, felt rather stupid & did not talk with much energy. Tried to tell them the fullness of the atonement & show them their certain doom if they continued in the state in which they now are. I think I gave them some new ideas & hope it will do them good . . .

SUNDAY 14. Did my part of worshipping with the Indians: gave them in the evening the account of the ten virgins [Matt. 25]. But still they do not attend very well. Have said as much as I could stand & talked to Mrs. W. for spending so much of the day in reading what was not intended for Sabbath reading.

SUNDAY 21. Not being well to day, did not feel much interest in speaking & do not know when I have talked with such little energy . . . The Indians are less interested than they appeared to be formerly. God alone can give them the hearing ear & the understanding heart & when he speaks, they will hear.

DECEMBER: SUNDAY 19. Felt remarkably dull to day & could not talk with any energy. Gave a description of the legion of Devils. Went to the lodge in the evening & found the Teacher at work on his snow shoes. [Hard at work transcribing the first vocabulary of the Spokane dialect, Walker constantly sought linguistic aid from willing Indians.]

WEDNESDAY 22. Commenced teaching the [Indian] children to day. They do not appear to be very anxious to attend & I expect they will not be very punctual.

SATURDAY 25. Taught the children in the morning. I had a request to let the Indians thrash the wheat of the Chief in the new house but did not consent . . .

FRIDAY 31. This is the last day of the year. One more year has gone its rounds & we have all been spared. I have been permitted to pursue our labors without molestation, but we can not say, so far as this people are concerned, that it has been a year of the right hand of the most high. Surely we can say that goodness & mercy have followed us all the days of this year.

I have not enjoyed so good health as some former years but think it is some improved from what it was in the spring. I have not lived as I ought but think I have had more enjoyment in religion than formerly & have felt more its importance. I have abundant reason for gratitude & praise.

## 1842

FEBRUARY: THURSDAY 24. It commenced snowing early this morning & continued to storm most of the day, a sort of

Professor W. D. Lyman delivers an address in memory of Elkanah Walker, October 29, 1908, at Tshimakain, site of the Eells-Walker Oregon mission.

rain snow. Made a shelter over the saw pit & then sent for the Indian. Fell & hurt my side very much & it is a mercy that it is no worse. Went & had some talk with my teacher. He seemed to understand very well about the people & said that they did not feel the least concern about their souls & that he was just like them. If we had a plenty of tobacco, we shall have people enough about us as long as that lasted.

SUNDAY 27. We laid some later this morning than common. Have felt unwell all day & my side has been more sore. But a few people present to day. Gave them the story contained in the seventh chapt. of second Kings. Tried to impress upon their minds the omnipotence of God. I fear they do not get or form correct impressions of God, that they think he is something like their Medicine men. It seems to me that they grow more stupid & less attentive to religion & they say they have no concern about their souls.

MARCH: WEDNESDAY 16 . . . Mrs. W. was safely delivered of a son this evening. We have every reason for gratitude from our heavenly father for his unnumbered mercies.

SUNDAY 6. Only a few people present to day at worship. Mr. Eells addressed them & made rather a poor speech & gave them some errors for want of language. I took the same subject at the evening worship.

THURSDAY 17. The snow was much gone in the plain. We had a very comfortable night, notwithstanding the sickness of Mrs. W. . . . [She is] as comfortable as we could expect & [I] find it quite hard to take care of the house.

[Between May and June of 1842 the missionaries held a meeting at Waiilatpu to settle their differences. The main source of conflict was the dissension between Whitman and Spalding, with Walker acting as a moderating influence.]

MAY: MONDAY 16. Commenced our session to day. Did not do much except make an organization . . .

TUESDAY 17. Did no business to day. Had Mr. McKinley with us [chief trader from Walla Walla]. Had our meeting this evening.

FRIDAY 20. It was agreed by all that we should without delay start for Clearwater. The move struck me as unfavorable & I consented merely as a matter of course & felt that I was wholly in the dark for what purpose we were going & set my thinkers to work to see if I could not think of some better way & hit upon a plan which met the approbation of all, which was to send our opinions clothed with the authority of the Mission.

TUESDAY 31. Had a hard session to day & there was so much bad feeling manifested that I said that I thought it was an abomination for us to meet to pray. We had no meeting this evening.

JUNE: SUNDAY 5. Had rather a sleepless night . . . I took two pills to make me sleep. Have been rather stupid to day & I suppose it might be expected, after so much excitement. I preached to day & preached my missionary sermon as it was the day before the monthly concert. I liked my sermon very well. Think it quite good.

SUNDAY 26. Made preparation to go & had worship with the natives at their encampment. I was three hours in going & two & one-half in coming. Had two worships with them & tried to give them earnest instruction. It does seem to me that they have no fear of death & hell & that they are wholly insensible to the love of God to them . . . It seems that neither horror nor love can move them.

MONDAY 27. Went to the [Spokane] river to day & had worship with the few Indians at that place. Got one piece of salmon.

SEPTEMBER: SATURDAY 17. Felt some better today but felt rather lonely. About noon the old Chief came in & I had considerable talk with him . . .

SUNDAY 18. Went out and caught my horse & thought of myself & concluded that my feelings were the suggestions of the evil one to destroy my peace & usefulness. This has relieved my mind in a measure & I pray that I may have the grace to serve God faithfully, let my end be when it may. Had worship with the Indians about noon & then again about four o'clock & went in the evening & had some talk with the Chief. He talked well . . .

NOVEMBER: TUESDAY 1. Wrote more in the book to day than yesterday. We were writing when the Indians came up with letters. We learned that Dr. W. [Whitman] left on the third of Oct. for the States without any letters from us . . .

WEDNESDAY 2. Took a good ride this morning before breakfast . . . Met Mr. E. soon after breakfast coming in with the letters & wanting to have more talk over them. I told him that I could not talk then as I was engaged about my potatoes. He stayed some time and then went off. I think I have good reason to think that he does not have much confidence in me. Even his wife said as much as this & I think that in order to get along with him, I must not offend him in any thing. My opinion is good for nothing— only when it accords with his & so it is good for nothing in his estimation . . . Had quite a number of Indians to work to day & have finished my potatoes . . .

THURSDAY 3. Have done something more to day at the book. I find that I can stand it longer than Mr. E. Finished my store house . . .

SATURDAY 5. Went after the horses this morning before breakfast. Found that I was going to have a headake. Have had it all day. Had one lesson only . . . Had some contention

with the old Chief but he yielded to me. I think he improves some in prayer.

SUNDAY 6 . . . Had the Chief come & had a long talk with him. Gave him to understand that they ought not to hope that God would bless them so long as they let their thieves go unpunished.

MONDAY 7. Started early this morning with an Indian after the cows. We hunted all day but could not find them, so we had to make up our minds to go without fresh meat one day longer.

SUNDAY 13 . . . Mr. E. talked to them in the morning & I did in the evening. Had no rehearser & I was glad of it. I find I can talk better without one than with one. Gave them one of my hardest talks I ever did & I think they did not much relish it. But I see no evidence that it did them any good & it seems they are bent on their destruction & they will work it unless God interferes & saves them. All we can do is vain.

DECEMBER: FRIDAY 2 . . . Finished setting the rest of the type [Walker printed 250 copies of the sixteen-page *Spokane Primer* on the mission printing press] & struck off the numbers & commenced setting up four pages more. I think we succeed well for new beginners. Rode out this evening on the Lawyer's horse. [The "Lawyer" was a learned Nez Perce chief who assisted Walker in his Nez Perce and Flathead language studies.] Had considerable talk with the Lawyer on the language.

SUNDAY 4 . . . Have had rather a listless day to day. I have some fears that Mr. S. does not give his people the best kind of instruction. I fear he is inclined to preach something else than Christ. It is snowing this evening.

TUESDAY 6. Got up in doubt what to do, whether to make a start to day or not. Thought some of getting all ready &

Two girls contemplate a parade in California.

Student evangelists amuse themselves by a river near Abilene, Texas.

Sunday picnickers stage a footrace in California.

Thomas Riggs and missionary workers pausing for a meal

Miss Lockheart, possibly on a Sunday stroll through a California forest

Students of the Baptist Normal School, Grand Island, Nebraska, pose during their Sunday outing.

A picnic on the Sabbath, near Monterey County, California

Trainee missionaries enjoy a Sunday meal, Pasadena, California.

make an early start the next morning but feared it would be too hard for my animals to go through in four days. Made a late start & came to the foot of the mountains. It was long after sunset when I got into camp.

THURSDAY 8. Made a pretty early start this morning . . .

SATURDAY 10. Thick fog this morning when we started . . . Was full of melancholy apprehensions, but reached home & found all well. A merciful Providence had carried me through many dangers & kept me & mine & wife . . .

SUNDAY 11. Felt dull and stupid all day. Was able to say something to the people in the afternoon. Mr. McPherson [a Hudson Bay man who frequently visited the Walkers] on his way to Colville made us a call & spent the day with [us] & gave us to understand that the priest was losing influence among the Indians & that they were interfering with the trade of the Company. God can, & we have assurance from his word, that he will bring all their plans & designs to naught.

[Only twenty-two Indians were converted by the Protestant missionaries. Unlike the nearby Catholics, the Protestants demanded an identifiable conversion experience before the Indians could become a part of the mission family. However, there was marked competition between the Catholic blackrobes, who lived without women and were perceived as more "holy," and the Protestant missionaries, who were engaged in family life.]

MONDAY 19. Went down & commenced the school; gave out eleven books. Drove up the horses & after that went to hauling fencing stuff although it was late. Made a good day of it. In the evening commenced [school] at the lodge here; had eight present. Heard to day that they were absent playing medicine at the lodge above us . . .

TUESDAY 20. Spent most of the day at the lodges. The old Chief was in the steam bath. I thought that he kept away

lest I should say something to him about this medicine.

THURSDAY 22 . . . The school has increased to sixteen . . .

FRIDAY 23 . . . Went to the school. Had a short lesson . . . Hauled poles in the afternoon.

SATURDAY 24. Went to the Chief's to day & talked to the people here. Gave them in the forenoon the ten commandments & in the afternoon the atonement made by Christ, which I think I did with more clearness & force than ever before . . .

MONDAY 26. Heard this morning that they were going to play the Nehian [part of the Spokane medicine rites] to night at the Chief's place which altered the arrangement of Mr. Eells. When will they learn not to trust in lying vanities . . .

FRIDAY 30 . . . Mr. E. thinks the old Chief is more strongly attached to his medicine than ever.

SATURDAY 31 . . . This is the last day of the year 1842. God in his mercy has seen fit to bring us all to see it in peace & comfort. It has been a year of peace & quiet as far as the Indians have been concerned & how great are our obligations to him for mercies past & what ought to be our confidence in him for time to come. How much reason I have for humiliation & self abasement . . . I have been so distrustful of his goodness . . . I have done so little for him. May his grace be sufficient for me that I may spend the year that is to come, if permitted to stay on earth, more to his glory, be more active in his cause & be the means of greater good that his name may be glorified.

# 1843

JANUARY: SUNDAY 1. This has been a day of deep interest to us. We have been permitted to come around the table of our dying Lord & celebrate his dying love. Still I have been quite stupid & not felt as I should & am compelled to cry, "My leanness, my leanness." Draw me, O Lord, & I shall run after Thee. Quicken Thou me for I hope in thy mercy.

In my address to the Indians I [spoke] with considerable freedom but they will not regard it . . . Mr. Eells addressed the Indians in the afternoon. It seemed to me that he was not much impressed with his subject & did not give them much that was new. I cannot see that he makes any advancement in the language . . .

TUESDAY 3. Went early this morning to instruct the children. Did not stay long, as we expected to kill another beef but did not, it was so late & was storming quite fast when I reached home. Heard after my return that they were going to play the medicine again at the Chief's. Felt somehow tried about it & thought we ought to do [something] about it . . .

WEDNESDAY 4. Kept the cattle last night & early this morning took down the beef & by noon had him about dressed. Went to the school, saw some with the sign of the Spirit on their heads. Some had their heads tied up, for what purpose I do not know, whether to keep their spirits from running off or to conceal them. Said nothing about their medicine. Opened the school with prayer & said as much as I could of the supremacy of God. Told them it was to no purpose that I came down, as they were so sleepy that they did not give any attention . . .

THURSDAY 5 . . . Started pretty good season this morning to go to the school. Had considerable talk with the old Chief about their medicine & was astonished that his belief was so strong . . . they were so full of the medicine that I came away as soon as I could get off. I am much in doubt what is best to do. It does not seem quite right to keep silent, & to come out boldly upon them, it seems to me, would do them no good . . .

FRIDAY 6. Quite cold this morning & I delayed to go down to the school till afternoon. Was determined to say nothing on any subject lest I should get into a controversy about their medicine—which I was convinced would do no good in the state they were then in. Had the school as soon as I could & came off after saying a few things to the old Queen, as we call her, being constantly at work. [I] thought that she ought to make the young women do more.

MONDAY 9. Have been quite down all day. Heard that they are playing the medicine at the Chief's. O foolish & wicked people . . . Went & taught the children this evening. Find that they have not made so much progress as I expected.

WEDNESDAY 11 . . . I have been more incensed with Mr. E. to day. I fear we shall have trouble about the language. Spent considerable time at the lodge this evening talking on the language. I find it very difficult to catch the sounds they make.

THURSDAY 12 . . . Went in the afternoon to the Chief's. Had some talk with him about the language. I am determined to keep writing & if I write any thing fit for the press, I will let him see it & make what changes he sees fit. I shall say no more to him for the present about writing a book, as I have spoken to him several times . . . If I had not drove it through [*The Spokane Primer*], we should not have had one now.

I was some what displeased with [Eells's] conduct to day . . . [O]ne of [the Indians'] little images was set up for some purpose (I know not what) and [he] carried it off a piece & threw it down. I told him I thought that such things were not the best. It was like pulling down the images in the time of the Reformation, which was so strongly condemned by the wise and prudent of those days.

But I suppose I must be careful how I disapprove of any

of his doings as he will not bear to be told of his faults.

The old Chief had considerable to say about their medicine. He put it in the background & God far ahead . . .

SUNDAY 15 . . . Went to the Chief's to address the people & found that he & his two sons were gone, so I had the pleasure of talking without a rehearser, which I found is much better. They seemed quite unmoved at the truth of the gospel & seemed more hard & stupid than ever . . . The only thing which seems to engross their attention is what shall we eat & drink & how to get it without laboring for it?

TUESDAY 17. Wrote till a late hour last night in a letter to Mr. Rogers. As Mrs. W. was washing [I] thought I might as well be writing as not, as I should not sleep if I went to bed.

WEDNESDAY 18. Went this morning to the school & found the old Chief quite unwell after his medicine. Did not say much to him. When I went in, I remarked that it rained. He made the reply that he could not get them to make medicine for snow. They all said their medicine was good for rain, that they might have some roots & a plenty of small fish. How easy it seemed to me to show me that the thing had happened just as they wanted but I presume there was no such thing said in their medicine for rain.

Confined to the house most of the afternoon to take care of the children, to let Mrs. W. fix for dipping candles.

FRIDAY 20. It was quite cold this morning, but as we had concluded to go en mass to the Chief's, we thought we would go. We did, & had a pretty cold time of it & found the Chief in no very agreeable mood to receive us. He appeared more unkind than we commonly see him. Spent considerable time there & did not reach home till sunset. The children well tired.

SATURDAY 21. We had one of the coldest nights we have

had this winter . . . It has been quite cold to day but more moderate this evening . . .

He [Eells] seems more engaged in doing other things [than] preparing himself for usefulness among the people & [it seems] to me that if we could get a good knowledge of the language, we would better do these things afterwards. We could do much more good with less labor among the people. But it may be that my course is such that he cannot meet me & labor with me on the language.

If I knew this was the case, I could reform when I knew I was wrong. I can see nothing new in his conduct which would lead me to suspect any such thing, for it ever has been so since we have been in the field. But it is more important that we should come together now than ever. Had we always made it a subject of conversation, we should have been much further advanced. We have now nothing settled about the language.

SUNDAY 22 . . . Rose earlier this morning than common. Made some preparation for the address to the Indians. Went & gave them quite a long talk . . . Found Mrs. W. reading newspapers when I returned both times from Indian worship. She said she had read nothing else all day. [Walker believed her to be breaking the Sabbath by reading newspapers.]

SUNDAY 29 . . . [Mr. Eells] did not close with prayer in Indian but I thought it may be because I some time ago spoke to him about some of his expressions not being grammatical. If I thought that this was the case, I should be exceedingly sorry, as I do not wish to have him think that I was his teacher in Indian, or that I wished to show that I knew more about the language than he did, but simply for his good, & for the good of the native.

I have a deep sense of my sins to day, even an apprehensive sense of them, as committed against God. But I think I was able to trust in Christ for pardon . . .

I addressed the Indians in the afternoon & think I was able to do it with more freedom & energy than common. Had no regular subject but attempted to show them that they were of the same disposition of heart as the murderers of Christ because they did not repent of their sins.

TUESDAY 31. Laid late this morning as Mrs. W. was up till past midnight washing. Considerable cold . . . It has been rather an unpleasant day to me, from Mr. Eells saying that he was in doubt about building here. I do not know what he intends, but one thing I have about determined in my own mind, is that I shall not oppose him, or say much one way or the other. I think I shall not give up here without higher authority than there is in the country.

I have been brought into difficulty in listening to his remarks and suffering them to have influence with me, & henceforth I am determined to pursue my business without shifting about. We had no meeting this evening as Mr. E. had the headake. Mrs. W. and myself had united prayers. What makes him have the headake so much on this evening?

FEBRUARY: SATURDAY 25 . . . Took quite a long walk on snow shoes & find it did not tire me so much as I expected but after walking three or four miles, I was quite ready to get on a horse. The Indians get plenty of deer & are as big & confident as they need to be. I was quite tired with them.

SUNDAY 26. Mr. Eells addressed the people this afternoon & took for his subject in the afternoon one of the verses in the last chapter of [Rev.] . . . but it did not appear to excite their anger or fear. How much we need the

Spirit's outpouring here to revive the working of our own hearts & to fasten a conviction upon the hearts of this people.

MARCH: WEDNESDAY I. It was the coldest night last night we have had. The ice in the trough about two [inches thick]. Went to see the horses & found them all well, but some poor & hungry. Have felt rather dull today. Do not know why, but all my religious services do not satisfy me. I seem to be hungering for something more; felt as though I wanted to see a revival among these Indians & am almost at times able to believe that God was about to pour out his Spirit here . . .

FRIDAY 24. The old Chief came about noon. We had a long talk. Mr. E. does not get very correct ideas of what the Indians say, or I am very much mistaken. He cannot give them in good language any nice statement of things.

TUESDAY 28 . . . Another creature found dead. We were very much dissatisfied with the conduct of the Indians. As it could not be decided whose it was, we took the meat . . . We had our meeting. Mr. E. took the lead.

APRIL: SUNDAY 2. Felt very dull this morning & ill prepared for the duties of the Sabbath. Addressed the people in the morning on the commandment to honor the Sabbath. Think Mrs. W. spends too much of her Sabbaths in reading newspapers, which as a general thing are not appropriate reading for [that day]. They were never designed to be read on the Sabbath unless for relaxation. No one who spends most of their time reading papers, although of a religious character, on that holy day, can have a very clear & exalted view of its sacredness & must suffer; if not in time, they will in eternity.

SATURDAY 8. Had two women helping to day & it relieved me of work in the house but I have been very busy in getting the Chief at work ploughing. He succeeds very well but they make foolish work of putting horses in & handling them.

SATURDAY 15. The old Chief planting potatoes. We gave him some seed. They made wretched work of it, planting too thick. Made out our bill for Vancouver. Felt more tired with Mr. E. to day in some remarks he made about sending to Boston his letter [concerning the problems with Spalding]. I fear we have seen our most harmonious days.

I am determined to yield to him in all things so far as I am able.

## 1844

FEBRUARY: SUNDAY 4 . . . It has thawed some. I addressed the people this forenoon of the duty of children honoring their parents. We had English worship at our house. Mr. E. took the lead. I had quite a ride after some stray horses but could not find them. I saw many wolves' tracks & one single horse. Mr. E. lost his mule last night so that he could not take his sled to worship.

SATURDAY 10. I set my Indians threshing my wheat & finished it. I have had more trouble with the Indians to day . . . Paid off one. I told him he need not work any more. Mrs. W. quite unwell & she thinks she may be confined before morning . . .

SUNDAY 11. Mrs. W.'s expectations were realized & she was delivered of a son about ten o'clock. [The baby was Joseph Elkanah, one of five children.]

Mrs. Eells and myself had to manage the affair & we felt considerable anxiety about it, but finally succeeded quite well with the child but the after birth was long in coming as her pains subsided. By stimulants, we were able to excite pains & to succeed . . .

What abundant cause we have for gratitude & praise & what reasons we have to humble ourselves before God and to trust him more faithfully. Mrs. W. has had quite a comfortable day of it . . . Mrs. Eells stayed with Mrs. W. while we were at Indian worship . . . We did not have any English service to day as we found that all our energies were needed in the other duties of the day, which has been a hard one to us.

FRIDAY 16. I was up but once last night. I have had the best night's rest I have had this long time . . . It has been a quiet day for us.

SATURDAY 17. We had a pretty good night of it last night. Mrs. W. is quite smart. As I was making my breakfast & toasting some bread, an Indian came in & blew his nose upon it. It so vexed me that I told him he was like the hogs, which caused him to leave the house & as he was going, I called him back to take his pay. After a while he came, & I paid him off. He asked if he was done work[ing]. I told him he was. There has been quite a number here from abroad to day.

TUESDAY 20. We were up rather earlier this morning than common of late . . . An Indian came & told me that the Indian whom Mr. E. offended yesterday said he would kill a cow. We took no notice of it & at night the same Indian came & said that the one who gave out the threats was ashamed & had thrown away his anger.

MARCH: TUESDAY 12. Started to day for Colville. We encamped at the Fool's place . . . Cyrus stood it well.

WEDNESDAY 13. Reached Colville to day & found all as well as common. Sat up late.

THURSDAY 14. I rested very bad last night on account of some treatment I received from Mr. McD. & determined that I would not give him an opportunity to treat me so again. We started for home to day but could not find Cyrus's horse. I am very much inclined to think that he is stolen. We encamped in the big plains.

SATURDAY 16. We had to wait a long time before our animals could be found. We traveled very fast & reached home, sun about two hours high & found all well. I have had one of the most unpleasant journeys to Colville that I ever made, & I think it will be long before I shall go there [again].

SUNDAY 17 . . . Mr. E. talked to the Indians in the morning. I conducted the English service at our house & talked to the Indians in the evening.

TUESDAY 19. Up quite early this morning & found the dogs had eaten up my whip.

APRIL: TUESDAY 16. I went to the river to get some one to go with me but could not obtain any one as all were gone away. [Then] I planted some more corn. Some strange Indians came in and attempted to smoke in the house. Mrs. W. was more moved with them than common for her.

JULY: TUESDAY 2. I did not rest much last night & of course I have had a miserable day of it. Talked some to an Indian on the duty of living for God & making eternity the great business of life.

WEDNESDAY 3. I have become so worn out with our guest [a biologist named Geyer, who stayed with the Walkers for a year] that I hardly know what to do. I hope he will soon leave us. We have come to the conclusion that we shall tell him to go soon if he does not leave without.

FRIDAY 5. The Chief came in to day & the others [who] had caused us some trouble left & we were glad that they are now gone. The Chief behaved very well, encamped a good distance from us & said he thought it well the people should not encamp too near. Some did not like it, but as for himself, he did not dislike it. I swapped cattle with him. We have given him a suit of clothes & allowed him to put some provisions in the hen house.

SUNDAY 7 . . . Mr. E. was intending to go to the river but I told him that if he would have an exercise with the children, I would go. He readily consented. I have had a pleasant time & think the people appeared more than usually interested . . . My subject was the conversion of Paul. I endeavored to impress upon their minds that what they did to his children, they did it to Christ & that he would revenge all insults done to his children just as they would any injury done to their children . . .

My patience is clean gone with Mr. Geyer . . .

MONDAY 8. After worship this morning, I told Mr. G. that it was not consistent for us to entertain him any longer, as our means were not given to support any but missionaries.

SATURDAY 13. I had a long ride after the horses. It seems singular that when it is my turn to hunt horses, they always get far away. Mr. E. left for the lower fishing place to spend the Sabbath with the Indians.

SUNDAY 25 . . . I hope it will still rain to clear off the smoke which is now so thick [a forest fire is in the area] to be disagreeable. Elkanah [was] coughing last night. It has been rather a gloomy day to me. I have had many thoughts about myself & some ardent desire that I might be Christ's indeed. I find it good to examine myself . . . If I am not deceived, I have an increasing desire for the salvation of souls. It is a grief to me that Mrs. W. is disposed to read so much that is not devotional on the Sabbath. I fear that her view of the sacredness of the day is very limited.

OCTOBER: TUESDAY 15 . . . We had our meeting this evening. Simpleton wanted [to] borrow the gun. I told him he might have it. He then wanted some powder. I told him no. I had already let him have twenty loads. He put the gun down & went off. He came [back] in the evening and talked in a very friendly manner. Mr. E. took the lead in our meeting.

WEDNESDAY 16. Simpleton came & wanted to borrow the gun to carry off with him to Colville & after some time he would come back with it. I told him no. We did not let our guns go away. When the people were encamped here, we let them [use the gun]. He was very much enraged & began to use abusive language. I left him & went off. Just as he was starting, I saw him take some fire. I expected he intended to burn the barn. When [he] got abreast of the house, he came & told me that he was going to burn the plain & to look out for our houses. I told him to do just as he was disposed. He set fire which burned up some important grass, but did not do much damage.

THURSDAY 17 . . . I commenced making a window in the dining room, but could not do much as I had to spend so much time hunting &c.

WEDNESDAY 23. We had a very quiet night last night. I told my Little Man [an Indian] some things I had against him & should have set him to work before, only I did not know his heart . . .

MONDAY 28. I did not mean to do much to day, but I got into the work before I knew it & have been busy all day. We commenced on the school house.

THURSDAY 31. We have been all brought to the close of another month. We have been highly favored through this month of God. We have been busy on the house & have got most of the roof on. I had rather an unpleasant affair with an Indian to day. He climbed over the fence & took a hoe out. I went out & took the hoe from him & told him when he wanted a hoe to ask for it. I had worship with the Indians but he did not attend.

DECEMBER: FRIDAY 27. It was some stormy this morning. I fixed up a mat over the saw pit so that the Indians could saw. I sent a boy after the horses who brought them back in due season. I took some of the children to ride out, & met Mr. E, contrary to my expectations . . .

SATURDAY 28. As I had rather a bad cold, I made my way to bed [in] pretty good season last night but was much disturbed by Mrs. W. who kept to work till a late hour . . . [Excerpt from Mary Richardson Walker's diary: ". . . Mr. W. loaded me with reproaches so that my night's rest was far from being quiet."]

I have felt much down to day at the sad desolation all around us & no prospect seemingly of being able to do any good to any one. But I feel that all opposition of [ours] is vain because God is on the throne of the universe. I feel I profess too much of a spirit to pray that fire might come down from heaven and destroy these idolaters.

TUESDAY 31 . . . We have been permitted to see the last day of another year. It has been a year of labor & toil & one of health to me & mine. I have experienced rich mercies for which, I hope, I am truly thankful.

# Benjamin Brown

"The manifestations of the goodness of God . . . ought not to be buried in oblivion or forgetfulness."
—Benjamin Brown,
*Testimonies for the Truth*

*Benjamin Brown, born in 1794 in Queensbury, New York, became a high priest in the Church of Jesus Christ of Latter-Day Saints and wrote* Testimonies for the Truth *in 1853 as a statement of his Mormon beliefs and of his faith in the extraordinary workings of God. Brown wrote ten years after the death of Joseph Smith and, along with his wife and children, was an active church member at the time of two of the sect's most significant historical events: the dedication of the Latter-Day Saints' temple in Kirtland, New York, and the flight to Nauvoo, Illinois, in which ten thousand church members escaped oppression in Missouri. As a preacher, his travels took him to Canada and England as well as through the United States. In the States he repeatedly suffered mob attacks led by ruffians who responded to the protectionist temper of the times and found Mormons fair game. Brown was utterly dedicated to his faith and "continued to preach, fearless of*

*opposition," hoping that each incident would "awaken attention" to the Latter-Day principles.*

*After finally migrating to Utah, he lived in Deseret— the Salt Lake Valley—for four more years, until 1852. Then he was called upon a mission to England, given a week's notice to leave, and sent forth with an optimistic prophecy for his success. He arrived in England January 5, 1853, "rejoicing in the mercies of [his] heavenly father." He died later that year.*

I was born on the 30th of September, in the year 1794, in the town of Queensbury, Washington county, state of New York. My father, Asa Brown, belonged to the denomination of "Friend Quakers." He [was a] farmer. I worked with him until I was twenty years of age.

During my boyhood I was much deprived of the benefits of education, owing to my father's moving from place to place and [buying cheap land] in new settlements. By these means he was able to have his children settle around him. Being thus raised . . . my ideas of religion were entirely Scriptur[al], with no priestcraft existing to diminish their force. Consequently, I believed in the Bible just as it read . . .

The idea that revelation from God was unattainable in this age, or that the ancient gifts of the gospel had ceased forever, never entered my head—until I gathered the notion from creeds of churches with which I became acquainted in after years. I can remember many times—while yet quite a boy—retiring to some barn on occasions of sickness among my relatives, and their being suddenly restored to health in answer to [my] prayers.

I continued thus until about fifteen years of age, when . . . I was unfortunate enough to hear [church] preaching. I soon began to lose my pure, simple ideas of God, and imbibe those more generally held. Shortly after, I found the hitherto simple Bible a perfect mystery.

I had previously been seriously and religiously in-clined, but the jarrings . . . of my new ideas shook [my] simple faith . . . A deep anxiety possessed me to find the truth.

About the age of twenty-five, I married and settled on a small farm of my own. Once, after a fatiguing day's labour, I returned home one evening, turned my back to the fire, as my custom was, and leaned with my head on my arms on the chair top to rest myself and dry my clothes . . . My wife tried to rest, expecting me to shortly follow. Thus left alone, I was musing on things generally, when a vision of my brother, who had died some fourteen or fifteen years previous, appeared before me, praying. I heard his voice clearly and distinctly, and listened atten-tively. He referred to a great work to be done on the earth during the last days, quoting several Scriptures . . . Soon he disappeared from my view, when suddenly . . . a sound . . . seemed to fill the house and myself, and I heard a voice saying, "This is the spirit of understanding." An open Bible appeared before me, so placed that I could see portions of . . . the Prophets and Apostles at once. Directly I heard the above words I began to read, [and] understand-ing and intelligence burst upon my mind . . . I seemed able to read a chapter in the time usually [spent] on one verse; and the contents of a whole book were laid before my mind as quickly as a single chapter . . . I never before saw such CONNECTION between the Scriptures. [I saw] what one Prophet had said on a subject, and directly, with the quick-ness of thought, I read what each of the other Prophets or Apostles had said about the same thing.

I saw the whole at a glance, perception . . . only the Holy Spirit can give.

I was disturbed . . . by my wife's calling to me. The vision left me, and I felt like a hungry man called away from a feast.

Five years more passed, and I was still unconnected with any religious party. At this time "Protracted Meet-ings" [camp meetings] were very popular in America . . . I felt unfavourable to these meetings, but such magnificent reports of their results—the wholesale conversion of souls—led me to attend one. Before going, I covenanted with the Lord. If He would reveal His mind and will to me, whatever sacrifice of duty He might require, I would do it.

As soon as I began to attend, I felt the Spirit of the Lord operating upon me, so that I seemed filled to overflowing with its teachings. A continual stream of glorious truths passed through my mind, my happiness was great, and my mind was so absorbed in spiritual things that all the time the meeting lasted, which was about fifteen days, I scarcely ate or drank anything . . . the Spirit of the Lord [removed] my desire to eat.

The subject of "Freemasonry" was just then agitating the public mind, so that many of the churches were di-

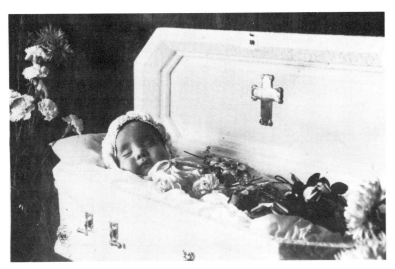

Young infant in burial casket, ca. 1920

Prayers at a grave site on the Lac Court Oreilles Chippewa Reservation, Reserve, Wisconsin, ca. 1910

Woman mourning "R. Tibb" near Jacksonville, Oregon, ca. 1870

Arthur Richardson's funeral, Wyoming

vided about it, into "Masons" and "Anti-Masons." [It] caused a great deal of quarreling and contention, and much anger and bad feeling, of which I knew but little until afterwards. I had heard of the two parties, but was not interested myself . . .

While [I was] sitting in the meeting, listening to the preaching . . . the Spirit of the Lord came upon me, and revealed that I was to visit the minister of the Anti-Masonic party, Judge Cushing, and tell him of his foolishness and wickedness in increasing the spirit of division between the brethren.

This mission was a very hard task. How was I, a man from the thrashing-floor to reprove a minister, and, moreover, a Judge? But the Word of the Lord came to me again with greater power than before, that I was to go AT ONCE! I had a covenant. I felt determined to fulfil it if it killed me. So I sprang to my feet, took my hat, and departed the meeting.

I found the Judge at a public inn, engaged in making some purchase. I requested to speak with him for a few minutes in private . . . I sat down, but the Spirit of the Lord was again upon me like fire in my bones, commanding me to deliver a message directly.

The Judge came, and the Spirit . . . filled my mouth with words, and I laid before him . . . his conduct. The Judge acknowledged his folly, said he would amend, and told me that he had had many sleepless nights on the same subject. He also said that . . . although I was a stranger to him, something told him why I came.

However, I had another trial to undergo, which occurred some days after, during the same meeting.

While the minister was preaching, it was revealed to me to rise up and declare to the congregation that they, before coming together to pray for others, ought first to be reconciled one to the other . . . Some were guilty of oppressing the poor, taking unlawful usury, oppressing the hirling in his wages, and many other sins.

I waited until the preacher had finished. The idea of having to rise and speak before this congregation of about fifteen hundred people [whom] I considered better persons than myself, filled me with fear, and the perspiration rolled.

I would sooner have given five hundred dollars than have buckled up to this task, but there was no escape, I had covenanted, and the moment the minister ceased speaking I delivered my message. I was received very well by the congregation, many fancying I was converted to their faith and, being blessed with such gifts, was a bit of a prize . . .

A whole year and a half I deferred my baptism, still waiting for my wife, who, although at first favourable to "Mormanism" had become a determined enemy to the Church. When I went to hear the "Mormons" preach at Westfield . . . I, with four others, was baptized . . . on the bank of the creek . . . My wife, who [was] present when I was going to the water, even threatened that she would not live with me . . . for she felt . . . it disgraced her to have her husband belong to a church that was so poor. [But a dream] and other confirmations so impressed her that she was baptized, and has remained firm to the Church ever since.

When I had been in the Church about a year and a half, I was ordained an Elder, under the hands of Jared Carter. The next day my wife and I went up to Kirtland [New York] to visit the Saints living there . . . While on the lakes, I was attacked by one of the lake fevers there, and became very ill indeed . . . The same day, two Elders of the Church called in to see me, and finding me in such a condition, they laid their hands upon me . . . I felt the disease remove from my body, commencing in the pit of my stomach, moving gradually upwards towards the hands of the Elders, and I was made perfectly whole . . . This was the first case of healing I had ever witnessed.

The succeeding winter I again went up to Kirtland to attend the dedication of the Temple . . . Hundreds of Elders spoke in tongues, but many of them being young in the Church . . . felt a little alarmed. This caused the prophet Joseph Smith to pray the Lord to withhold the Spirit. Joseph then instructed them on the nature of the gift of tongues, and the operation of the Spirit generally.

We had the most glorious and never-to-be-forgotten time . . .

By this time most of the members of the Pomphret Branch, into which I had been baptized, were gathered up to Kirtland, the first gathering-place of the Saints; and I was left without anyone to counsel or direct me as to the way in which I should devote my labours . . . when one day the Word of the Lord, by the power of the Spirit, came unto me, saying, "I have fourteen sheep in Portland: go and gather them also." I then began to preach for the first time, and for that purpose procured the schoolroom in Portland, and, through my friends, circulated a notice that I was going to preach. This gathered a small congregation of some thirty or forty people. At the time appointed I stood up to address them . . .

I continued preaching at Portland until the winter came on, when, having baptized a few out of the place, they met at my house . . . on the Sundays; and on the week days I extended my labours in the South . . .

Not long after receiving the office of Elder, I was called to lay hands on a sister named Crowell, in Chautauque county, New York, who was afflicted with a cancer . . . I visited her in the morning, and found her head, where the cancer had broken out, a dreadful sight, full of cancer worms, which were eating into the scull—three pieces of which had come out! I anointed her head with oil, and prayed the Lord on her behalf and . . . left to attend to my hay. The next time I saw her . . . she pulled off her cap and showed me her head. It was entirely healed, and the flesh was sound as ever . . .

[Brown emigrated from New York to Missouri along with his wife.]

I felt a great desire to gather up and live with the body of the Church. With this idea I endeavoured to dispose of my farm, but failed—the only thing that saved me from a share in the Missouri persecutions. The winter previous . . . I sold my farm, and the time for me to vacate expired just before this took place.

For several months I was preparing to remove, getting teams, waggons &c. When the time arrived, my wife, children and I . . . journeyed until we came to Springfield, about a hundred miles from Nauvoo, where we met with some brethren who had been driven out of Missouri. [They] told us that the Church was collecting in Nauvoo, then called Commerce. We turned our course in that direction, and arrived there in June—the weather being warm at that time. We found brothers Joseph Smith and Sydney Ridge there, with a few others. The rest were coming in daily in a most distressed condition. Many of them were sick, and they had no house to enter when they arrived. The nature of the climate, combined with the hardships they endured, soon made those ill who were not so before.

Numbers of the sick and dying had to lie on the ground, with only a blanket over them. No springs or wells were handy, and the Mississippi waters were unfit to drink, so that many had to go miles for water to give to the afflicted. Sometimes one would go on horseback with a jug, and fetch a little for the sick and take it round to them . . . The persecutions in Missouri [seemed] small matters compared to the miseries endured at this period in Nauvoo.

My family, with myself, were also taken sick, and I laid so for two or three weeks. I was so far gone that I was quite senseless, and all thought I was dying. Doubtless I should have died, but one day Joseph Smith was passing by my door . . . and . . . laid his hands upon me, and commanded me to rise and walk in the name of the Lord . . . I found myself walking on the floor, and within ten minutes I was out of the house visiting my daughter, whom I had not seen for nearly a month. I felt full of joy and happiness . . . This was the second time that I had been healed instantly by the power of God, through His servants. This man, Joseph Smith, was one the world [calls] an imposter, and a false prophet . . . Was it the power of imagination over my body that cured me, when I did not even hear Joseph's voice? . . . The honest in heart will [know].

During this period [I obtained] several missions, one to the North of Albany, another to the Eastern States [and] Nova Scotia. Our route lay through Chicago, a distance of two hundred miles, which we walked. Then by steamer we passed down the northern lakes to Buffalo, a journey of at least a thousand miles, and again took steamers on Lake Ontario, about four hundred miles further, and arrived at Sackett's Harbour. As we were destitute . . . we stopped to preach awhile, until we could procure means to go on. But the waters froze up, and we were compelled to spend the winter in this place. This brought me to a region where I had lived for ten years when a young man. [In] Lime, New York, we procured a school house as usual. The custom in America in laying out townships, which are usually about six miles square, is in every two-mile lot to apportion a piece of land for a school house. When the school house is

built, it is public property, and vested in the hands of three trustees. This enabled us to sound the Gospel in America easier, in some respects, than in England.

Two ministers who usually occupied the room greatly opposed us at the close of our preaching. They [tried] to set the people against us, but these ministers displayed such a weak, mean spirit that their congregation left them. We confined our labours chiefly to Jefferson county . . . where we managed to raise up some six Branches of 200 members. These were absolutely blessed with the gift of tongues, prophecy, healings, &c., and became very strong in faith . . .

Spring was coming on, and the river began to clear from ice, so that we were able to continue our journey to Nova Scotia. [At] a farewell meeting . . . a little boy stood up and spoke in tongues, the tears rolling down his face all the time. The interpretation stated that I should be mobbed and left for dead, and that the blood should run down from my head on my clothes and the ground. I took this for a timely warning, and thought that I might escape. [Thus] with great caution, I kept clear of much that I might have suffered.

[Brown and his partner met a man floating on a raft in the Saint John's River. He invited them twenty miles downstream to his home, where they stayed for some months.]

We commenced to baptize soon after arrival . . . [and] all manner of lies began to circulate about our conduct and intention. It was stated that we [interrupted] public meetings, and [this information] was given to the Governor of New Brunswick by the ministers and other enemies. This led him to send down an order to convene a meeting and procure evidence, either for or against, and report accordingly.

Mrs. Albert Manwaring and children in Springville, Utah, 1903

First Presidency of the Church of Jesus Christ of Latter-day Saints, 1901–1911

... These Justices ... had been searching law books for something to lay hold of us with, and found an old Statute, applying to the whole of the province, forbidding all Dissenters to hold public religious services without a written license from the Governer.

The day of the meeting arrived, and all manner of witnesses were raked together—amongst others a negro's evidence was taken, who had previously been convicted of lying.

I quickly discovered it was high time to stir in the matter, or possibly the next discovery would be that we were inmates of a jail: I [approached] Judge Nardsley, who had attended our meetings, and procured a certificate from him that he had done so, and had heard nothing injurious to the people or the government. And with this ... I went to the Governer's residence ... [He] was terribly prejudiced against us, and very ignorant of law and gospel. He broke down, however, before the arguments of his aid-de-camp, who pleaded on our behalf.

This enraged our enemies so much that our lives became endangered, and to escape their violence, we had to sleep in the woods, and do our baptizing in the night, as they [wanted] to mob us at the first opportunity. Unfortunately, one of the mobbers heard me promise to visit one of the brethren after I had been preaching one day. This mobber, with a party of about ten others, waylaid me. Some of them held me while the rest beat me about the head with their fists: but not being able to bruise me sufficiently in this manner, one of them took off one of my boots, and belaboured me about the head with the heel of it, until I was covered with blood, which ran down onto my clothes and the ground. Some of them then threw me down, and jumped upon me with their knees, until they broke several of my ribs. All this while I had been calling out loudly, whenever they did not stop my mouth. But it suddenly occurred to me that, if I feigned death, they would leave me, thinking their murderous work accomplished.

So I groaned loudly as if dying, and resigned myself into their hands, holding my breast as much as possible. This succeeded ... they left me, and ran off as fast as they could. Directly as they were gone I arose, though with great difficulty, and went into a house not far from there, where I washed the blood off my person, and Elder Crosby, who also came there, laid hands upon me. The mob, however, [somehow] discovering I was not dead, resolved to attack the house that night . . . They proposed to cut Elder Crosby's ears, tar and feather us, carry us out into the middle of St. John's river, and, after tying stones to our feet, sink us both.

First . . . a wooden rail [was] hurled against the window. The rail broke through the window and came in upon the bed where we were sleeping, and awoke us both. We immediately sprang up, and Elder Crosby rushed to the door where they were hammering to get in. He held it as well as he could, but in another moment they would have succeeded, had not Mrs. Shelton, who had been alarmed by the noise, come upon them unexpectedly with a lighted candle, and surprised them in the act. This frightened them [and], alarmed lest they be known, they fled the house.

We were quiet after this for about an hour, and Justice Shelton, at whose house we were stopping, went to alarm the neighbours, and his son who lived some distance off, so that we might have assistance in case of the mob returning.

They [did] return. They made a second attack upon the house, trying another door this time. But Elder Crosby held the door with an iron grasp and the resolution of a lion, and they were again unsuccessful. After drinking round, one of them managed to get his arm through the door opening, but . . . was caught round the waist in the arms of Mr. Shelton's son, who, with several others, entered the place at the moment.

And thus the Lord delivered us out of their hands . . .

Several of them were recognized by their friends. These Mr. Shelton put under bonds, but they threatened to burn his house and barn if he attempted to prosecute. Fearing the government . . . would refuse to back him up, he was compelled to let them go, and we remained without redress . . .

Notwithstanding, we did not leave the country, but continued to preach, fearless of opposition, until we had baptized about fifty, out of which we organized two branches. These were also visited abundantly with the signs following, and the Saints rejoiced greatly in the work.

. . . The work in New Brunswick rolled on prosperously, but the time came when we had calculated to be at home. We had heard too that our beloved Prophet had been murdered in Carthage gaol, and we naturally felt anxious to know how things were with our families and friends at Nauvoo. Our parting with the Saints in New Brunswick was not very pleasant, as may be supposed . . .

I arrived at Nauvoo safely, but I had scarcely been there three weeks before I was again sent to Jefferson county, again on a tithing mission. I got back in about four months, carrying with me about a thousand dollars which the Saints had donated towards building the temple of the Lord.

While I was on my mission to New Brunswick the Church agreed with the mobs to leave Nauvoo by the next grass time—spring, so that when I returned the second time, the city was all in excitement. All that could were selling out; some were disposing of their things by auction for whatever could be got, while others would take cartloads of furniture out into the country and "swap" it for money or cattle: for, ready or not ready, the mob meant to have the Saints out by the time stated.

My property was rather more pleasantly situated than many others, and I succeeded in getting 250 dollars for my house and orchard, the nursery to which contained six thousand grafted young fruit trees, and was worth three thousand dollars, at least. Many of the Saints would have been glad to have got off with no greater sacrifice than myself, but as the time drew near, the prices offered for our property fell in proportion. Some of the Saints did not get half as much as I did, for property equally valuable. Others got nothing at all, but had to leave their houses just as they were, and those living in the outskirts were saved the sacrifice of SELLING their houses for less than their worth, for the mob burned about three hundred of them down, and destroyed the property of the owners.

In February, 1846, the authorities took the lead, crossed the river Mississippi with a large camp, and stopped some seven or eight miles from the water, on the other side, waiting for the snow to go off, which just then had fallen heavily. Thus, they had no food for their cattle, and had great difficulty procuring any food, but as soon as possible they were on the move.

When the general emigration of the main body of the Church came on, it was pretty much all at once. On the Nauvoo side of the river, two or three hundred waggons were waiting at one time for the ferry. In these wagons the Saints had to sleep, cooking their food on the beach. Although all the boats and ferries that could be had were employed, this state of things continued for a month.

All the opposite shore was covered with waggons, in which the Saints were living, but multitudes were without any protection from the weather, except tents made with blankets, under one of which a whole family had to live. A scene of human suffering and endurance for the gospel's sake on so large a scale has seldom been seen on the earth.

Here were twenty thousand people, starting to locate a thousand miles beyond the borders of civilized life, over . . . impassable mountains. Reports had arrived of Colonel Fremont's exploration, and the hardships he had suffered, but there were not only men, but thousands of women and children, starting on the same hazardous journey, not only temporarily to endure these difficulties, but proposing to make a settled home in those dreary wilds, where not a spear of wheat could be raised.

Shortly the first camp moved on. But when the first camp had crossed the Missouri River, the command was, "Stop and raise grain to go on with next year." We had a thousand miles' journey ahead, and not a settlement on the road: besides, unless we wished to starve, we must have grain to sow our lands when we got there. So a spot was selected, and, before many weeks had passed, lands were fenced in, and a city, composed of roughly-built houses and waggons, and called "Winter Quarters," sprang into existence.

As the winter was just coming on, we could not put in any grain until the spring. We began, more than ever, to feel the destitution of our position; for want of vegetables had brought on the scurvy, the provisions of many were exhausted, and our prospects of a fresh supply seemed distant.

The city was laid out in wards, over each of which a Bishop was appointed. One of these wards was committed to me, and this gave me, of course, the care of the poor. The little stock I had of my own was soon gone, and still the poor had not done eating. What was to be done? I went to President Young, and very pathetically told him that all my grain was gone, and I had not the first shilling to get any more grain.

All the consolation I got from him was some instruction to "feed them well, and take care they have enough to eat," and it would not do for a Saint to say he could not.

So I had to scheme. I borrowed ten dollars from a sister who possessed a small store. I then crossed the Missouri River, and laid the money out in meal and some meat. But when this was gone I had to borrow of some one else to pay her, and then of someone else to pay him. I borrowed until I made my debt up to fifty dollars, and no more chance of payment appeared than at the first. Who would not have been a Bishop then? Fortunately, just then, the lost cattle of one who had died in my ward came to me, and I sold them for fifty dollars. I paid my debt, and I was just right, and ready to begin borrowing again with a clear conscience.

In those times the Bishops had plenty of work, if no one else had, and some of it sorrowful enough, for our grave yards began to fill up rapidly. Our situation began to resemble that of our entrance into Nauvoo at the first, for stagnant waters that had been left on the banks through an overflow of the river, combined with the rotting of over-luxurious vegetation, filled the air with death.

After a time, the black leg scurvy began to cease, for we had obtained vegetables from Missouri, and as the spring came on we procured fresh fish, which further varied our diet.

The Pioneers started for the [Wasatch] mountains to seek out a resting place for the Saints, and the body of those remained to raise grain. I and many others left our

*Benjamin Brown*

families, went down into Missouri, and hired ourselves out to obtain means to buy teams, clothes, flour, &c., so that we might follow the Pioneers' camp when the time arrived . . .

. . . We were instructed to use none but our old clothes, and save the best, for [we believed] that we should be driven to wear deer and sheep skins. This did not shake our faith and resolution. Such matters were light work for men who had tried and proved the Divinity of the Church on whose behalf they suffered.

When the time arrived, the Saints moved out . . . and, after crossing the Elk Horn River, were organised into two large divisions called Brigham and Heber's companies. These were subdivided into smaller companies of hundreds, fifties, and tens, and in this way the Saints proceeded across the plains . . .

In September, 1847, we found that the Pioneers . . . that had gone into the Valley [of the Great Salt Lake] had been hard at work, sowing all winter; for every waggon had taken about two bushels of grain, thus most of the wheat the crickets had not harvested on their own, the people had, [along with] many vegetables to boot . . .

Such numbers, however, had arrived in the Valley that the vegetables raised went but a little way . . . It was a rarity to get any vegetables until the following June, fourteen months from the time we left our winter quarters . . . Our bread also became scarce . . . Some persons lived for three months on their cattle, which they had to kill for food, and on roots which they dug up. Of course, after a time, our clothes and farming tools began to wear out, and we [began to] wear sheep skins. Stocks of tea and coffee were exhausted, [and] the first shop was a thousand miles off, and some began to doubt, and wonder what could [come] of all this. There we were, completely shut out from the world, with scarcely any knowledge of its proceedings . . . Our boots, shoes, hats, coats, vests, and material to make them of were either fast going, or altogether gone. Our waggons were becoming scarce, many had broken in the kanyons, and we had no timber to make more, nor iron work necessary for making them—or ploughs, shovels, &c.

In fact, naturally speaking, things looked alarming.

Matters were at this crisis when one day Elder Heber Kimball stood up and prophesied that "in a short time" we would be able to buy clothing and utensils cheaper in the valley than in the States. [We] only hoped it may be so, but without an absolute miracle, there seemed no human probability of fulfilment.

However, Elder Kimball's prophecy was fulfilled in a few months. Information about the great gold discovery in California reached the States, and large companies were formed to supply gold diggers with food and clothing and tools. These companies expected tremendous profits, and no expense was spared . . . When these companies, after crossing the plains, arrived within a short distance of Salt Lake City, news reached them that ships had been sent from many parts of the world with goods for California. This threatened to flood the market . . . The companies were in a fix. They were too far from the States to take their goods back, and it would not pay to carry them through. And the companies were half crazy to become gold diggers themselves. Accordingly, they brought them into the Valley and sold them for just what could be got—at least half the price paid in the States.

. . . Thus were the Saints amply provided, even to overflowing, with every one of the necessaries and many of the luxuries of which they had been so destitute, and thus was the prediction of the servant of the Lord fulfilled.

# Bert Foster

"On the frontier there was no idle capital, nor surplus funds . . . so the church building, like the new dress, and the better times, was off in the distance. A thing to be longed for, and bye and bye secured—but not just now."
—Bert Foster

D*r. Bert Foster was born on the high seas en route to England on April 14, 1861. He traveled in Burma with his parents, and came to America as a young Episcopalian minister in 1889. He was ordained a priest in 1890 by Bishop Talbot of Utah.*

*Foster's mission field was the intermountain region of Idaho, Utah, and Wyoming, the heart of the country's hard-rock mining and deep-shaft coal excavation. A brand-new train system in the area increased his ministerial radius to several hundred miles, and he often traveled without an overnight stop because he had no money for lodging.*

*Foster represented the Episcopal church in America: a "high" church, unremittingly formal and often viewed as a sideshow curiosity by uneducated coal and lead miners. They were a hardened, impoverished lot who were ex-*

*posed daily to the toxic by-products of charcoal. Foster, in his trailing white "nightgown" and surplice, ministered to them in railroad cars, in schoolhouses, and in the open air. He was always present at miners' funerals and at the scene of mine disasters, organizing mercy benefits and making sure that widows and orphans were cared for.*

*Foster's parishioners were often ex-Mormons, newly freed from the strictures of their local elder and highly resistant to tithing or pastoral direction. He sought their loyalty through prayer and home visits, yet often received their insults in return.*

*Foster was continually shocked at the disloyalty of his Western parishioners. Men and women flocked after "personalities"; they changed churches on a whim. They were unwilling to support a pastor who did not entertain them.*

*When Foster published his autobiography in 1940, at the close of his fifty-year career, he was commended by his best friend, W. Bertrand Stevens, the Episcopal bishop of Los Angeles, as a "devoted pastor and thorough Christian." Bishop Stevens said that Foster drew on "the meekness of Moses, the patience of Job, the wisdom of Solomon . . . and the shrewdness of Saint Paul" to maintain his difficult Western ministry. He died in Upland, California, on September 5, 1940.*

Nothing is too good for the miner when he is flush. He eats of the best.

One day, I visited [a miner] supposed to be very ill with typhoid fever. The fellow was as wild as the West can provide . . . He had not sent for us, and did not want us, but his wife had dared to send, which we dared not let him know.

The missionary longed to minister to him, and after reading some well-chosen verses and saying a few gentle words, called upon me to pray. We knelt on the soiled floor, and while I prayed the sick man raised himself on his elbow and began discharging tobacco juice, studying how near he could shoot without hitting me "for fair."

. . . He recovered, probably on the principle that "it's hard to kill a bad thing," and while he showed no great sign of improvement morally, he was always pleased to meet the parson and glad to serve him a turn.

Medicine Bow is ten miles east of Carbon [Wyoming] on a down grade. The population is sometimes thirty people in all. It was my privilege to lecture there once to raise money to meet the missionary's traveling expenses. The meeting was to be at seven o'clock if we could get there so soon. Train service was very irregular, though we always had a timetable . . . "subject to change without notice."

We got there on time in a freight caboose, guiding ourselves with the hand brake. The freight train had broken away from us, but it being a clear stretch we kept moving, and drew up on the level near the settlement without accident. The boys were out in goodly numbers, and I still see their long legs—too long for their cramped quarters—

stretched out into the passageway between the rows of desks [in the schoolhouse].

There might be but one train West in the next twenty-four hours, and that might come along at any time, so toward the close of my lecture one of the boys was dispatched to give notice of the approach of the train, as it could be sighted some miles down the track.

The lecture was over and the offering [was] being lifted when a man brought word the train was in sight. Immediately all was confusion. One man cried, "Give him the hat!" Another, "Take the dough and run for it!" Another, "Here boys, if you haven't chipped in, follow the parson to the cars!"

[My] people were not church people. In all my district—covering fully two hundred miles of railroad and both sides of the railroad—I do not remember . . . more than one family born and brought up in the Episcopal Church and very few in any faith other than Mormon . . .

It is harder for our Church at first than for many others, because we have a form of public worship. In a new country people . . . care very little for religious services of any kind . . . and care less for public worship such as reading and responding . . . This part of the missionary's work is hard at first, both on the people and himself. It is likely to create feelings of irritability . . .

The few people attached to the Church in the settlement where we first set up housekeeping had been Mormons who . . . desired to show their independence of clerical constraint.

I expected more of them than was reasonable, so in my first mission I proved an utter failure.

After Bishop Tuttle had been transferred to another diocese and his large missionary field divided into several jurisdictions, these people, having drifted out of Utah

153
଼ঌ

*Bert*
*Foster*

Homesteaders of the intermountain West, typical of those encountered along Bert Foster's circuit in Utah, Wyoming, and Colorado

. . . were for a long time without a visit from Bishop, Priest, or Deacon. They were held together to some extent by the oldest member and were all related through the polygamous marriages of their parents.

In their new settlement . . . a kind of tribal community life had grown up; this again was unexpected, and proved a barrier from the beginning.

I did hope, however, to overcome in time, and believed my wife would easily win her way into their hearts. But this, too, must be put down to my ignorance. My wife had left a comfortable home. My desire was that in our very limited quarters she should have such comforts as might be possible, so [I] had furnished our two rooms with a great deal of care.

We had taken with us china, linen, glass, and bric-a-brac enough for a much larger house; and selecting a few simple pieces, I displayed them to the best of my knowledge, and was proud of the first home to which I was bringing my young wife.

But there, too, I was in error. At once we were put down as proud; as putting on style, as dudes; and the Indians who went through the house crying "Wyno, wyno" were the only friends who rejoiced in our few home touches, and the dainty hand-work and ornaments. And yet we had put out these little ornaments as much for the pleasure of our people as ourselves, thinking—God help our foolishness—our people would rejoice in the comfort of their minister's home.

When they first called, to show them how welcome they were, we made tea and my wife served it in her best hand-painted china, that our people might see we wished to treat them with the utmost courtesy . . .

The picture is with me still: Our little home, our visitors, my young wife anxious to please. She is handing the cup of tea and I am following with the plate of cookies. The cup is offered to our first guest, who, making no motion to take it, says in the voice of a phonograph, "I don't drink tea." . . . I see a look of surprise, and then a look of pain: my wife had failed, we had both failed, to gain the goodwill of our very first mission people . . .

I remember once when a cloudburst and sudden thaw sent a flood into the town and shut off the school house on a little island of its own and the boys ran wagons into the streams and set planks against them for bridges to carry the people over to the service; I remember Tom, with his long gumboots up to his hips, lifted me on his shoulder and carried me across the stream, saying, "Damn it, we can't afford to let the parson get wet."

The town did nobly by the Church and generously supported [me], but one day—after a few years—[I was summoned] to conduct a funeral over [a man] who had lost his life in the hills. I found that the town [was] gone.

Water had failed them, and the people had lifted the buildings bodily onto flat cars, and the railroad company had carried the whole business—houses, stores, and people—twelve miles farther north, where I found them.

The funeral was also an odd experience. At the service was a man who believed himself to be President Cleveland and in charge of the town. He sang with all his might when a hymn was announced, but his voice was like a bass viol out of tune. I thought for a moment it was a joke the boys were "putting on" me, but soon learned the truth . . . Arriving at the grave, we found it too small for the casket, and though it was intensely cold, there was nothing to do but wait until the frozen earth could be dug out. We were out on the prairie with no accommodations at hand, and there was no place to leave the body—it must be buried that afternoon. Men were in the excavation picking and shoveling out as best they could when the lad who thought himself President called out, "Let me in there." Someone pushed him back and he appealed to me . . . I told the President to take off his coat, which he did, and alone he soon dug out that grave large enough for its purpose. I could not get a train back until two o'clock the next morning, so I announced an evening service . . . [The President] was so pleased at being permitted to dig the grave that he determined to attend and help with the singing.

But the boys had enough of his singing. [They] called out, "You shut up, you can't sing."

Down went the hymn-book on the desk with a bang and out of the school house stamped our grave-digger, muttering dreadful things, but nobody paid any attention to him and the service went off without further incident of note.

Our first home was in a town depending upon sunk wells and water brought from the foothills in ditches. [The wells] . . . depended upon the winter snows for their summer supply.

In the winter . . . things began to look parched. Except for the alfalfa, which is able to care for itself, the outlook for cattle and crops was very discouraging, and long before summer arrived the wells and ditches began to give out.

There having been so little snow, we looked for a rainfall—but it failed to appear. Sometimes a heavy cloud would loom up in the southeast . . . and every heart would be filled with expectation, every inhabitant [would be] out on the road bareheaded watching the dark cloud traveling our way, and then with a rush it was upon us. Into the house we ran, bang went the windows and doors. Imagine . . . our disappointment when not a drop of rain fell, but dust—thick, blinding, penetrating dust—filled the air; every crack, cupboard, and room covered with alkali dust,

so fine that no crack had been undiscovered, no corner had been unfilled.

Knowing how much rain was needed, men almost cried with disappointment, while women stormed at the dirt on beds, gables, chairs, and on everything in the house.

At last the wells ran dry, the ditches contained only stagnant water, and scarlet fever and typhoid invaded many a home. The school was closed; church services were prohibited; my other missions wrote me to stay away from them; and the little mission was practically quarantined.

Some people were terribly afraid of any kind of disease, and rather than go near a house where there is sickness they would let the afflicted die unattended . . . Our pioneers were good-natured enough, but frightened beyond reason at the very beginning of the outbreak, and knowing I had called at a house where there was fever, refused to admit me to their homes no matter how long after, whether I had changed my clothes, or taken proper precautions against spreading disease . . .

There was one family on the outskirts of the town, where three of the four children were tossing with fever at one time. The father was away from home looking for work and the mother was single-handed nursing the children.

We were able to provide food for her and no fire was needed. One of the little ones died, and as I went in to carry it out—we had no undertaker and no one cared to venture into the house—the mother asked me if she could not go with me to the grave with her baby. "I'll see if I can manage it," I said and, leaving the body with the mother, hurried away home.

My wife could not refuse and at once went with me, and stayed with the other children while the mother and I

Reverend Bert Foster, Rector Emeritus of St. Mark's Church, Upland, California; previously Vicar of Emmanuel Church, Grass Valley, California

went with two men who waited without the house, and she had the sad satisfaction of seeing her baby reverently laid away.

At last, toward the close of summer, I took down with typhoid, but our Indian friends, who had stuck to us through it all, were perhaps the cause of my breakdown.

When water was plentiful we taught them to wash and gave them soap for that purpose. Now for weeks we had had no water except a very little in the ditch outside our gate, on the street. It was stagnant, of course, [with] a scum coated over it, hiding it from the sun and saving it for us. Every morning, before the sun was well up, I would go out with a can and, pushing the scum with my left hand, dip up with a quick motion all the mud bottom. This we would boil thoroughly and it served as our supply for the day for drinking purposes. We had none to wash in for weeks, and had to learn to take sand baths and dry rubs.

But we had taught Johnny and Joe [the Indian friends] to use soap and water, and they found out our small reservoir. One morning I went out as usual for our day's supply and found our two friends sitting over the hole washing themselves in all the water we had.

At the height of the quarantine the railway company arranged to send us water on a freight train, which was a Godsend.

My fever ran its course, and left me almost at death's door. But a generous, faithful physician, the best of nurses and the love of God brought me through.

On a Tuesday I was carried to the train and sent off to Mineral Springs to gain strength, and so quickly did I pick up that on Sunday I was able to hold a service in the school house there—the first service ever held in that locality.

There was a beautiful shepherd dog in our settlement, and during my long fever [he] walked through the town twice a day to our home, scratched at the door, came in and went to my bed and stood there a moment, and then walked out and home. His mistress would watch for him and say: "Well, Shep, how is Mr. Foster now?" She knew by the wagging of the dog's tail the minister was still alive, and when one time they reported me dead, she was assured by Shep that the report was incorrect.

"Don't come. School house occupied by theatre troup. J.L."

This was the telegram I received one morning as I was starting off for a [mission].

I planned to visit this town every two weeks, and [had] arranged for the use of the school house in advance. The town was twenty-six miles north and was the nearest of three towns which I took regularly. This town on Wednesday; the next on Thursday; the third on Friday, spending all day Saturday traveling home for Sunday.

Each town was supposed to meet its part of the railroad or stage fare, so that if I could not end my journey at the first place, I had to travel [the entire] fifty-eight miles at my own expense.

Yet J—— L—— was [an] Eastern churchman I [hoped] would protect our interests in that town. Because he "so seldom had an opportunity to visit a theatre" he had allowed our appointment to go by the board . . .

I have no ill will toward the footlight artists; they have been very kind to me. I have [even] been taken for a theatre troupe agent because the shape of my coat [vestment] is peculiar, or because I am obliged to rustle round to advertise our services. Once a man on the train, after looking at me quite a while, came up and asked, touching my vest, "Say, is that the new kind of chest-protector that is being sold along the line? Have you any of them along?"

*Bert
Foster*

Funeral procession for mine victims in Tonopah, Nevada, ca. 1909

An acting troupe struck the town one Sunday afternoon . . . but finding we had the first claim on the school house, decided to stay until Monday. The manager proposed that his troupe would sing a couple of anthems for me if I would announce their play for the following night. I [told] him we would be glad of his help in the service, but it would hardly be proper to announce a play from the altar.

He decided not to attend church, but as he had announced [the songs] before he spoke to me, the crowd was there, and we had a good service.

The next night the play was given, and in putting up their stage, beams were run up through the muslin ceiling to the rafters so that when the beams were removed the ceiling was in tatters, and the next time I held service there the muslin hung about me like the unkempt mustache of some open-mouthed giant reaching up to swallow me with one mouthful.

It became necessary for me, after some months, to move to a new town being started some thirty miles southeast.

This was Indian territory, but owing to [a nearby] railway junction, the people flocked in and every available . . . house contained two families, or one family and roomers.

Shelter became a serious problem. The railway company would have given us a box car, but as [it] would have been on a siding some distance from town we were not anxious . . .

Fortunately one of the railroad men gave us two rooms in his house, [which] we moved into at once lest they be snapped up by some employee with a better claim. One room was very small and filled with our surplus belong-

ings, while the larger room became our home. Perhaps no one but a parson's wife—and few of them—could have made so cozy and attractive a home in one room, thirteen by eighteen feet. At one end was a folding bed, looking when closed like a writing desk. This end of the room . . . was our parlor by day and our bedroom at night. At the other end stood the dining table . . . a few chairs, sewing room, and [the] general living apartment . . .

One night a missionary called at two A.M., demanding we keep him till morning as there was no place vacant in town. He insisted upon staying, so I pulled down a mattress and laid it half in the store-room and half in the living room, and told him to get to bed with his head to the south and not rise until I called him. We kept him to breakfast and dinner and he moved on further west before sundown.

The time came when this little . . . room could not be spared to us . . . Again the railroad company stood good for a box car if nothing better was offered. It was an anxious time, for the life of the mission almost depended upon [my] presence in the settlement. One church member offered to fit up a barn he owned. He would make two good rooms in it, if we would pay him fifteen dollars a month and lease it for a year.

And so it came out, that the "boys" built us a five-room house costing six hundred and fifty dollars, and . . . as the Indians had given us permission to build, they felt a pride in the place and gathered in our yard to gamble and play cards . . .

For some years my work lay in a silver and lead camp. I resided there in a rectory which I planned myself in a hole in the ground on the side of a hill.

The town was . . . in a canyon, with side streets on the hills parallel with the main street at the bottom of the canyon.

The church was on the lower side of the upper street . . . Between the built-up church and the built-up side street was a hole in the ground, owned by the church.

The people promised me a house if I would go and live with them, and the house we eventually built in this hole. We could not build up even with the street because we could not shut out the light from the church. [We had to] build low enough to avoid interfering with the church windows. This we did, and with sixteen steps down to our hall door and twelve steps more to our back yard, managed to erect a house whose roof was about even with the front and side streets.

It was a cozy home, and many a good time we had in it, and sometimes not so good.

[One day] a new family moved into the lower part of the house next door. They had to back down the furniture wagon on the side street, which inclined at a slight angle to the back of the house. As the horses were backing down from the street, the weight of the load began to carry them with it . . . They snapped their traces, and the wagon broke at the same moment, [swerving] towards our [house]. The wagon, with all its contents, driver included, turned over into our lot, carrying down our porch, also smashing our windows and throwing some of the goods into our parlor.

As soon as I could gather myself together, I made my way to the door to see what had happened, for it might have been an earthquake or mine explosion for all I knew. At the front lawn lay the large barn wagon upside down and underneath the wreck lay, buried, the driver.

Some people do not believe in Providence. Some do. Our house being lower than the street, we had to dig a trench across the front to carry off the rain and snow water. Into this trench the man had fallen lengthwise, and over him had fallen the kitchen stove crosswise, and in a little while out crept the man without a scratch, but, like myself, very much frightened . . .

I was caring for a widow and five children through a long siege of diphtheria one winter. The snow was very deep and I had to take food already cooked to them. Their home was on the highest point where no road had yet been made. I had to climb up to the house on my hands and toes, and slide down again as best I could. I had given the grocer and druggist my word for all bills, and after the sickness was past, I [had to] raise at least seventy dollars to meet the bills incurred. During this time the "boys" [local miners] had paid the expenses of one funeral and I felt a delicacy about asking them for more money. But it was a case of necessity. So I arranged to deliver a lecture and take up a collection. Unfortunately, many of the men had to go to work at 9 P.M., and our meeting could not open until eight o'clock. However, we went right along and when it came time for the men on the night shift to leave, they each left their offering on the seat next the door. The amount taken in that night amounted to ninety-three dollars.

Before paying any of the bills, I gave the family twenty-five dollars to help them out, and then paid the bills in full, adding the small balance necessary out of my own funds.

But while I was feeling most grateful to the [miners] and thinking how good everyone had been to Mrs. A. and her family, she was not grateful at all, for she came to me and demanded the whole of the ninety-three dollars, claiming that I had given the lecture for her and that the whole sum raised belonged to her. Of course I could not

159
&

*Bert*
*Foster*

No 3.

Chinese Mission School, Monterey County, California, ca. 1885–1900

Nun presiding over a lesson at St. Michael's School on the Navajo Reservation, St. Michaels, Arizona, ca. 1910

*Bert*
*Foster*

Class picture from the Shoshone Indian Mission School, Wind River, Wyoming, 1896

Sioux pupils and teachers at Congregational mission school, Oahe, South Dakota, 1908–1909

agree with her and did not give her any more of the fund. In fact the bills were paid and the money was gone.

One afternoon . . . as the men were leaving the mines, something happened. The men were on the incline making their way up. Some few had already reached the surface when there was a report like a cannon, or sharp clap of thunder, then a tongue of flame, or flash of lightning, and then in the sudden darkness and unearthly stillness, the falling of debris and human bodies. Men were blown by the force of the explosion clear up the main way and out across the plain . . . There were no narrow escapes that I remember; death and destruction swept all before them.

The cause of the explosion was said to be spontaneous combustion, caused by the setting in motion of the dry dust lying along the car track, but as all the persons immediately responsible for the mine were among the dead, no full inquiry could be made.

Forty-six widows and hundreds of orphans were left penniless and without credit in any store. Relief was tendered from all over the West, and carloads of clothing and provisions were immediately forwarded to the relief committee. In the silver camp men were eager to do something. The merchants gave generously in provisions of all kinds and a subscription was started at all the mines. It fell to my lot to be one of the collectors on the main street from the offices and saloons, and in two days' time our committee had collected from all sources in cash $952.70, which was handed over to me [for] the distressed camp.

The Methodist minister [accompanied] me. We spent one full day going from house to house distributing in gold and silver the sums allotted to each person or family. It was an awful day. Rain fell incessantly and the yellow clay clogged and slipped, until the five-mile tramp and all

day contact with poverty of the saddest kind, and going in and out amongst a people who had forgotten to smile if they ever had known, now made the single bunk we were to share as acceptable as a bed of down. From each person . . . we requested a receipt. As I look at that old receipt book today, I find the Finlanders and Swedes signed their names while the English and Scotch only made a cross.

The Mormon church stepped in and distributed the families throughout their many settlements and I was assured that within one year . . . every one of the widows was married again.

But the men left behind did not forget the kindness shown them . . . I was but the agent, yet the people treated me as if I had myself done them a favor, and when some time later I was [near] the coal camp they invited me over to preach to them and promised me the use of their church.

. . . I went, and the boys met me at the entrance of town with a brass band, and played me up to the church door. Here I found a good congregation, the full Mormon choir and the "bishop of the ward" ready to assist me in every way. Later, they sent me a $50 note with the following letter:

October 29, 18—

Dear Sir and Brother:
Never in the history of our lodge has such a scene been witnessed as tonight at our meeting. Brother after brother, English-speaking as well as Finnish-speaking, rose in their places and testified of their regard and respect of you as a brother, counsellor and friend . . .

This letter was written and composed by the [men]

themselves and they were just the kind of men we might have been proud of. But while one of our missionaries had labored in the camp for two years . . . the bishop was never able to send in a [permanent] man, because of [lack of] permanent support from within, and the owners of the mines felt no obligation to care for the spiritual welfare of their human machines.

I had been in the mission field about two years when I found myself at the end of my financial resources, and no visible prospect of any funds coming in, though they were overdue.

The salary promised me would have been sufficient had it been paid with any kind of regularity. But, the bishop . . . promised in good faith, hoping it would come in, and when it did not . . . the bishop's private purse had to provide. No one knew outside the bishop's house the sacrifice made and the ingratitude returned. We had spent our last dollar and . . . things looked black enough when the "general merchant" came over to make a proposition to me. His bookkeeper had left him, and he [had] no one to take his place—railroad men, tradesmen and laborers were plenty, but men for clerkships were very scarce, and for them wages were good. If I would accept the position of bookkeeper he would give me $125 a month. Here I was, living at haphazard, with only $300 per year certain, and only $1,000 if all had been paid, and within my reach was the certainty of $1,500 a year, paid monthly, and only one man to please, instead of a congregation.

Fortunately, the merchant did not know how tempting his offer was just then, and more fortunate still, I had a wife to whom the honor of my priesthood was more than life itself, and with her support and the grace of God I had no great difficulty in refusing, though I felt grateful for the confidence placed in me by this Western merchant . . .

The missionary cannot obtain his support from the people he labors for . . .

My appointment included the promise of a definite salary, no mention being made of "perhaps" or "maybe," and childlike, I never dreamed of anything but a literal interpretation of the "I am now prepared to offer you $1,000 per year."

The bishop tried hard to keep his promise for a while, but as the work was increasing and new men were required, and the bishop's income . . . was inadequate, the promise failed.

The church missionary society in time placed me on its payroll at a salary of $200; the bishop assessed my Mission $500, and he agreed to be accountable for the balance of $1,000, this being $300 per year. The missionary society paid regularly; the mission paid, when it did pay; and the bishop paid when he could pay, so that my "regular" salary was $200 a year, paid quarterly, and my "irregular" salary was $800, paid as I could get it. My traveling expenses were supposed to be met by the people I served, and if not met by them, I had no claim on any fund . . . New towns were springing up and my ambition was to "get in on the ground floor."

As it took days, often weeks, to get a letter to the bishop and back, I often had to act on my own initiative; and when my journey proved expensive and financially unprofitable, I had no one to blame, as I had no one to advise [me].

More than once I have taken our last dollar and started off literally without purse or scrips, except for my vestments and service books, and spent my little all on railroad fare, trusting God to open homes to me. In this way, I opened Missions in new camps and towns, and returned to them as often as possible. I had one such Mission 104 miles east. I left on the 4 A.M. train, reaching my destination about 9:30. I spent the day going in and out amongst the people, held service in the evening, and sat up in the depot for the return train, due to leave at midnight.

This saved me hotel expenses, and I could generally get at least one meal at some home.

The offerings were not large, and in some places there was no offering, because the people were mostly Mormons, and they never have an offering taken at any of their services. For two years I visited [a] town, at an expense of more than $7, each two weeks. There was not one member of the Episcopal Church in the Mission, and the people were "as sheep without a shepherd." For months, . . . I had to put up at the saloon hotel, and of course this added to my expense account. Yet the bishop thought it well to hold on, and eventually he placed a missionary there . . . The burden was more than the bishop's purse could bear, and when the missionary resigned, no one could take his place, and the Mission died out.

# Mary Collins

"Children are taken into the Boarding schools too young. A child under no circumstances should be taken from its home and its mother's constant care at so early an age . . ."

—Mary Collins,
September 1904

*Mary Collins was known among the Dakota Sioux as a healer, teacher, and woman of the Bible. She spoke their language and lived in near isolation in a tiny hut on the Standing Rock Indian Reservation, nearly two hundred miles from the territorial capital of Yankton. With affection they called her Winona, or "Oldest Daughter."*

*Collins was unusually gifted with empathy, vision, and the grace to change her mind. Her extensive writings make clear that her first, more traditional view of Indians as childlike dependents altered over the years. By 1915 she staunchly objected to government-sponsored Indian boarding schools and had become a spokeswoman for Indian rights at every policy-forming conference she could attend.*

*Born April 18, 1846, in Alton, Illinois, Collins grew up in Keokuk, Iowa, attending public schools and Bible classes in the local church. Her first missionary interest was Micronesia, but in 1875 she and a close friend, Emmarette J. Whipple, were asked to settle in Dakota Territory by the American Board of Commissioners for Foreign Missions. Matter-of-factly, she proceeded to learn the Dakota language, recruit young men to form a YMCA branch, and minister to the sick. Her task grew more difficult yearly: no sooner had she convinced the Indians to accept allotment (the government's division of Indian land into privately owned parcels) than white cattlemen moved in and quickly reduced Indian herds. Likewise, she soon found that most Bureau of Indian Affairs policy only increased the poverty and misery of the Sioux. Homesteaders endlessly usurped Indian land, forcing the mission to preempt 160 acres of land on the Standing Rock Indian Reservation simply to shield it from the onslaught.*

*Collins knew Chief Sitting Bull and came to understand the warrior as few other whites ever had. In the 1890s she tried to dissuade him from his fateful participation in the Ghost Dance, in which thousands of Indians across the country began to dance, fast, and pray for the*

*return of their dead, the vanished buffalo, and a lost way
of life. She was unsuccessful. Sitting Bull continued in the
ill-fated movement and was killed by a Sioux policeman
employed by the authorities on December 15, 1890.*

*In her later years, Collins returned to Keokuk, where
she served as a missionary in the First Congregational
church until her death in 1920.*

My father and mother came west in an early day . . . when
I was born, moving to Keokuk [Iowa] . . . My father kept
horses and I learned to ride . . . and to harness and drive
a team when so young that I scarcely remember when it
was. I was fearless and this was a great help to me in my
life on the plains . . .

My religious training at home consisted largely in
. . . Sunday School . . . and always as a child going to church
with my parents . . . One Sunday night when I was five
years old the minister asked all who wanted to follow
Jesus to stand up. I looked at Mother and she bowed her
head so I stood up . . . I knew what I had done. It had great
influence on my child life. I was appointed by . . . the
American Board as a missionary to the Indians in June
1875, and in October of the same year Miss [Emmarette]
Whipple and I . . . were ordained . . .

We traveled by rail as far as Yankton, SD, then the
Capitol of Dakota Territory . . . From Yankton we took
teams, [a] large wagon with our supplies and a smaller one
for the family . . . Following the Missouri River, we saw no
more White Settlements . . . until we reached Fort Thompson at the mouth of Crow Creek . . . We were a happy group,
Mr. Riggs and his most beautiful and winsome wife and
the dear baby boy . . . The tent was pitched by us all helping
. . . Our belongings [were] parceled out and placed in our

little spot and the beds spread down . . . Sometimes Mr.
Riggs would kill a duck or grouse, and then we had to get
those ready for the next day. In the morning all was hurry
and bustle to get ready for an early start on our way. The
tent [was] taken down and folded up and put on one of the
seats . . . cooking utensils put away and tent poles tied
under the wagon . . .

About the middle of the afternoon we reached the Missouri and unloaded the wagons and started in on our life
work [at the] Cheyenne [River] Agency . . .

Soon after our arrival Mr. Riggs opened the various
schools. I taught the children in the morning . . . Then Miss
Whipple taught the men at night. We taught in the Dakota
language at the same time we were learning it.

One Sunday, while all was yet new to me, I was surprised to see three or four great stalwart men come into
church clothed only in breech cloth, moccasins and blanket. They had come to the Missouri River, and finding no
boat and wanting to come to church, they swam across and
so walked into church with all the dignity of well clothed
gentlemen. I became used to such things, but the first sight
of the unclothed in church was rather startling . . .

When Mr. Riggs decided we ought to have a chapel
. . . he explained it to the congregation and then asked for
a collection. They were poor. They had almost no money,
but many of the women had pennies or nickels in their
ears or around their necks for ornaments. We would see
blankets go up over their heads, and men too had pieces of
money tied to their braid; but when the blankets came
down and heads were uncovered, all the copper and silver
had disappeared and were dropped into the collection basket. I thought how God must bless the gift, for they plainly
said by their actions, "Such as I have give I unto thee."

In 1876 our annual meeting [of Congregational mission-

A studio photograph in Pierre, South Dakota (from left to right: unidentified woman, Elizabeth Winyan, missionary Mary C. Collins, Elida Scott)

aries] was to be held at Sisseton Agency, a long ride across the state and no white settlement all the way, only . . . Indian country . . . We drove on and on. By and by we thought we saw a lake ahead and when near, we stopped and unhitched the horses . . . [but] it was a mirage and no water. We opened canned tomatoes, ate our dinner and drank tomato juice for water. All the afternoon and evening we drove on and on. No water . . . We rode on till near midnight when [we] came to a bluff, where we knew there would be water . . . The [next] night we camped near a stream in high grass where the mosquitos almost devoured us and the horses. The others could cover their heads with the blanket and sleep, but I could not breathe with my head covered, so I volunteered to keep them off the baby as I could not sleep and had to fight them anyway . . . We traveled on from there and reached the Reservation and the meeting . . .

It was my first experience with Christian Indians and was a splendid lesson for me. I could see what could be done for Indians if the Missionary learned their language and did not get tired and leave the field.

[Mary, Emmarette Whipple, and the Riggses continued to travel throughout the Dakotas by buggy, ministering and teaching.]

We had now extended the work, and a little school for women was started . . . and I taught it, going on Horseback. One cold day the wind began to blow hard and the snow to fly and a real blizzard was on. I tried to hurry the horse but facing the storm was hard work and he would not hurry. An Indian, Bears-Ears, was driving along in a wagon, overtook me, jumped out and put me into his wagon wrapped in a Buffalo robe. He carried me to the schoolhouse, rubbed my frozen ears with snow and built

a fire for me. He was only an Indian. Not a Christian Indian either, but he cared for me most tenderly . . .

This year, 1878 . . . the Government had allowed the Indians to live on the Peoria Bottom on the Missouri River simply by Presidential Proclamation but now they were ordered to go across to the West side of the river and the land was thrown open to settlement. Now we were stranded far away from the Indians with the Missouri River between us and our people, only a few families remaining near us. It was thought best by Mr. Riggs . . . to build a small school where young children could be brought in to prepare for our great school at Santee Agency, but I did not feel the call. I left the dear old home . . . [g]oing to Standing Rock Agency in mid winter and starting my work among the Sitting Bull people.

We left Oahe crossing the river on the ice. We had two teams. I drove my ponies and the Indian woman and I rode in my buckboard. Mr. Riggs and Wakanna, the Indian man, had a large team and a road wagon carrying my winter supplies, household furniture etc. After crossing the Cheyenne River the weather began to grow colder and a high wind began to blow. It increased [so] that by the time we were well on our way across the plains a heavy storm was on. Snow and cold wind. Toward evening it was impossible to proceed further as the snow was so deep the horses could make no progress. Then the Indian began to look for a place where we could stop. There was plenty of snow, so we could melt that for water, but we must have wood.

Finally we came near a bluff and some ravines . . . where there was a little wood. The wagons could not be taken down there but the men carried [a few supplies] . . . and led the horses down. About three feet of snow was shoveled out by the two men and the tent was pitched.

During all this time I was sitting on some buffalo robes trying to keep warm . . .

This awful storm did not abate . . . for three days. At night Mr. Riggs read the scriptures and we sang a hymn and prayed and retired. At the end of the third day we found our supplies getting short. There was danger of the horse fee[d] giving out. So we determined to try to start the next morning, hoping to go to the Moreau River which was twelve miles away. We had to abandon the big wagon. [We] hitched the big horses to my Buckboard and Wakanna, riding my pony Bessie, went ahead, leading my pony Jumbo. He partially broke the track. Mr. Riggs walked and drove our team.

After an all day trip we covered the twelve miles and reached the Moreau. We found a cabin with a stove and a bedstead in it and went in where we could keep warm after the Indian woman had thoroughly cleaned by sweeping all the corners. We were all glad to retire after eating our suppers. And the next day the two men spent making a sled out of poles. The day after . . . the two men took the sled to go after our supplies, for food and horsefee[d] was growing scarce.

After they had gone, an old woman came to our cabin and brought us some shelled corn. Wakanna's wife took ashes and made lye, and with the corn she proceeded to make a kettle of lye hominy, or as a yankee would say, hulled corn. She and I lived on this for two days, and on the third day the men returned. When we saw them coming we took the little piece of Bacon that we had left and the little coffee we had and by the time they reached us the appetizing odors of coffee, bacon and hominy filled the air and gave new strength . . .

We stayed three days longer and then made our way to Grand River which was to be my future home. Soon after, Mr. Riggs and the Indians returned and I was left alone. Alone with Sitting Bull's people, thirty two miles from the Post Office and the nearest white neighbors. [Her home was in Running Antelope's village, thirty-two miles southwest of Fort Yates.]

It was a hard long winter . . . living in a room about fourteen by twelve feet . . . [The] large room was used for the church services and school room and office. One of my interesting cares that winter was a man who had smashed his knee . . . I had to have clean rags and bandages. As I had brought only a few they were soon gone, and nowhere to get any more. The deep snow made the road to the Fort impassable so I had no way to obtain anything . . .

I tore up one of my aprons. I had only two. Then I took one pillow case, [t]hen another, leaving . . . only one, and then a sheet and later another sheet . . . for [he] had cut an artery in his leg. I was . . . reduced to the necessity of washing and drying and ironing all the same day. But the Lord knew all about it and I said in my prayers, "If it is thy will, and I need the schooling, I can endure it. [A]nd I will." Toward spring when I received my mail . . . there was a package containing two sheets, two pillow cases and two towels. [There was] no name, and to this day I do not know who sent them. But God had sent to some servant of his a wireless Message and I was supplied.

This incident gave me the Assurance that God had sent me there and that he was taking a personal interest in me. I was sure of his loving protection.

And he never failed me in all the years.

[After 1882, Thomas Riggs established an outstation near

Grand River, 32 miles southwest of Standing Rock Agency. Collins moved here and, over the years, became friendly with Sitting Bull.]

One day Sitting Bull called at my home. He stopped outside the gate and called me. I paid no attention to him, and after calling several times he tied his great white horse [a gift from William Cody] to the fence and came to the door. I had seen him but did not know him yet.

He said, "Do you know who I am?"

"Yes," I said, "you are Sitting Bull."

"Then," said he, "why did you not come out when I called?"

I replied, "You are a man, and I am a woman. If a man wishes to speak to a woman, it is his place to go to her. It is not the woman's place to go to the man."

He at once removed his hat and said, "Ho, I did not know." So ever after when he came he removed his hat and rapped at the door.

Soon after, he came with eleven other leading men to call. They filled my little room. He was spokesman. He said, "Winona [the name given to Collins by the Sioux] . . . we have come to see you and have a talk . . . are you going to live here?"

I responded that I was.

He then said, "Shall your horses eat our grass and drink our water, and shall you live on our land?"

I said, "Is the grass yours?"

"Yes."

"Is the water yours?"

"Yes." It was pouring down a rain.

"Is this rain that is falling yours?"

"It is."

I said, "Then I have something to say. I have spent money to have my garden plowed. And money for seeds and paid one of you to plant it. Your rain is ruining my garden, and if it is yours I want you to keep it off my garden."

For a moment they all looked at me as [if] I were insane. Then a smile broke out [on] their faces. And they laughed, came forward and shook hands with me and departed . . .

I took my regular trip to Thunder-Hawk in June, and the day was miserably hot. The sun [was] shining in that clear atmosphere, not a leaf for shade, not a breath of air stirring . . . About twenty miles from home I met the old chief Crawler [a Blackfoot Sioux]. The poor old man, on a little pony, almost overcome with the heat, stopped me. He was almost weeping. A few days before this, a man [had come] up from the Cheyenne Agency and his wife was ill. They were relatives of Crawler. When they started home it was raining . . . so Crawler gave them an old blanket. It had been issued to him the fall previous. It was reported to the Agent and the Agent had ordered [Crawler to come in] to punish him for giving away his blanket. Then he told me of the twenty miles he had already ridden and the forty he had still to ride to reach Fort Yates. He said, "Winona, I am not able."

So I wrote a letter to the Agent and gave [it] to the policeman and sent Crawler to his sons a few miles away. The Agent never sent for him again . . .

We had now started a number of Mission Stations. The work had grown from a few young one[s] to a large Congregation of Christians. When my Bible class used to meet and learn to read and learn the will of Christ toward us, I found three of the young men very anxious to learn . . . One Wauketemani had a most wonderful memory . . . [and] was my right hand in all my work . . . He studied the Bible very carefully, always marking the verses which especially interested him and asking me to

Missionaries in camp—probably Thomas Riggs, his wife Nina Foster Riggs, and Mary C. Collins as they traveled through Dakota Territory

Chas. Frazier. Rev. John Eastman. The late Dr. A. L. Riggs. Rev. C. L. Hall. Dr. T. L. Riggs. Rev. G. W. Reed. Dr. John P. Williamson. Rev. A. F. Johnson. Prof. F. B. Riggs. Rev. M. C. Collins. (Winona)

Missionary meeting at Fort Yates, North Dakota, on the Standing Rock Reservation

Mary Collins's small frame house on the Grand River, surrounded by log buildings and a cribbed circular earth lodge

explain them. He became an ordained Minister. Years after, I heard him tell the story of his conversion to an audience of two thousand Indians at our Annual Conference. He said . . .

"I have been asked many times . . . how to become a Christian. Years ago I asked Winona the same question and . . . she said, '. . . I cannot tell you; no one can tell you. Just pray and pray and pray and bye and bye you will know that God has heard you.' So I tell you, you must pray and do not get weary. God will answer and you will know it. When Winona told me that, I would go out on the prairie for my horses. When I was away off where no one could see me, I got off my horse and knelt down and prayed. Again and again I did this, but I felt no different. I soon found that in the morning I was in haste to go after the horses, and then I discovered that it was so that I could pray, and God came into my heart and I knew that I was in touch with His heart."

When I heard his story for the first time I thought of Christ's words "O ye of little Faith" and was so sorry that I had been so unfaithful. Had I always been careful and been faithful to try to lead these precious souls into the light[?] . . .

In the early days there was no church organization and I felt that it would be impossible to meet all these Dakota societies [without] an organization. So we formed from my Bible class . . . a young men's society. Only three of those who could read were willing to join . . . The three had prayers outside . . . every night. They read the scriptures and prayed and sang. This was something new and it attracted a good deal of attention. Soon other young men joined and they held a meeting once a week . . .

One day I was walking along the road, rather discouraged and with bowed head. My horses had disappeared. The people were still dancing day and night and mourners were making the nights hideous with wailing. I had no white neighbor within thirty miles and I wondered if it paid. Then, hearing a wagon coming down the road, I looked up to see a common road wagon with the box on it and six chairs in the wagon. Six young men [were] sitting in the chairs and an attempt had been made to dress in a white man's clothes. Indian young men seldom rode in a wagon, always on horseback, and then the dress! One had in some way come into possession of a suit of clothes, and had divided it among the others. One had on a hat, another a pair of boots, another a vest, one a shirt, and another a coat, and another a pair of trousers. I at once knew it must be some very formal occasion and . . . asked them where they were going. "We are going down to Flying-By's to organize a young men's society. They have called us." I felt strengthened, no longer discouraged. Six fine young men to help me. This society merged into the National YMCA, and in later years was my right hand . . .

[I] was now very busy visiting churches and colleges in the East, speaking in behalf of the Indians and working on the reservation. [I was] trying to teach them everything from washing clothes to making dresses, from scrubbing floors to leading meetings. I loved the people and I loved the work.

I went to Winona, Minnesota, to speak at a State Asso[ciation]. When I was about to leave the platform . . . a telegram was handed to the president . . . It said, "Winona . . . Minnesota sends greetings to Winona of Dakota. We raised money to build her a house last night."

My little mission home was built . . .

During the building . . . a man was hired to draw some lumber and I sent one of the best Christian men with him for lumber and to show the white man the way. As they returned from the river . . . there came up a dreadful storm. The road was dim and night was coming on. The man kept swearing terrible at the horses and at the weather and everything else . . . The next morning he came to me and told me that the Indian left him about five miles back and he had a hard time to find his way. I called the [Indian] and asked him why he left him. He said, "Winona, I was afraid. He kept making such wicked prayers. I was afraid God would answer him and I did not want to be near him." When I told the white man what he said, he looked much ashamed and said no more. I hope it was a lesson to him. The Indians cannot swear in their own language. They must learn English to be able to swear.

The Standing Rock Reservation is not an agricultural district. It was therefore necessary that the Indians should only try to raise vegetables and grain enough for personal use and depend upon stock to make a living. I began at once to insist upon the people scattering out from the densely populated villages . . . It took several years to make them see the necessity of living so isolated. But one by one I succeeded in inspiring them with the idea of a permanent home and its ownership . . .

[E]very man who chose his land [had to] be taught to know his corners, and he would mark them himself. This was so thoroughly done that in after years, when the allotting agent came to allot the land, he did not have to urge them to take homesteads. The Indians swarmed about him asking . . . to be first allotted, and they could show him their corners . . . [H]e repeatedly said that it was not half the work there that it had been on other Reservations . . .

Their herds grew very rapidly and they were almost self supporting when the cattlemen came in with their great herds . . . [I]t soon became evident, as the Indians

Formal portrait of an unidentified California women's music group

Red, gold, and yellow "chariot" built to soothe the saddlesores of Salvation Army evangelists, who previously traveled throughout California on horseback

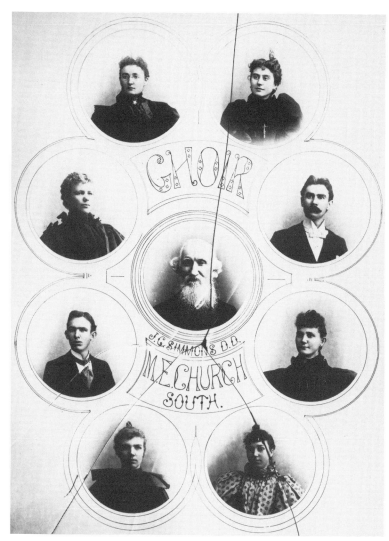

*Mary
Collins*

ABOVE: Choristers of the Methodist Episcopal Church, South, in an unnamed California town

TOP RIGHT: Group of musicians and singers with their songbooks

BOTTOM RIGHT: Music students practicing hymns in California, 1896

expressed it, that the cattlemen's cows often had twin calves and many of the Indians' cows had no calves at all. So at the present time the Indians do not have as many cattle as they had ten years ago. It is so easy to ship other cattle off and sell them, and no one know of it . . .

There was a time when the people throughout the country were greatly interested in the Indians, when they were wild and picturesque, but a [half] civilized people are far from being either, so that many have lost interest. I attended a meeting of the National Educational Association and one of the leading Scholars of the country read a paper in which he favored keeping the Indians in their native condition . . . that ethnologists might study their customs and their manners, with their ideas of life . . . It seemed to me such an absurd idea that any intelligent person should think at this late day we could turn back the wheels of time so as to provide a place for a wild nomadic race to live his natural life in . . . Civilization was coming to him. There was no question of that. The only thing that Christian men, or even civilized men and women, could do was to see to it that these wards of our Government had the best civilization that we had to give, and that was to give them the Gospel of Jesus Christ . . .

Elizabeth Winyan . . . an Indian woman of great intelligence and d[is]cernment, [told me of] "an old man named Longfeather, dressed in Indian dress paint and feather [who was] teaching some boys the Indian dance and song. There were three boys: One with long hair and painted face and Indian dress; one with long hair and shirt and leggins and a white boy's shoes and stockings on; the third dressed well in entire white men's clothes. One represents the past, the second the present, and the third one the future. I know it has to be, but to me the one dressed all in the Indian child's clothing looked the best. But I am only an Indian."

Elizabeth had a little granddaughter of whom she was very fond. When she was about three years old she was visiting her grandmother. They were sleeping in a tent next to my own tent. Elizabeth snored so loudly that no one near could sleep. Little Pilgrim awoke and said, "Grandmother, sleep softly. Sleep softly."

Their expressions are very beautiful when correctly translated, but many interpreters . . . are illiterate and know very little English and . . . depend upon slang largely to express themselves . . .

It is impossible to do thorough work as a Missionary through an interpreter. If one does not learn the language of the people . . . it would be better for him to have some other calling. If he does not know what the Indian is thinking about, he can do little to change those thoughts. No Indian will tell his heart life to a Missionary if he has to do it through an interpreter. And he will not welcome advice or help from a Missionary that comes to him through the interpreter. Speaking . . . face to face and heart to heart will accomplish much and will win friends for the church.

# Annie Bidwell

"Suddenly the realization came to me—it was mine to obey and trust Him, as did the seabird, resting in his love without a care, effort or fear."

—Annie Bidwell,
in a personal letter
describing a religious vision

*A*nnie Ellicott Kennedy, born in 1841, was the great granddaughter of the surveyor who laid out Washington, D.C., in 1790. Her father, Joseph Camp Griffith Kennedy, was federal census director as well as a recognized agricultural expert. Her own social circle included American presidents and the political elite. Little in Annie's early years gave indication of the course her life was to follow. But in 1868 she married California rancher and politician John Bidwell, a man twenty years her senior who was later to found the city of Chico. After meeting Bidwell, Annie left her distinguished Washington family for Rancho Chico, a twenty-two-thousand-acre ranch in Butte County, California—a dusty site already inhabited by the Chilcat tribe of California Indians, who gathered acorns

in the brushy chaparral and lived in smoke-filled domed houses of tule, weeds, and sticks. Both Bidwells felt intensely responsible for the fate of this tribe, eventually ceding 250 acres of their estate for the tribe's permanent use.

Annie and John Bidwell were staunch Presbyterians. They built a chapel on the grounds, near their residence, so the Chilcat tribe would have a church. In 1875 Bidwell organized a school for the Chilcat as well. The curriculum was reading, oral and written arithmetic, spelling, and geography; music was nightly hymns and the enthusiastic symphony of a native brass band. Sunday services were attended by thirty-five or forty local Indians.

After years of lay ministry to the Indians, conducting church offices that would normally have been carried out by a (male) cleric, Annie Bidwell became a Presbyterian minister. Clerical duties, however, never interfered with her civic responsibilities. She became an ardent conservationist, lobbying against the destruction of forestland, especially uncontrolled felling of the coastal redwoods.

In 1884 her health partially failed, and she turned the Indian School over to the Presbyterian Board of Foreign

*Missions. Despite her frail condition, she championed many causes—women's rights, prohibition, and Indian welfare—until her death on March 9, 1918.*

When I arrived in 1868, I found the Indians located on my husband's grounds within a stone's throw of his residence, where he had brought them and protected them.

Rancho Chico was not the home of these Indians, they being located on other land, but my husband recognized that his coming drove away their game and placed them under bad influence, and that it was due them to remedy the evil as far as possible. There was not anything on Rancho Chico which was so dear to my husband as this little band of about two hundred and fifty Indians or less. [He took me to] see the little village early in the morning after my arrival. I can never forget the soft whisper in which he said he had something to show me, and the tender expression of his face, mingled with some merriment, as he [showed me] the village spread out in full view, the houses like old fashioned dome-shaped straw bee-hives with no opening save the one on the top.

I was always careful to conceal myself from their view. If I approached the village there was a general stampede, some dropping down the hole in the roof as skillfully as frogs into the water, and others disappearing into the shrubbery . . .

The men were always off at work, except at night, so I did not see them when in the village . . .

This characteristic made it very difficult for me to become acquainted with them, or to carry out the desire which I had from the first, to give them the blessings of the gospel and teach them a better mode of living.

However, after years of fruitless attempts to become

Annie Ellicott Bidwell, wife of California agriculturist and statesman John Bidwell, and missionary to the Indians on the Bidwell estate

Christmas festivities at the Bidwell's Rancho Chico Indian Mission School

California Indians holding a "morning concert" on the Merced River

acquainted with them, I decided to try a play successfully used in mission work in the East, that of giving clothing to those who would make it, provided they would come to the mission school. So by taking the cotton goods to the village and holding [them] up in a way to excite their curiosity and retain their interest; and by gestures and words, I made them understand that if they would come up to the "Mansion" (as our home was called), I would show them how to make clothing which they could have for the making.

My husband [offered] his office building near the residence, and, to my great joy, the following morning about seven women and a few children appeared. From that moment we were friends. But it was some time still before they could speak English, I having to teach them the language by means of pictures, and arithmetic by using pebbles and sticks for teaching numbers, addition and subtraction. The first half hour was given to devotional exercises: the next to reading with the women and girls, and the rest of the morning to sewing while the boys had lessons in the rudiments of English.

They would come as early as half past seven in the morning, and sometimes remain until twelve. Whenever they came, I had to open school, lest they would leave, and they were always reluctant to put their sewing away, even continuing to sew as they carried their work to the closet. My husband had given them thread and needles of coarse size to make their calico dresses with, and they had mended sacks in the mill, but they had never seen such sewing as I expected of them, and at first, by signs and murmurings in their language, protested against such fine work: but with amazing rapidity, they equaled any I could do . . . and a weary woman I was, cutting out garments to keep their needles busy. I had to devise puffs and ruffles

and a great deal of hemstitching to keep them supplied with work. I even had to puff the men's shirts as the Spanish did (at least my husband told me they did).

In an amazingly short time women over forty years of age could read ordinary literature, and were especially fond of the Bible, and when they first heard the story of our Savior's crucifixion, many a head was bowed and buried in their aprons with which they wiped away their tears. The first hymn I taught them they learned so readily and sang so perfectly on their first effort, that I was overcome with amazement and emotion.

. . . My husband John had long tried to induce them to live in wooden houses, but they were not as comfortable as their underground-ones, and they would not change. They could not accustom themselves to the idea of [the] exposure of the windows. The roof was their first step forward, and when I saw a house built with a window by the side of the door, great was my joy. This was built by one of my pupils, and now all have a parlor in their homes. Even several aged, blind couples have had the bedrooms attached to their kitchen, which they keep tidy by sweeping and dusting with buzzard's wings, feeling the floor with their hands to see if they have removed all the dust.

When I first knew them, death was terrible. Day and night for several days the wailing resembled in sound a great band of cattle and drivers mingled in wild confusion, and could be heard a mile distant. Those especially bereaved covered their hair with tar made from "tar weed," over which they threw ashes . . .

The first time that I witnessed a burial I saw the most magnificent Indian baskets laid into a grave as a tribute of affection, and was shocked to see a strong man take a spade and crush the baskets, that they might be better disposed of in the grave. "What a waste," I said to myself.

In an instant . . . I thought, "IS it a waste? Is not the self-sacrificing love which has offered these baskets more precious than the baskets themselves?" I have seen a mother leave the grave and go to the house to bring something more that had been forgotten, wailing as she performed this errand. Clocks and all sorts of small household wares, together with the clothing of the deceased, and all the bedding used during the illness, and garments contributed by loving friends, all went into the grave.

Recently a Christian Indian said he was going to die, going to his Good Father, and told his wife not to cry much for him, because he was going to his good home . . . he spoke little English but understood it, and was very fond of visiting us . . . at the "churchee house." He had in his rooms the most marvelous display of bear skins, flicker feather ornaments and Indian belts. I think he had seven belts made of scarlet feathers of the woodpecker, breast feathers of the mallard duck and white beads all woven together with fine cord made of wild hemp. Some of these belts must have been a yard and a half long. The medium sized ones were valued at one hundred and fifty dollars, but are never sold. The feathers are arranged in blocks, separated by rows of little white beads . . .

I did not expect him to sell me a belt, but when I told him and his wife how many years I had wished one, they talked it over in Indian, and he let me have this at a moderate price, saying, "I never sell belt to Indian or white man: many Indian like to get this belt, no sell 'em, but you have 'em forty dollars." He had a great display of curios, and had them all locked in a valise before his funeral and buried with him. I could but long for that valise with its many treasures.

Day after day, [the Indians] came from a great distance to mourn, and to give offerings . . . I saw a large circle of men and women seated on the ground, heads bowed, bitterly weeping aloud, while three aged women walked around the outside of the circle, also weeping bitterly, bending over the bowed forms of the men and women and wiping tears from their eyes, till they had completed the circle—which was a slow process. So slowly and solemnly did they walk, now and then stopping to wipe their eyes. In the center of this group stood one of my pupils (an Indian girl of about twelve years) dressed in scarlet, with her arms outstretched heavenward in pleading attitude, and her eyes lifted upward . . . As I looked on at these women pacing around the graves of their dead, I thought . . . it heart-breaking to witness. Later I asked this young girl what was the meaning of the group in which she stood, and the meaning of her attitude. She explained that the weeping Indians represented life here: or, to use her words, they were "thinking of them down here," while she was "thinking of them in heaven."

I never attempted to interfere with these customs, but simply tried to give them the gospel. I begged them to ask God to let them know [the difference between] right and wrong. Then He would surely show them the way . . .

It was about 1876 when the first casket was used for an Indian burial—by request of one of the men who said he was going to the white man's God, and he wished to be buried like a white man. He wished our carpenter to make the casket, and ever since caskets have been supplied to all the Indians, with the exception of two or three who wished to buy their own. They have been much comforted by Christian burial. A friend who was assisting them in dressing the little chapel for a funeral told me that one of the Indian men, whom she was helping . . . said, "We hope we will all die before Mrs. Bidwell, so she can bury us," for it had been my office to bury them ever since I have had charge of this mission . . .

We are so inconsistent with the Indians . . . We have implicit faith in God's wonderful dealings with the Jews, and we also believe the prophecy that in the latter days God's people, men and women, would see visions and dream dreams through the out-pourings of the Holy Spirit; yet if [God] gives the Indian such guidance as he gave Abraham or Elijah, we think that it is a superstition to be discouraged . . .

They had implicit faith in a Great Spirit who rewarded or punished according to their works. It was a religion of legality without the Redeemer, yet with a consciousness of God's goodness in giving them blessings with which they were surrounded.

They ask a blessing at their public meals, and some tell me they never ate without thanking God for what they had. Once they had a great feast here, attended by Indians who had no Christian instruction. A great table was spread out of doors and a very tempting repast was served by the Rancho Chico Indians, who cooked in their houses and out of doors to meet the great demand upon them. As there were too many for the first table, many servings were to follow, and the cooking was to continue. When these guests seated themselves at the first big table, one stood at the head. All was silence. The merry chatting ceased, and all assumed an attitude of reverence, bowing their heads, while the man who stood at the head of the table made a little speech in Indian language, which proved to be a prayer. When he had finished, all at the table began to eat heartily, and the chatting was resumed . . . I asked one of the Indians what [the speaker] said while standing, and she replied: "To eat what was before them . . . and to thank God for it."

They had a certain amount of light, but lacked the knowledge of a Savior, which they realize has brought to them a blessing. One said to me, "We don't cry now like we used to cry, because we know about heaven, and about God."

It was this knowledge that led them to abandon the great wailings and the tar and ashes in their hair; but their affection has not grown any less, and is to me a constant source or admiration and wonder. One has to be with them intimately to understand their deep emotion controlled by a trust in God.

Referring to the special intervention of God, I will give you an incident. When my health gave way under the strain of the day school, the doctor ordered it discontinued. My husband . . . used the building for other purposes, which obliged me to go to the village to instruct them. [Thus I met] the men, who came around to hear the singing and the other services, as we held the services out of doors. My brother, before I arrived in California, had a Sabbath class of young men, which, for good reasons, he was obliged to discontinue. But he had sown some good seed.

One day I was asked to see a man and his wife who were dying. The woman lay on the floor unconscious, and the man [named Tokeeno] was propped up against the wall, seemingly dying of consumption. I tried to lead him to the Savior, but he could not understand—though he struggled to do so. The next day I called and saw a fine clock on the mantel. [The sick man's] cousin, [a woman named No-panny], seeing me look at it in surprise, explained that [Tokeeno], in his effort to recall what my brother had taught him, [had] sent her to town to buy a clock, as my brother had taught him so to tell the time of day, and he had an idea it would help him to remember the rest.

I said, "Let us pray." [Nopanny], who was a member of my school and who had become a Christian, said, "Not in this house. That woman doesn't believe," referring to [Tokeeno's] wife. After a brief consultation in Indian language with . . . Tokeeno, she said, "I wish I had my cousin in [my] house," whereupon several men moved toward him, indicating they would carry him. So this woman, Nopanny, said that she would run ahead and get her house ready to receive him and the rest of us, where we would have a service, for we had long been promising to build them a little chapel at the village. I told them, on this occasion, that pretty soon we would have it built. Said Nopanny, in indignant tones: "Pretty soon! Pretty soon! All the time 'pretty soon!' Never have it! My cousin wants that church-house." Nopanny built a nice fire in her fireplace, drew out a big rocking chair and laid a quilt over it, and the men brought Tokeeno in their arms and tenderly seated him in the chair, and the little congregation crowded into the room. Suddenly a ghastliness overspread his face: his eyes became glazed and wide-open. His jaw fell and his whole appearance was that of death. I was horror stricken, as were all the others, and knew not what to say. We had had services before in Nopanny's house for our little school band, but this was the first time the men had come, and I was afraid his death would prejudice them against having any more services there, and, besides, I was full of horror at the event.

Usually, when death comes, a terrific wail is instantly heard, but today they seemed transformed to stone. In my despair, I said, "Let us pray." At the close of the prayer, not knowing what to do next, all of us gazing at Tokeeno, a sudden violent trembling passed over his body. The light came back into his eyes, the pallor of death passed away, and the fallen jaw suddenly rose to its place, and this thin, terribly emaciated man, though still thin, had the appearance of health. I gave a little scripture lesson and after a prayer, left the house, too overpowered at the strange 'event to remain, and turned homeward, but was overtaken by Nopanny, who, with great excitement and earnestness, said, "My cousin says he died and went to God and the good lady prayed and God sent him back to see that church house built, and we want that church house."

On reaching home, I said to my husband that the church must begin tomorrow, even if it should be but an ordinary room. On Monday morning, our carpenters were at work and a little chapel was erected. This proved too small, the men having to stand and hold the children in their arms, so we had to erect another. Tokeeno walked out of Nopanny's house that Sunday, and for six months at least, while not strong enough to work, seemed entirely free from disease, and walked around like any of the other Indians, radiantly happy, [until] one day, without any seeming reason, [he] died. Nopanny, until her death recently, always called the little chapel "My cousin's church": and I admit it was. I feel that God did send him to force us to do our duty, we waiting till we could build them something ornate, while he knew a humbler building, like their own homes, was much better.

. . . When I came here in 1868 I saw this young man plowing. My husband drove to where he was and said to me, "I want to introduce you to an Indian boy who has never done anything wrong." My husband assured me that from the time he took him as a youth to assist him around his home, that he had never known Billie to do anything

Westward-bound missionaries pose on front steps of an Episcopal Church Mission House, 1908.

Two Presbyterian missionaries visiting an aged Apache woman, Anadarko, Oklahoma, 1898

wrong. He had no education, yet he taught about the evils of gambling and drinking, and was their "pastor." It was he who had prayed and talked to God on the top of the sweat house, when the dances were held—these dances being sacred as much as were those of David and Miriam and Jeptha's daughter.

When Billie's wife became a Christian, she asked for a Bible, for she had learned to read very well. [Billie's wife, Nopanny, was the daughter of the Indian who was chief when John Bidwell took over the ranch.] I gave her a large family Bible which she carefully kept wrapped in flannel on her mantel. This was before she returned the Bible to me saying, "My husband doesn't believe that Book and I can't keep it." He had not forbidden it, but she felt it was too sacred to be subjected to his disapproval. Not very long after this she came to me for the Bible, saying, "My husband died and went to God and God showed him that Book and told him it was His Book, and he must believe it." From that day to this, Billie has been a loyal Christian. [Billie had not actually passed away, only "died" in the sense of experiencing a vision.]

An anti-Chinese movement was inaugurated in Chico, and my husband's property was threatened with destruction if he did not dismiss the few Chinese he had. [In 1862 an "Anti-Coolie Club" was founded in San Francisco to promote discriminatory legislation against the Chinese. These feelings peaked in the mid-1880s, when mass demonstrations were held in the Sacramento Valley—and in Chico.] This alarmed the Indians for the safety of the church, and Billie would get up every night and walk around to see that there was not an incendiary about. As Billie had work all day, and lost so much sleep at night, it became a serious question, but I could not dissuade him.

One day at an Indian funeral, a peculiar flag was carried in the procession to the grave, and then taken to Billie's house. I . . . asked what it meant . . . Nopanny said that Billie awakened her one night saying:

"The house is full of light. The house is full of light and God wants me to go out and talk to Him."

[Nopanny] said, "There is no light here. It is all dark."

But he said, "No, it is all light."

And he got up and went out and was gone some time. When he came back he walked like it was light through the house, and said to [Nopanny,] "When I go out I see flag flying in village. God said: 'You see that flag? I got one like it. I watch church house.'"

So Billie, in the morning, [went to town for calico to make a flag].

It was evident that Billie had seen plainly such a light as Abraham when God showed him the stars.

Someone had poisoned all the dogs in the village, and the Indians were crying about it, and she had said to them, with a laugh, "What do you want dogs for? My husband watches better than any dogs." When Nopanny died recently, Billie laid in her casket a duplicate of the flag . . . He had carried the flag at another funeral at the request of a man who had heard of Billie's revelation, and had seen the flag made. To them, it was a symbol of God's care over them. I have never seen it carried at any other funeral, nor a duplicate used of it except for Nopanny.

Nopanny was the daughter of the Indian who was chief when my husband took possession of Rancho Chico. Nopanny and I were devoted friends . . . When she was taken suddenly ill and unconscious, I was sent for. We did everything possible for her, especially the doctor. Suddenly Billie, who was seated by her bedside, lifted up his voice in one of the most pitiful cries that I have ever heard. The

*Annie Bidwell*

doctor said, "If Billie cries that way I cannot do anything. It unnerves me." [Billie] looked at my face and said, "Mrs. Bidwell, my wife is gone. I saw her go."

Evidently he had, for . . . she was dead; yet she had been seemingly breathing when Billie saw her go.

The Indians are not spiritualists, for they have no mediums. But they have visions. Or, what is more real to them, appearances of those who have left . . . I have not baptized many because I do not wish to seem antagonistic to customs. But I had taken that work up, contrary to customs, for, at that time in our church, no woman dared to pray in public. And when Tokeeno demanded the church house, I tried to get some man to take charge of the services, for the Indians would not have Sunday School, they wished "church." Finding that I had to assume charge, I thought I would call it Sunday School anyway, even if it was church, when it seemed to me God said to me, "Will you lie to the Holy Spirit? This is a CHURCH." I have often wept all the way from home to the little church because of my insufficiency, and because I did not think it was proper that I, a woman, should teach men, especially Indians. For I thought they had less regard for women than white men.

[But I was so ignorant.] From that day to this, the men have stood by me to such an extent as to be the marvel of those who attend the service. Only the other day an army officer said to me, "This is the first church I have ever seen where the men were in the majority."

I feel justified before God in baptizing, for Saul was baptized by a disciple, and not by a clergyman, and Philip was a deacon who was to look after merely the material wants of the church . . . I ought to have the right officially given me to perform these services, that these Indians whom I baptize may be duly accredited to the church, of which this is a mission branch. I have never dared urge, as a matter of conscience, that these old Indians be baptized . . . But where they have insisted, whether young or old, I have obeyed God rather than man.

# A. J. McNemee

"I failed to get to Alaska. That made the third time I had missed a good appointment because I did not have a wife."
—A. J. McNemee

With good reason, A. J. McNemee called his autobiography the Iliad. Throughout his ministerial life he bore hardships that seem little short of epic—near-starvation, alienation, self-doubt, and rugged treks of hundreds of miles on foot, often without the welcome assurance of food or shelter at journey's end.

He was born in Portland, Oregon, on March 5, 1848. By the time he had decided to become a minister, the opening of the Northwest Passage had brought to Oregon and Washington scores of Protestant missionaries hoping to win back the Indian population from Catholic influence.

McNemee, with his awkward temperance speeches, outspoken criticism of weak Christians, and weather-beaten visage, seemed unable to strike a happy balance in communities. He was an unmarried traveling circuit preacher at a time when the settled, married pastor received more local support. And he tended to antagonize leading citizens by insisting on stopping all commerce on Sunday.

During his early years, McNemee built churches by hand, working as a cooper or hod carrier to pay off church debts. He forged swollen rivers and traveled, hungry and cold, through the Goose Lake Valley in southern Oregon and the seventy-five-mile Whatcom County circuit in Washington. Once he quit the ministry in despair, only to return after seven years to the Squak Mission in 1885. In 1886 the presiding elder reported that though McNemee was not a "great preacher" he knew how to "rustle."

By 1889 McNemee was forty-one years old. He had finally passed the Methodist Course of Study to become the oldest deacon in the state. After his ordination, his brother paid his fifteen-dollar ticket to the San Juan circuit. He arrived wearing a new suit—also paid for by his brother.

In April 1909 Brother Mack arrived in Langley, Washington, one of his last mission sites. He worked there for a year, holding revivals and collecting funds to build a church. McNemee admitted he was a "nervous wreck and needed a change," but was shocked when, at year's end, his presiding elder asked that he retire. After twenty-five *years of ministry, McNemee was offered eighty-two dollars as a token of esteem, along with the position of missionary pastor at a nearby hamlet for the less than grand sum of fourteen dollars annually. He complained and was later reassigned to Dungeness, on the Langley circuit, then finally back to Langley. By then he had saved five hundred dollars and retired from the ministry for good, taking pleasure in an active Sunday school following and "the good will of the people." He finished his journal in August 1924, at the age of seventy-six. He died in 1936.*

I was born in Portland, Oregon, March 5th, 1848, in a small house on the S.W. corner of Yamhill and Front streets.

My grandfather was David Cochrane. He was born in Virginia, moved to Kentucky, where he hunted with Boone and Kenton, and later moved to Ohio . . . In 1845 my father sold his claim for $400 and eight horses and started across the plains with an ox team. My uncle Fred Waymire and his brother John, with their families, were in this train . . .

They finally reached the Dalles [Oregon] almost destitute . . . [and] in the spring of 1846 my father moved to what is now called Portland. At that time it was a small Indian trading post of three log cabins. Father bought two lots and built the fourth house in Portland . . .

In 1866 our family moved down the Columbia River to the Chinook fishing grounds, where my mother died, September 1, 1872. Father died in Portland, October 1, 1872.

My first religious impressions came when I was a very small boy. I attended church with my mother . . . a strange feeling came over me and I felt as if I could not move. During the class meeting that followed, the preacher asked me if I did not want to be a Christian. This question

broke the spell and I ran for home, crying all the way . . .

When I was about 13 years old I used to carry milk over to Father Royals. When I went to the front door the old gentleman would generally meet me and often would give me some tracts and along with them some good advice. When I went to the back door Grandma Royal would give me an apple, or some cookies. I always liked her kind of religion . . .

On the evening of March 16, 1868, at nine o'clock, I picked up a tract that had been given me . . . I wanted peace, and [to] believe. Suddenly there came a sweet peace in my soul and I cried out, "Blessed Jesus, Blessed Jesus, Abba Father." The burden of sin was rolled away and my soul was filled with great joy. I did not realize that this experience was what was called "conversion"—it seemed too good to be true. It was so easy and quick . . .

One night I was sleeping on a bed of straw in my cabin home in Chinook, Washington, when all at once I seemed wide awake and felt an unseen presence at the side of the bed and heard that still small voice saying, "Andrew, I have set thee apart for the Holy Ministry . . ." The presence seemed to depart from me, but I felt a great peace in my soul and from that time felt that I was called into the ministry . . .

[McNemee was given a scholarship to Willamette University for twenty-five dollars. He lived with two friends and worked as a cooper to support them.]

In January, 1870, I started to school. Oh how hungry I was for an education. I felt as if I wanted to study night and day . . . I lived on 25 cents a week and . . . fasted more days than feasted, but I was so eager to get an education that I was willing to go ragged, hungry and pay almost any price for the privilege of attending school . . .

In August, 1872, I took sick and went to Chinook and

staid two weeks with my mother. She looked well and seemed happy. She said she had received the second blessing [further evidence of conversion, or the "born again" experience] and was now able to cast all of her cares and troubles on Him . . . She urged me to stay longer, but I felt I must get back to work. I am sorry now I did not give up school and try to make her last days more comfortable, for she had led a lonely life without Christian fellowship of any kind near her. She passed away September 1st, praising God.

I continued at school, but lost my ambition and interest in life. For six months after her death, as I walked the streets of Salem I often felt as though I would like to "curse God and die."

[McNemee had received his license to preach in 1871, but continued to attend school and support himself. He carried a hod and built scaffolding at the Salem state penitentiary, worked as a janitor at Bishop Scott's Academy in Portland, and in 1876 labored at a fishery to finance his studies at the Boston School of Theology, to "better fit [him]self for the ministry." At the Annual Conference in 1876 he was accepted as a supply preacher, sent to the Whatcom County circuit, and given part of the allotted seventy-five dollars in missionary funds.]

Going to Sehome in 1876 was quite different from what it is now. Then it was kind of a tri-weekly affair. The steamer went down one week and tried to get back the next. The Presiding Elder came with me, down to the steamer, and [said] . . . "My young brother, I want you to be sure to keep up your ministerial dignity." I did not fully comprehend what he meant, but learned later that [he meant] when traveling on boat to be sure to ask for a clergyman's half fare, and if you can get a meal without paying for it by telling that you are a poor Methodist preacher,

be sure to do it . . . At home I had been taught that wherever I went I was expected to play the man, and this idea of playing the dead beat because I was a Methodist preacher was not pleasant to me. So, as I went aboard the steamer to go to Sehome, I had a fierce battle to fight, that is, whether I should pay full fare or . . . ask for half fare. As it happened, the Purser . . . was an old school mate of mine, so when I told him I was a preacher, he gladly gave me half fare. We also had a pleasant visit talking over old times . . .

Sehome was a coal mining camp of 150 men and there were two families living in the old town of Whatcom . . . When I arrived . . . a messenger came and notified me that a child was dead and they wanted me to conduct the funeral. I had heard ministers talk of their labors and I had made light of it, but now, could I have had my choice, I would rather have cut wood or carried a hod than to have had to preach, especially a funeral sermon. However . . . I gave a better talk than I did the evening before. At the close of the service a man offered me five dollars, but I refused to accept it, telling him that preachers did not make a charge for a funeral service. He insisted that I should take it . . . so I took it. It was needed, too, as I only had $1.50 and was among strangers and a long way from home. I thanked the Lord and took courage . . . but it was many a long day before I ever saw another five dollars. This gold piece I intended to keep as a souvenir, but six months later I met a Methodist preacher's wife who only had a little bread and tea for her family, so I made her a present of my gold piece . . .

The next day I started . . . for Semiahmoo . . . I reached the home of Thomas Hoskins that night . . . and the next day, hastened on my journey. Thomas Hoskins went with me through the woods, as there was no trail for several miles and only a blaze to follow for six miles . . . At the first cabin I came to I asked how far it was to Semiahmoo and was told that this was it. I was looking for a town, or at least a village. My courage went down to a low ebb as I thought this was the most desolate looking country I had ever seen . . . I asked myself why on earth would white people ever settle in such a place, and the Presiding Elder had told me that this place was to be the head of my circuit. He also said he was sending me to a good circuit . . .

That night I reached the main settlement . . . and [on Sunday] a large crowd came to hear the new preacher. They came from miles around, by foot and by boat. I had intended to preach the same sermon that I had used at Sehome and, as I had studied it over again carefully, I felt better prepared. But just as I began the service, in came Capt. and Mrs. Conway from Sehome, who had heard me when I tried to preach there. So I changed off and selected another text that I had not studied, and my second sermon seemed to be more of a failure than the first.

The plan of the circuit was as follows: First Sunday morning at Blain . . . Second Sunday, Mountain View; Third Sunday at Ferndale School House; and Fourth Sunday, Lynden and [the] upper crossing of Nooksack. The way I had to travel from Blain to Lynden was called fifty miles, and then I had to return to Blain, which made one hundred miles every four weeks for me through the brush, over logs and through the swamps and trails, for there was no road except from Sehome to the Nooksack Crossing. With a pack of books and clothing on my back, I made the rounds for twelve months, for the Presiding Elder had told me that I must read and study as they needed educated men in the ministry.

For six months I never staid two nights in the same house but kept on the move, boarding around the circuit until I felt it was a burden on the people to keep me. So I concluded to try housekeeping. Having saved up $3.50, I sent to Portland for some blankets and then borrowed a camp kettle and frying pan. I rented a cabin. As it was getting late in the evening . . . I boiled some potatoes in the camp kettle, placed them on a board and made some tea in the same kettle. With some crackers, that was my meal, but I felt glad to think that now at last I was in a home of my own. However, in the middle of the night I was taken very sick and thought surely I would die, and I concluded to make my will. As I took a look at my possessions it struck me as very funny, for I could not have sold the whole outfit, I suppose, for $15. I had a good laugh over it and then went to sleep. In the morning I found out what was the trouble. I had used salt water in my cooking and, when I went to the well to get water, I found a dead skunk in it. Of course I had to move off into another cabin, where I spent weeks with nothing but bread and water and at last only water, as I dreaded to go boarding around again. At last I was so starved I had to move. One day, while in the cabin, I borrowed a shotgun and tried to kill some pigeons, but they were too wild so I shot a blue-jay and a red squirrel, expecting to have a feast on them. But the squirrel was so poor I couldn't skin it (Guess he had been boarding around like the preacher), so I threw it away. I then cleaned the blue-jay and put it in the pot and boiled it for two hours. The longer I boiled it, the tougher it got. It was like trying to put a fork in a rubber ball, so I threw it away and drank some of the soup, after which I had a good cry, for my dinner was all gone and I was faint with hunger.

The result was that I had to go boarding around the

Reverend John L. Dyer (right), affectionately known as "The Snowshoe Itinerant" throughout his Colorado circuit

circuit again, as there was no work to be obtained and I felt like a soldier who had been sent to hold the fort. But I often wished that God would call me home . . .

On my first visit to Lynden I was told of a family, Mr. and Mrs. Bertrands, who lived three miles across what was called Bertrands Prairie, but I found it more like a swamp, as the water and mud would almost come up to the top of my boots when I tramped across that marsh. I only had a blaze to follow, and, as it was getting dark, I lost the blaze and thought I would have to camp in the swamp all night. As I went to step over a root, my foot caught and I fell head first in the mud and water. As I picked myself up, I felt like having a good cry, for I was so tired and hungry. Then I thought, "Young man, you must have been hard pushed for employment to travel 400 miles to get a job like this with the promise of $100 salary and the privilege of boarding around among a lot of poor people who themselves were on the verge of starvation." The thought struck me as something to laugh at. When I had rested a bit, I started on, and about a hundred yards ahead of me I saw a light and found it was Mr. Bertrand's house, and he and his wife gave me a royal welcome. As Mr. Bertrand had just killed a bear, we had that for supper and it did taste good to me after my long hard tramp. Mr. Bertrand was an old hunter and trapper and his wife was a sister of an Indian Chief . . . and a better Christian woman I never knew. They gave me the best they had.

Their house was small and they had a large family of small children and I was puzzled where I should sleep. But after prayers, they pulled out a trundle bed for the children and laid the fresh bear skin in one corner of the room for me and, with a blanket and my boots for a pillow, I dreamed of the promised land and the next morning felt renewed strength and courage to go on in my work . . .

In October, 1876, my Presiding Elder, Reverend A. C. Fairchilds, came to Blain to hold my first Quarterly Meeting . . . At this Quarterly Meeting the Presiding Elder preached twice and the collections for the two meetings were $1.25. He had an appointment to preach in the school house on California Creek, but as it was a stormy day . . . he sent me to preach with instructions if there was a large crowd I was to take up a collection. There were only five persons present and it was so cold I did not preach. The second time that I went there they only had a small crowd. I did not take up a collection this time either. When my Presiding Elder went back to Seattle, he said he would send me my second quarter missionary money, but instead of sending me the $18.75 that was due me, he only sent me $13.75, stating that he had kept $5 of this money, as he thought my collection on California Creek would amount to that much . . . I never did get that five dollars. It was only a small amount; but, as I only received $25 in ten months on that circuit, five dollars meant a good deal to me at that time.

The last of December, 1876, Rev. Magill and I went over to Skagit County to hold a meeting . . . Our meeting was a failure from the start. We tried holding meetings in an old deserted cabin. The weather was very cold and stormy. Very few people attended and no interest was taken. This was before the land had been diked and ditched and it was bad traveling in winter . . .

In June, 1877, we arranged to hold a Camp Meeting on the south bank of the Nooksack River in a grove of maple trees. We made brush tents and I covered mine with maple boughs, which was good protection from the sun, but a poor protection from the rain which came a few days later, while we were in the midst of our meeting.

Between Ferndale and Semiahmoo there was no road,

only a blazed trail through the woods. But Grandma Cain of Semiahmoo said she wanted to attend one more camp meeting before she died and, as it was too far for her to walk, her four sons . . . slashed and made a sled road to Ferndale. Making a sled, they loaded it with bed and blankets, seated Grandma Cain on top of it, and with a yoke of yearling steers for a team they brought her to the meeting with many a song and shout along the way. Most of the others who came walked or came in canoes, and a few from British Columbia came on horse back. The Presiding Elder came to take charge of the meeting and Rev. Thomas Magill was to assist and he did a splendid work. I walked . . . twenty-five miles to meet the Presiding Elder, for I had been then on the circuit for ten months and I felt hungry to talk with a Methodist preacher, as I felt the need of a word of comfort and cheer. About the first thing he said to me was, "Have you taken up the benevolence collections?" I said, "No, the people are so poor I did not like to ask them." Then he said that I would never succeed as a Methodist preacher. That I must take up the collection . . .

A great crowd gathered at the camp meeting . . . and I was notified to preach on Saturday morning. However, Friday evening a crowd came in . . . among them Rev. Jos. Hall, said to be the best preacher in British Columbia . . . fine men, all of them. I was told by a friend the Presiding Elder had invited Rev. Jos. Hall to preach in my place, so I made no further preparation for preaching, but was busy helping to build tents and make these new comers comfortable. At 10 o'clock Saturday morning someone asked me who was to preach and I said I had been appointed . . . but Rev. Hall would preach in my place. The Presiding Elder heard my answer and said that was not true, that he had appointed me to preach and that he was expecting me to do it. I was all broken up by the way he had spoken to me, and as then I only had one hour to prepare to preach, I quit work and went off alone in the woods and had one of the fieriest battles of my life. I was tempted to pack up my blankets and go over into British Columbia and never again tell anyone that I was a Methodist preacher. Then I thought I never yet had run away from a hard job and that it was a poor time to begin now. So I selected a text and that was about all the preparation I made. When I stood up before that large crowd with so many preachers present and tried to preach, it was indeed a hard place. I talked perhaps five minutes and then broke down. Rev. Taite followed me and gave us an excellent sermon. I at least had the sympathy of the people, who realized how hard it was for me to preach when there were three good preachers present who had traveled 60 miles for the purpose of helping in the meeting. God who answers prayers poured out His Holy Spirit and many souls were converted . . .

At the camp meeting we held our last quarterly conference. I had been ten months on the circuit and had received $25 from the people. When I told Rev. Magill the amount received, he said he thought I "ought to thank God and take courage." When the question was asked about the pastor being returned, some of my members objected, stating that they wanted a man that could preach and one that also had a wife . . . I was asked if I did not want to join the Oregon Conference, but I said no, for I thought if I did, I would have to serve under the same Presiding Elder . . . A heavy rain came during the meeting but the people were so deeply interested that they paid little heed to it. At last our provisions ran short so we were compelled to close the meeting, as many of the people had come a long ways from home to attend. There were about 150 Indians . . . many of

Chinese immigrants encounter American missionaries aboard ship in San Francisco harbor.

Schoolchildren in front of First Presbyterian Chinese Church

RIGHT: Ellen Su Moon, Japanese girl dressed for graduation, possibly from a Southern California mission school

197
෴

A. J.
McNemee

Chinese mission school in Monterey County, California

Parade in Chinatown, possibly at Eastertide, in San Francisco,
California.

whom were converted. It was a joy to hear them speak of their religious experiences, and listen to them sing the songs of Zion . . .

After resting a few days, I made arrangements to go to the Springfield Circuit under Presiding Elder McCain, but [was] advised not to go, as it was a worn out circuit. Rev. John Wolfe advised me to go to the Goose Lake Circuit, saying I was a Western boy and they were Western people who were just hungry for the Gospel . . . I said all right, and . . . Elder McCain had no objection. But I had to get permission of Rev. George Nickerson, who was stationed there in charge . . .

I borrowed $15 and started for my Circuit, going to Eugene by the railroad. From there I started afoot with a pack of books and clothes for the Klamath Agency two hundred miles away. On the second evening I reached Mountain House, or the last house between there and the Agency, which was one hundred thirty miles further . . . That night I reached the Deschutes River . . . After supper, however, it turned intensely cold and, as I had no blankets, I could not sleep. so I concluded that as long as there was a full moon I might as well try to keep warm by traveling on the road. I had been told at the Mountain Hotel that when I was half way, I was to leave the Military Road and take the Old Immigrant Road to the Agency, as the Military Road ended in the Klamath Marsh where no one lived and I could never find my way out . . .

So I kept a keen lookout for the Old Immigrant Road. About midnight I saw a dim trail leading off from the Military Road. At first I thought this certainly could not be the Immigrant Road and passed on . . . But the thought came to me, if I have made a mistake, I certainly will die in that wilderness, so I returned and followed the dim trail until I came to some wagon tracks and I rejoiced greatly,

although I was still in doubt as to whether this was the road to the Klamath Agency. I became very tired and sat down, leaning against a pine tree. It was very lonely and still at this hour of the night. Suddenly I heard the howl of a wolf that sounded far away. I listened to find out if he was on my track. Then all at once it seemed as if I could hear a thousand wolves howling all around me. I had a heavy pack on my back but I did not stop to remove it. I climbed up that tree in a hurry, nearly to the top, as it was a small tree. I took off my belt and fastened myself to the tree for fear I should fall out, as my hands and feet were almost frozen. After a while the wolves left me. I was so cold that I could hardly stand, but I started again on the road.

Fortunately the full moon made it almost as light as day. I had only gone a few hundred yards when I saw the track of a big cougar in the road. As I stopped, I saw a large animal standing in the shadow of a big tree. I could not make out at first what it was but thought it was a grizzly bear. I looked for a tree to climb, but they were all large and [had] no limbs within reach. I was about half way then to the Agency and it was as dangerous going back as going forward, so I took my cloak and waved it in the air, yelling as loud as I could. Immediately the animal broke and ran and I saw it was a large elk.

It was so cold that, when I stopped to drink, my mustache and whiskers froze together. My nose was clogged up with ice so that I had difficulty in breathing. I took my knife and cut my whiskers and mustache apart and could then breathe out of my mouth at least. When daylight came the weather became very hot and I had to travel many miles without water. I had often gone without food for days, but that suffering was nothing to that of thirst. My blood seemed to be all on fire. My tongue was swollen and felt as large as my wrist. I became delirious and then insensible to pain, imagining that I saw a beautiful lake on the bank of which birds were singing and flowers blooming. Three times I left the road to go to this enchanted ground, but I managed to have sense enough left to realize that it was only a mirage that was leading me to death. About four in the afternoon I reached Sand Creek and I was so crazy for water that I plunged headlong into the stream. I then had a strange experience. It seemed that [the] cold water burnt my face, as if I had plunged into a flame of fire. I could not drink, as my tongue was swollen and hanging out of my mouth, so I sat there bathing my tongue and face in that cold water until the swelling went down and I was able to drink a little water at a time. While I was doing this, a band of antelope came within a few yards of me and they seemed much interested in seeing what the young preacher from Oregon was doing off there in the wilderness. After walking a short distance, I was so faint I laid down by a log and slept two hours, then traveled on until nine that night. I came to the Williams River and found a camp of Indians who were out on a hunt. I never was so glad to see an Indian in all my life. They gave me water to drink and told me I was ten miles to the Klamath Agency. As I had then traveled one hundred twenty miles in two days and one night—38 hours in all—I asked if they could loan me a pair of blankets. Two Indians gave me theirs and I tried to sleep while they sat up all night. But I was so worn out I could not sleep. It seemed as though every bone was aching and my feet were so badly swollen I could scarcely stand up, so I gave an Indian the last dollar I had for a horse to ride into the Agency, where I expected a cordial greeting from Mr. Nickerson and Rev. J. M. Roorak, as I had been well acquainted with them in Salem, Oregon . . .

My greeting was not as cordial as I had expected. When I told Rev. Nickerson the object of my visit he said I was a fool for going to Goose Lake, as there was no missionary money for that circuit and it was a hard field. However, if I wanted to go and take charge of Goose Lake Circuit, I could have his permission.

. . . I then started for Goose Lake by the way of the Yanix Indian Reservation. I met many of the Modoc Indians, as only one-half of the tribe had gone on the warpath . . . I had enjoyed my work among the Indians on the Nooksack River in British Columbia, but these Klamath Indians were different. They had been spoiled by contact with bad white men . . . I told them I had no money, and they thought I was telling them false stories and would laugh at me and call me all kinds of hard names. The preachers they had met were under the Government and received good salaries, so could travel horse-back or in buggies. It was very hard for me to keep up my ministerial dignity when I met such people as the Modoc Indians.

At last, after nearly a week of hard traveling, I crossed the mountains and came in sight of Goose Lake Valley, which I thought the most beautiful place that I had ever seen. I felt so happy that I sat down and cried for joy, as I thought that now I was at last at the end of my journey, having gone 125 miles by railroad and 400 miles afoot to get here. I thought that all I would have to do now was to preach and visit and pray as I went around my circuit . . .

As I descended the mountains, there came a blinding snow storm. That first night in Goose Lake I found shelter with Mr. and Mrs. McDonel, good people who were very cordial. I was very glad to find that they were also Methodists . . .

When I arrived at Rev. Harrow's home, he informed me that they already had a pastor, Rev. John Vineyard, and at

*A. J.*
*McNemee*

this point [he] was on the California side of the valley. Harrow advised me to go back on the Oregon side and preach in Lake View, organizing my circuit from there. Lake County had just been organized, with Lake View as the County seat. Only a few families lived there, but it was quite a business point for the cattle and sheep men. I arrived on Friday afternoon, put up at the hotel and gave out notice that I would preach in the Court House at 11 o'clock Sunday morning. I spent the time visiting among the people, but no one invited me to a meal or to stay all night, or gave me the least encouragement. On Sunday morning I went over to the Court House, a rough board house about twenty by thirty feet, and found it crowded to the doors. A few women were present, but most of the crowd there were cowboys just in from the range with long hair down their shoulders. Each one carried two revolvers in his belt and a bowie knife in his boots. These fellows had come to hear what the young preacher from Oregon had to say. I certainly was a stranger in a strange land. I gave them a talk on the parable of the Prodigal Son, and, while I was talking, the thought kept coming to me that I was the young man in the far country, etc. After the service a poor woman invited me to dinner, for which I was very grateful, as it was the only meal that I had been invited to in Lake View and I felt as though nearly every one had treated me like a tramp and dead beat. When I paid my hotel bill I found that preaching my first sermon in Lake View had cost me $3.50.

I then took a tramp around Crooked Creek and through the Chewcan County and back again down the Goose Lake Valley until I had spent the last dollar. Then, like the Prodigal, I hired out to a citizen of that country and he sent me up into the mountains to split rails in the midst of snow and sleet, living in a log cabin.

This ended my career as pastor of the Goose Lake Circuit in 1877, for which I never received one dollar in salary. But I had this thought to cheer and comfort me—the Lord Jesus was present with me . . . When I was a boy, I often wondered why men truly called of God to the ministry quit and went into secular business. I now knew why one man quit, after the hardest year's work of his life . . .

After working my way for six years through school and college and then two Circuits . . . I yielded up to despair. I saw no way opened for me in the ministry. I had to go to work at whatever I could find to do, so I split rails up in the mountains for two months and a half. Then I went to Modoc County and opened up a cooper shop, as I had worked in that trade . . .

I was doing well, working at my trade, when Rev. John N. Denison . . . wrote me in 1884 that the Presiding Elder of the Seattle District had a good circuit for me near Seattle, and that I could make my home with him (Denison). It seemed the Lord had once more opened up the way for me . . . so I sold my ranch and almost gave my cooper tools away, closed up my shop and headed for Seattle May 26, 1885. I arrived sick and worn out. After I went to my room in the hotel, I tried to pray to God for help but felt utterly unfit to enter the ministry again. My prayers seemed cold and formal, but . . . I said, "Lord, if you will open the door, I will try and enter once more into the work of the ministry."

For years after, this promise was like an anchor to my soul, in times of doubt and danger.

I was in poor health. My eyes were weak, I had trouble with my voice and my teeth were all badly decayed. Brother Denison advised me to have them all extracted. The year before, I had been thrown out of a wagon and had injured my back, so here I was with weak eyes, voice and teeth gone, and a lame back, once more offering to go out to preach. It was with trembling and faintness of heart that I looked forward to my work in the future . . .

I stayed with Rev. Denison until the Puget Sound Conference met in Tacoma, August 12, 1885. I dreaded to attend as I had little money and was poorly dressed. But the Presiding Elder urged me to come to the Conference, stating that he would give me a circuit. There were then twenty-four members of the Conference and five probationers.

The last day of the Conference my Presiding Elder said, "Mack, I intended to have given you a circuit, but Bishop Walden is opposed to sending out local preachers, especially old men (I was then thirty-seven years old). So don't blame me if you are left without an appointment . . . I had traveled 1,200 miles and spent $120 on the trip with the promise of a circuit. Sure enough, when the appointments were read off I was not given a circuit. I had spent all my money and knew not what to do. The first thought was to go off into the wilderness and live on fish and clams among the Indians. My second thought was, "Well, if the Lord has said, 'Behold, I have set before thee an open door and no man can shut it,' then neither the Bishop or Presiding Elder can shut it." So I rested on that promise . . .

After the Conference adjourned, the Presiding Elder . . . said to me, "Brother Mack, the Bishop is going to transfer twenty young men into this Conference, but it will be three months before they arrive here. Now, if you will take charge of the Squak Mission for three months . . . I will pay you the missionary money due for the first quarter of the year." I agreed to comply with the request, for well I knew, even if [they] did not know, that it would be a long time before they found a better man than A. J. McNemee. The next day the Presiding Elder gave me a certificate to preach, which I consider my first ordination papers.

The Presiding Elder asked the members to fix my salary. After a long delay they finally voted to give me $50 for the year from the entire Circuit. Before I came, they had [said] they would pay a preacher $300, but after I had preached for them for two months, they concluded that $50 would be about right to pay . . .

I have found this to be true—the less people pay in salary, the louder they talk about the preacher preaching for money. I had preached out on the Pill Chuck . . . before I received any salary. They then took up a collection and I received one dollar and fifteen cents. After this, as I had only a small congregation, I sent them word that I would not come again as I had a larger circuit. They were indignant and said that McNemee was like all the preachers, only preaching for the money, in spite of the fact that I had received only one dollar and fifteen cents. I'm sure that if anyone would walk four miles for four months, often through rain and storm and mud as I did . . . he would think I certainly earned my salary of one dollar and fifteen cents.

I stayed on the Circuit, traveling and preaching, from September until June and had received but a few dollars for my work. After living on crackers and water for three weeks, I concluded that the good people on my Circuit were entitled to a little rest. As the Northern Pacific Railroad Company was building a bridge across the Snohomish River, I applied for a position . . . [I was set] to work planing heavy timber by hand, and in three days I was made foreman of this crew at $3 per day. We planed one hundred thirty thousand feet of this heavy timber by hand. It was hard, but I was in debt so I stayed on the job for seven weeks. After paying my debt, I again started to round my circuit. My first Sunday at Marysville, old Brother John Spenser handed me $7.50 [saying], "It's your

A. J.
McNemee

salary. I had much more than this subscribed but when the people heard that you were at work on the bridge they demanded the money back." I then handed him back the $7.50 and said, "If that is the kind of people you have here, people who starve a preacher and then get angry because he goes to work, you can keep your money. I don't want any of it." Spenser refused to take back the $7.50, but I certainly thought I had run up against a hard crowd . . .

During the winter, in a blinding storm, I was called to go to Tualco to conduct a funeral for one of the old pioneers who had died. They had sent for Rev. Marcellus, but his wife would not let him go, so I took his place, walking seven miles in the snowstorm. The Skykomish River was frozen over but it was dangerous to cross. At every step you could hear the ice cracking. I didn't know whether I would live to get across, but I got over and conducted the funeral. There was a large crowd, but no one asked me to dinner nor to stay all night, so I started back for Snohomish. Upon reaching the other side of the River I met a friend who gave me dinner and I found a place to sleep. I was not even thanked for making that trip and it was one of the most dangerous I had ever taken. Yet if I had refused to go, it would have been noised abroad all over Snohomish County that I was too lazy to work and out for revenue only. I [had] preached at this point for one whole year and never received a dollar from them for my year's work. It was a rich farming community, too. My salary received from the entire Snohomish Circuit from the people was $28, and $160 from the Missionary Society . . .

The next year, 1889 . . . I did not have money enough to pay my expenses [to Conference] and only had an old suit of second-hand clothes to wear, as I spent all my money building the church . . . When I reached Portland, my brother bought me a new suit of clothes and a complete outfit. That year I came close to quitting the ministry . . . but my good friend Rev. John Denison advised me not to do it, but to go on to Conference, pass in my Conference Course of Study and be ordained. When I told my brother this he said, "That is all right. What you owe me is a present to you, and if you want to preach don't stop for want of money for I will let you have what you may need." So he gave me the new suit of clothes and money to go to Conference, where I passed in my studies and was ordained a deacon in 1889. I then started for my circuit and my brother gave me $15 to pay my way to San Juan and Lopez. If I have done any good in the ministry since then, I owe it all to that good brother, who . . . gave me between four and five hundred dollars to keep me in the ministry and he was only a poor, hard-working man, and not even a church member.

# William Robinson

"It was the height of my ambition to be a political orator for I had in me that retaliating spirit . . . and [I wanted to] tongue-lash the Southern people in politics. But I saw that I had the wrong spirit. If I accomplished anything it must be through the spirit of love and not of vengeance.
—William Robinson

Born in midnineteenth-century North Carolina, William Robinson experienced in his boyhood the last harsh years of Southern slavery, with its stringent Black Codes that regulated every aspect of slave life. President Lincoln issued the Emancipation Proclamation in 1863, when Robinson was a fifteen-year-old youth enlisted in the Confederate army. "May God forever bless . . . Abraham Lincoln, who led us across the Red Sea of slavery into the promised land of liberty," Robinson later wrote.

After the war Robinson became a fireman in Nashville. He later worked as an advertising minstrel for Hanlon's Wizard Oil Company, touring the "leading cities" of Indiana, Illinois, and Michigan to tout the oil company's products. Eventually, because of his success, he traveled to England on an eleven-month promotional journey.

There, for the first time in his life, Robinson experienced the world of ideas. He attended school in England, rapidly learned to read, and discovered that he had an "uncommon verbal memory." Upon his return to America, Robinson continued the pursuit of education, gradually discovering the desire and ability to minister. In 1877 he had a conversion experience and dedicated his life to God. In La Porte, Indiana, he joined the missionary Baptist church—although he was a Methodist. There was no other church in town.

Robinson later married and had children. He was a minister of the African Methodist Episcopal Church in Albia, Iowa, but little is known of his clerical years, save for some messages delivered from the pulpit. (It is certain that he had a congregation, as there had been a large influx of blacks into Iowa after the Civil War.) During the years of Robinson's service, the African Methodist Episcopal Church sought to conduct more restrained services, overcoming the stigma of emotional excess in so-called slave religion. It pressed for greater education, formalized Bible study, and individual improvement. Robinson, with his incisive rhetoric and obvious education, must have represented his denomination well.

I was born in Wilmington, a town in North Carolina, March 11, 1848 . . . My parents, Peter and Rosy, belonged to a very wealthy ship and slave holder, who owned two farms and over five hundred slaves.

My father was an engineer and towed vessels in and out of the Wilmington harbor into the Atlantic ocean. My mother was a cook at the great house, but hired her time from her mistress, for which she paid three dollars per month . . .

Father enjoyed the friendship of two very distinguished Quakers, Mr. Fuller and Elliott, who owned oyster sloops, and stood at the head of what is known in our country as the underground railroad, an organization filled with love of freedom for suffering humanity, that had for its end the liberation of slaves.

Father was with Mr. Fuller and Elliott every day, towing them in and out. This gave them an opportunity to devise plans for getting many into Canada . . . and my father was an important factor in this line.

The system of deliverance by the underground railroad was to divide the country off into sections, and at every fifteen or twenty miles would be a station or depot. One man would haul the slaves at night to the end of his station and get back home before daylight, undiscovered: then the slaves would be conveyed the next night in wagons from that station to the next, and so on, until they reached Canada.

Often the wagons had double linings with corn or wheat visible, while the cavity was filled with mothers and children.

Father . . . grew weary of the life of a slave, and with the assistance of his Quaker friends, plans were laid for him to purchase his own freedom and go to Canada; then

Baptism by water in the South

Reverend and Mrs. Thomas Towns. Towns was a chaplain in Fremont's army who settled in Monterey and, later, near San Jose, California.

his family would be sent to him by the underground railroad. If any one connected with the railroad was caught, the penalty was a heavy fine, and expulsion from the state . . .

The plans to free father were put into execution in 1858 . . . His Master immediately suspected these two Quakers. Father finally succeeded in convincing him that no white man was implicated. [In 1875 Robinson met the son of one of his father's benefactors, and discovered that the slaver had killed Mr. Fuller for his involvement in the underground railroad.] The master agreed to take $1,150 for [my father], who was to pay on the installment plan, paying $450 down . . . In 1859 my father went to California with a surveying company: staying one year he returned during the holidays, paying $350 more on himself, making a total of $800 paid on his debt. He went back to California, then news came to us that he was returning in chains. We knew exactly what that meant: to rob him of what he had paid, and sell him away from us. And we were not mistaken, for this was the exact purpose.

. . . That night I saw my mother in every attitude of prayer a human being could assume. Sometimes she would be prostrate on her face on the floor: sometimes on her knees and again in a sitting posture, imploring God to use his power in some way to keep father from being sold from us . . .

About three A.M. mother concluded we had better go to the jail, so we went, and saw father standing at the window . . . He shook my hands and kissed me good bye through the iron bars. Then three sisters and two brothers climbed upon the wheel and told him good bye. Mother climbed upon the wheel, and father said, "Rosy, I'm bound for Richmond, VA., and from there to some Southern market . . . We may never meet again this side of the shores of time, but keep the faith in God, and meet me in heaven . . . "

This was the beginning of sorrow in our home. It was not but three weeks from the time that father was sold away, until mother and three children were taken to the great house, and the other children scattered around on the different farms.

About a month [later] the master died sitting there in his chair. It was a custom to have the older slaves come and view the remains of their masters while they lay in state, and if the master was a man of any humanity, they would actually shed tears over his body. So as usual they called the slaves in, but mistress did not know that Master Tom had incurred the ill-will of every slave on the place by selling my father.

Father was almost a prophet among my people . . . [and] when they came, just outside the door they wet their fingers with saliva and made "crocodile tears" and passed on, pretending to be crying and saying, "Poor Mr. Tom is gone." Of course they didn't say where he had gone.

This may appear as a deception, but had we not made some demonstration of grief, our very lives would have been in danger . . .

In the will, we found that we had fallen to Scott Cowens—the meanest of all the Cowens family . . . A few days later, he found fault with my mother's biscuits . . . jumped up from the table . . . and knocked [mother] down from the porch to the ground. This was more than I could endure. An axe handle was on the opposite side . . . and I knocked him down with the axe handle.

I knew my only hope of escape was to run away, so I started at once. I had often heard ex-runaway slaves, men and women, tell the adventures of the woods, and their hiding places. I had heard [them] told so often . . . that I knew almost directly where [a hiding place] was . . . so I started to look for it . . . I went to an old mother—we were taught to call each woman mother, and they would call us son or daughter. It seemed there was a natural degree of sympathy existing in the heart of every woman for the children of others—[and] I told her what I had done. She gave me a chunk of fat and a half corn dodger and directed me to the hiding place. Then with her hand on my head she prayed one of those fervent prayers for God to hasten the day when the cruel chains of slavery would fall . . .

[Robinson joined a group of twelve other runaways, lived for some weeks on wild rabbits and small game, and was finally captured by a group of hunters and returned to his master.]

When I arrived home I found that my mother, one brother and one sister had been sold to negro traders . . . and no one could tell me their whereabouts. Of course my master wouldn't tell me. This was an hour of great sorrow and distress with me . . . One day the master sent me to get some goods, and in the packages there was a cow hide in its crude state . . . My master asked me how I liked the looks of it. I told him I didn't like it at all. We were in the bed room. He stood between me and the door. His wife came in with a decanter of whiskey [and a] glass and water, and he locked the door, then . . . tied my hands behind me . . . and whipped and cursed me until he had cut my back to pieces, and was so drunk he could whip me no more . . .

After four or five weeks my back had somewhat healed up, and . . . he sent me to the traders' pen. He ordered me in a cell and closed the big iron door, which told me that

I was bound for Richmond or some other slave market, and I was truly glad, for I now hated the soil upon which I was born.

[He was purchased by a new master who whipped his slaves and was also in debt. Robinson determined to run away again.]

I would often talk about running away . . . and ultimately, I made up my mind to leave. One morning my master sent me to the field to gather corn: I carried a basket and two sacks, and at noon I was to fill them and hitch up the mule cart and bring them home. I got the corn ready and sat down in the corn row. I realized then for the first time there must be some efficacy in prayer. My mother had taught me to get on my knees and say my prayers so far back as I could remember, yet I never knew the power there was in prayer, but on this memorial morning I went down on my knees in a corn row and prayed with fervent, childlike simplicity for God in some way to get me back to my mother or into Canada or let me die and go to heaven. While I was thus in prayer, it seemed that all nature was in sympathy with me, for there could not be heard even the rustling of the leaves . . . God seemed to be saying to me, "I am in deep sympathy with you." Reasoning came to me as audibly as though some one was speaking to me, saying, "You shall see your mother again."

I jumped up . . . emptied the corn out of the two sacks, put the sacks in the basket on my arm and left the field with full intentions to go back to Richmond . . .

I went about seven or eight miles that day through the woods, and about dusk I came in sight of a cabin in the distance. I was satisfied this was the home of some old mother or father . . . and found an old woman eighty years old . . . She went into the cabin and prepared supper, and as I ate, she sat with her hands on my head telling me how to get along in the world and pointed me to that friend that sticketh closer than a brother, and she said, "If God be for you it was more than all the world against you." She also gave me four or five onions and told me . . . not to eat them, they would make me sleepy. But I learned how to decoy the blood hounds, for she told me whenever I heard the baying of hounds on my trail, to rub the onions on the bottom of my feet and run, and after running a certain distance to stop and apply the onions again, then when I came to a large bushy tree, to rub the trunk as high up as I could reach, then climb the tree.

[Robinson had been sold to Scott Cowens by a trader in Richmond named Lee. Briefly kept by two others during his exodus to freedom, Robinson was finally captured near Richmond and was again spotted by Lee, who knew Robinson's mother's owner—a Mr. Hadley. Lee arranged for Hadley to purchase the son, and six weeks later Robinson was on his way to Tennessee to be reunited with his mother.]

Mr. Hadley was a very kind, fatherly acting man. He bought me a nice suit of clothes, and gave me money, told me to buy my mother, brothers and sisters some presents . . . I was anxious to meet my mother again, and was constantly inquiring, "How much further is it?" The words were scarcely out of my mouth when I saw coming down the road my mother and new mistress. Mother came up on the side of the buggy, and almost dragged me out of the buggy across my master . . . rejoicing and blessing the master for his deeds of kindness. In a few minutes my new mistress came up on the other side of the buggy, and pulled me over and to my surprise, and for the first time in my life, a white woman kissed me. This was a very new

*William
Robinson*

feature to me and naturally embarrassed me very much so that I mentioned it many times afterwards . . . I had just learned that not all white people were mean and cruel . . .

I had a glorious time in that home and felt almost as if I was free. My master owned a large farm three miles from Greenville, where we lived . . .

About this time in February, 1861, delegates from South Carolina, Alabama, Georgia, Louisiana and Texas met at Montgomery, Ala, and formed a government called the Confederate States of America. Jefferson Davis of Mississippi was chosen president . . . About this time the laws were very strict on the slave, and they were not allowed a pass to go to any public gathering of any kind . . . but the slaves would slip off to church and frolics and the patrollers were continually after them, but the slaves would play all kinds of tricks on them . . . The slaves would have to devise many schemes in order to serve God. Of course they had church once or twice a month, but some white man would do the preaching and his text would always be, "Servants obey your masters." But this was not what our people wanted to hear, so they would congregate after the white people had retired. Then you would see them with their cooking utensils, pots and kettles, go into a swamp and put the pots and kettles on the fence with the mouth turned toward the worshippers. Then they would sing and pray: the kettles catching the sound. And in this way they were not detected.

After the death of my master I remained as cook for a company until November, 1863, when at Blue Springs, Tennessee, Generals Thomas and Burnside routed Hood and Forrest after a short contest: and in the retreat I, with many others, was captured. There were fifty of us, and each one was riding one of those long-eared fellows that lean against the fence and say, "I have no one to love me." My long-eared friend's feet fell . . . and down in the ditch we went, such a scramble you never saw. But I found there were many rebel soldiers in there, who were tired of the Yankee lead and wanted to be captured. I was scuffling to get out but they told me to lie still, and in a few minutes Yankee soldiers seemed to have popped up out of the earth . . . The Rebels were sent to the prison and the cooks and colored servants were brought before General Thomas to be disposed of . . .

[Robinson took an oath of allegiance, and was drafted into the Union army.]

I enlisted in the 54th Massachusetts, where I remained nine months, [then] was transferred to the 28th Indiana, on account of having an uncle in that regiment.

I was mustered out on December 22, 1865, with no home to go to, no starting point or object in life . . . I [last] saw my mother in 1863 when I left her in the little log cabin in Knoxville, and I never saw her again for thirteen years. The medium then used in finding any of our people was the church. Any one looking for a lost relative would send letters of inquiry to all the different churches in the United States and Canada, describing the person and giving names of the last master they belonged to. So I tried to find my mother . . . but finally had to give it up as futile.

During this time I learned that I had a brother in Philadelphia, Pennsylvania. It proved to be my oldest brother, who was educated by the Presbyterian church and is now a minister in the same . . . Together we began a zealous search for mother, and ultimately found her . . . in Knoxville. And when she saw me she exclaimed, "I have seen William, now Lord let me die in peace."

I returned to Nashville—which I considered home—after several weeks' visit with mother. I re-entered on my duties as a fireman, for I was a member of the City Fire Department, and had been engaged as a hose-cart driver for eight months. While fighting [a] fire the captain called to "Jim Cowans," and that attracted my attention. I looked to see who would answer, and seeing a man on top of the house answering, I immediately climbed on the building.

I inquired of Jim where he came from, and it was but a few minutes until we recognized each other as brothers ... It went to the City Council of the City of Nashville that two brothers who had served eight months in No. 2 hose company had just recognized each other as brothers—having been separated for sixteen years. In honor of our meeting they gave us a public reception.

One extreme always follows another, for in three weeks ... my brother was thrown seventy feet from the hook and ladder against the stone custom house, and every bone in his body was broken: he died instantly.

I served seventeen months in the fire department and resigned to accept a position as singer and banjo player in a troupe ... known as the "Tennessee Singers." We sang nothing but the Southern melodies—songs composed by our fathers and mothers in the days of slavery. We disbanded in November, 1868.

In January, 1869, I hired to what is known as the Hanlon's Wizard Oil Company, with seven others, at twelve dollars per month and board. The contract was for one year. If there was any one thing I was accomplished in, it was picking the banjo and singing, and I soon became the center of attraction along these lines. We gave free street concerts for advertising the oil.

Everyone treated me so differently from what I was used to during the time of slavery that I forgot to some degree the hardships through which I had passed, and more than once stopped and inquired of myself, "Is this heaven and am I in it?"

[Robinson traveled to London, where he was sheltered by a wealthy gentleman, Lord Beckworth. There he was taught to read, encouraged to express his thoughts, and instructed in the fundamentals of gracious living. He wore his first velvet dressing gown and entertained Lord Beckworth's friends with plantation songs for eleven months. Overjoyed with his position, Robinson wrote his first letter, which looked as if a "chicken had walked across the page," to President Grant, informing him of his rise in status from a runaway to a respected gentleman; Grant replied, commending Robinson as a soldier, a citizen, and useful man "to his race and nation." Robinson returned to the United States with high aspirations.]

I worked one year—taking care of three different persons' horses and making fires in the winter. I saved my money, and when school opened the next year, I started again. After that term I went to night school, and in 1874 I entered the freshman class in college. I met here with embarrassment, for every one in the class was ahead of me ... But I had a spirit of determination and studied with a will, and by the close of the term had caught up with the class save three, had made many friends and was considered by all far from being the dullest boy in the class ...

Later I was hired at Lebanon, TN, as [a] teacher. I had a class of forty. The majority of them were old people forty five and fifty years old. I taught them two terms ... The other eight months I worked at most anything I could catch ... Through a friend I was given a situation as porter for the Woodruff Sleeping Car Company, which was afterwards bought out by the Pullman Company . . .

In 1877, while cooking at the New England Hotel, in Clark Street Chicago, I was one night in the third story of a gambling den owned by two brothers, Dan and Jim Scott, two very wealthy colored men. They kept a hotel, roomers, and ran a gambling den all in one building. I had drifted away during my railroad career into a class of company that led me to this miserable life. It seemed for a time that all the good that had been accomplished through my many friends and my self denial and perseverance, were all over, shadowed with darkness, in immorality and sin. But thank God, on New Year's night, 1877, while standing at the very gambling table, I heard my mother's voice, as I thought, as audibly as I ever heard it in my life, saying, "My son, is this what you promised me when you were wearing the shackles of bondage?"

I remembered . . . when she said, "Son . . . get the religion of Jesus in your heart and if we never meet again on earth, meet me in heaven." I resolved that night that I would not stop until I was converted. All the entreaties and prayers of my mother came rushing upon my mind, and I decided at once that they should not be in vain. My mind fully made up, I left the gambling den that night, never to enter it again.

The next day I accepted a situation as head cook in Evanston, Illinois . . . I was deeply convicted and began to reason of righteousness, temperance and the judgement to come. The more I reasoned, the deeper was my conviction, until it seemed that the clock on the wall as it ticked said, "Repent." I became so interested concerning my soul's welfare that I could not keep my mind on my business, so I began to seek the Lord in prayer. In June of the same year

I walked out of the hotel about eleven o'clock [and] didn't stop to draw my money: the train was due for Chicago and was at the depot when I arrived there. I was so completely absorbed in thought and stirred about the salvation of my soul that I walked by the train up the track towards Chicago. It seemed as though a voice was constantly saying to me to "Repent." I had not walked very far when a voice said, "You had better pray."

Of course it was the reasoning of the spirit within. I walked down the embankment and for the first time since I was ten years old, I called on God for redemption through the blood of Jesus. I became so intensely earnest that I did not notice the section hands working near by . . . My soul was crying for deliverance. I left, and bought a ticket for La Porte, as I thought of a Baptist preacher I knew about three miles from there. It was midnight and very dark when I got off the train. I inquired of the depot agent the way to this preacher's home. The road lay through a dense thick wood, and after wandering until about two o'clock in the morning, I found the place.

I remained at his home about three weeks, and would go each day to the woods with him and help him pile up brush and trim trees, etc. I imagined all the while that a tree was going to fall upon me and kill me. The very axe the preacher was chopping with seemed to be crying, "Repent," and I became so troubled until all hunger and thirst seemed to have left me. There was but one thought uppermost in my mind and that was that I might find peace with God.

One day the preacher persuaded me to stay at the house, saying I was too weak to go with him to the woods. He knew what was ailing me. I could tell that in his morning and evening devotion, as he would offer me to the throne of grace with so much fervor. After he was gone, I took the shot gun, saying that I would go hunting. I had gone but a short distance when something seemed to say to me, "You had as well take that gun and blow your brains out." Of course this was the reasoning of the devil making his last great effort to destroy my soul. But God has promised in His word that He would be a help in every time of need.

I hid the gun beneath a brush pile and started to a man's house about two miles away. As soon as I went into the house he told his wife to hurry dinner and clean up the dinner dishes and they would have a word of prayer. I knelt down behind a big drum stove in that log cabin with my mind fully made up to stay there until God converted me: and in less time than it will take me to tell it, I was happily converted to Christ.

It seemed as though I had been wearing a heavy log about my body, and in a moment it fell from me . . . Christ handed me a little testament and pointed towards a large body of woods, saying, "Preach my word to these people." In a moment every tree was transformed into a vast multitude of people and I stepped upon a stump and began to preach from Romans, First Chapter and sixteenth verse— "Now I'm not ashamed of the gospel of Christ: for it is the power of God unto salvation to every one that believeth: to the Jew first, and also to the Greek."

I had worn the shackles of a literal bondage for fifteen years, but in due season God emancipated me . . .

Sunday morning the preacher Rev. Bailey and myself started for La Porte. There were no trains on Sunday morning, so we rode half the distance on a hand-car with the section men, and walked the remainder of the way. We sat on a fence to rest, facing a beech wood, and I rested my head in my hands and closed my eyes. I had a repetition of the same vision . . . and I was satisfied that it was a Divine call to the ministry of the Lord Jesus. Ultimately an old minister of the A.M.E. church, who was traveling the La Porte circuit, after hearing me talk in class meeting several times, asked me to tell him exactly how I was converted. After two years I told him the whole story, and he said, "Son, I knew God had called you to the ministry." However I could not afford to give up my occupation of cooking, making from seventy-five to a hundred dollars per month, for an uncertainty. I knew how hard it was to raise money for the ministers, and like Jonah, I went for nearly five years before I entered the field of labor which God would have me do . . .

211

&

*William Robinson*

Bed tents for housing camp meeting attendees near Shoshone, Wyoming

# Notes to the Introduction

1. James Hennesey, S.J., *American Catholics* (New York, Oxford: Oxford University Press, 1981), 18.
2. Martin E. Marty, *Pilgrims in Their Own Land* (New York: Penguin, 1928), 98.
3. W. C. Anderson, *The Public and the Duties of Its Citizens* (Berkeley: University of California Press), cited in Ted C. Hinckley, "American Anti-Catholicism During the Mexican War," *Pacific Historical Review*, Vol. 31, May 1962, 124.
4. Susan Peterson, "Holy Women and Housekeepers: Women Teachers on South Dakota Reservations, 1885–1910," *South Dakota History*, 13:3, Fall 1983, 246.
5. Robert T. Handy, *A History of the Churches in the United States and Canada* (Oxford, Toronto, Melbourne, New York: Oxford University Press, 1976), 327.
6. Gerald Shaughnessy, S.M., A.B., S.T.D., *Has the Immigrant Kept the Faith?* (New York: Macmillan Co., 1925), 211.
7. Richard Hofstadter, *Anti-Intellectualism in America* (New York: Charles Scribners & Sons, 1944), 95–97.
8. Wade Crawford Barclay, *Early American Methodism, 1769–1844,* Vol. II (New York, 1950), 336.
9. Peter Cartwright, *Autobiography,* ed. W. P. Strickland (New York, 1856), 79, 360.
10. Julie Roy Jeffrey, *Frontier Women* (New York: Hill and Wang, 1979), 103.
11. Cathy Luchetti, *Women of the West* (St. George Utah: Antelope Island Press), 35.
12. Isaac Owen, Papers and Letters, 1857–1860, January 25, 1851, Bancroft Library, Berkeley, California.
13. Beverly W. Bond, Jr., *The Civilization of the Old Northwest* (New York: Books for Libraries Press, 1934), 484.
14. Leon Loofbourow, *In Search of God's Gold: A Story of Continued Christian Pioneering in California* (San Francisco: The Historical Society of the California-Nevada Annual Conference, 1950), 233–238.
15. William G. Lennon, *The Health and Turnover of Missionaries* (New York: Foreign Missions Conference of North America, 1933), 28.
16. American Board of Foreign Missions Annual Report, 1820–1830.
17. Lennon, op. cit., 28.
18. Clifford Merrill Drury, *Presbyterian Panorama* (Philadelphia: Presbyterian Church in the United States of America, 1952), 148.
19. Elmer Sandmeyer, *The Anti-Chinese Movement in California* (Urbana: University of Illinois Press, 1973), 17.
20. Handy, op. cit., 302.

Camp meeting kitchen being readied for the Mennonite General Conference, Oklahoma, 1914

# Selective Chronology of Significant Dates in Frontier Christian History

1610—Spanish found Sante Fe, New Mexico, on the site of ancient Indian ruins.

1611—First Presbyterian colony established in Virginia.

1620—Pilgrims establish Plymouth Colony in Massachusetts.

1626—Presbyterians first arrive in America as members of the Dutch Reformed Church, settling in New Amsterdam on the Hudson River.

1628—Puritans arrive at Massachusetts Bay.

1634—Roman Catholic colony founded in Maryland.

1639—English and Welsh Baptists first gathered by Roger Williams in a Separatist community at Providence, Rhode Island.

1640—John Eliot gathers New England Pequot Indians into "praying towns" to teach them trades, agriculture, and academic subjects.

1648—George Fox founds the Society of Friends.

1649—The Society for the Propagation of the Gospel in New England is founded to support evangelist John Eliot's work. The society continues until the American Revolution.

1663—Evangelist John Eliot masters the Pequot language, translating the Bible into that tongue. As a result of his efforts, New England claims fourteen "praying towns," twenty-four Indian evangelists, and four hundred Christian Indians.

1673—Jacques Marquette explores the Mississippi River.

1686—Father Kino, a Jesuit and skilled explorer, physician, architect, and astronomer enters southern Arizona to educate and Christianize the Pima Indians.

1687—First Anglican service held in Boston.

1690—Franciscans under Father Damien Massanet found short-lived missions in eastern Texas.

1723—Jonathan Edwards, the American philosopher and theologian under whose preaching the Great Awakening broke out in Northampton, Massachusetts, dedicates himself to God's service.

1730—First Great Awakening, noted for strengthening direct ties between the individual and God, and loosening the traditional ties to church, state, and family, spreads throughout England and America.

1740—Conversion of Samuel Occom, a Montauck Indian from Long Island who became a licensed Presbyterian minister to the Pequot Nation.

1741—Scottish evangelist David Brainerd begins his work among the American Indians. His short-lived missions spark Methodism to a greater commitment to evangelizing non-whites.

1758—First American Indian reservation is established in Philadelphia by an Anglican missionary group.

1766—The first Methodist church is established in New York City.

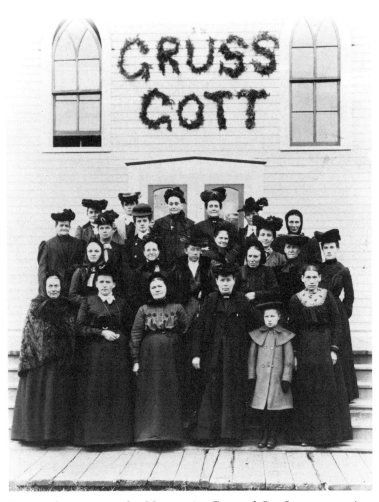

Group of women at the Mennonite General Conference sessions
in Mountain Lake, Minnesota, 1905

1768—Spain explores Lower California, sending two hundred soldiers, fourteen missionaries, and Father Junipero Serra north from Mexico.

1769—Jefferson's Virginia Bill for establishing religious freedom is passed.

—Junipero Serra leaves for Upper California and founds the first California mission, in San Diego.

1776—Congress adopts the Declaration of Independence as drafted by Thomas Jefferson.

1780—The Methodist Annual Conference in Baltimore affirms that all preachers should rise at 4:00 or 5:00; to stay in bed until 6:00 A.M. is "shameful."

1782—First Catholic parochial school erected by Saint Mary's Church, Philadelphia.

1784—First Methodist Episcopal church organized in Baltimore.

1785—First instance of Methodists denying communion to slave-holders.

1787—The first African Methodist church in America is founded by Richard Allen.

1792—Methodist circuit riders allowed to accept payment for performing marriages, provided that the fee be divided among other preachers in the district who had not been fully reimbursed for expenses.

1799—Revivalism begins at James McGready's Red River Church in Kentucky.

1800—Methodists rule to expel local members through majority vote rather than clerical discretion alone.

1801—A Presbyterian camp meeting in Cane Ridge, Kentucky, heralds the Great Revival of the West.

1802—Revival in Cane Ridge, Kentucky, heralds communal religion.

1803—Methodist hierarchy voices opposition to married circuit riders.

1805—Baptists and Presbyterians draw back from camp meetings because of their unruly aspects.

1812—Congress declares war on Great Britain.

—The American Board of Commissioners for Foreign Missions organized by the Congregational church.

1816—The American Bible Society is founded in New York.

—The African Methodist Episcopal church is established in Philadelphia.

—The annual salary of a Methodist itinerant is raised from sixty-four dollars to one hundred dollars.

1821—Beginning of the famous Week of Debates among clerical representatives from the East and the West, putting on trial the practice of revivals.

1822—Joseph Smith is led by the angel Moroni to discover the golden tablets—one of the founding events for the Church of Jesus Christ of the Latter-Day Saints.

1824—The American Sunday School Union is founded.

—The General Conference of the Methodist Episcopal church exhorts traveling preachers to recruit for Sunday schools.

1825—The American Tract Society is founded.

1826—Establishment of the Home Missionary Society.

—Founding of the American Society for the Promotion of Temperance. Ten years later it claimed eight thousand auxiliaries and more than one and one-half million practicing members.

1828—The Christian party began a short-lived attempt to organize evangelicals for political ends.

1830—First meeting of the Church of Jesus Christ of the Latter-Day Saints called by the church's founder and leader, Joseph Smith.

1831—Teachers of sacred music Thomas Hastings and Lowell Mason publish *Spiritual Songs for Social Worship,* a dignified alternative to the street songs, love songs, and circus music widely used at camp meetings.

—The first national convention of black people in the United States is organized by Richard Allen and held at the Mother Bethel Church, Philadelphia.

1833—The American Anti-Slavery Society organized in Philadelphia promotes abolition; attracts a quarter of a million membership and over 1,300 auxiliaries by 1838.

—Mormon "Word of Wisdom" advises against the use of tobacco, alcoholic beverages, tea, and coffee.

Mystic healer Teresita Urrea Nina de Caborca, who ministered throughout New Mexico, Texas, and Arizona in the 1890s

1834—Ursuline Convent at Charlestown, Massachusetts, burned by anti-Catholic demonstrators.

1836—The American Sunday School Union and the American Tract Society distribute a total of seventy-three million pages of printed material. Together, they develop a system whereby a new tract could be personally delivered monthly to every household in New York.

1840—The combined budgets of all Protestant voluntary societies estimated to exceed that of the federal government.

1842—The American Protestant Association founded to halt the spread of Catholicism.

1844—The Southern Methodist Church formed after a denominational dispute over slavery.

—John Quincy Adams presides over a national Sabbath observance convention attended by 1,700 delegates from eleven states.

1845—Pro and con slavery views cause a rift in Baptist ranks; the Southern Baptist Convention is formed.

—Temperance and abolitionist dramas are introduced by evangelists to counter "immoral" theater presentations. An example: *Uncle Tom's Cabin,* by Harriet Beecher Stowe.

1846—Mormons begin pilgrimage from Nauvoo, Illinois, to Utah.

1849—Oregon legislature passes bill to prohibit blacks and mulattoes from settling in the territory.

—The California Gold Rush; by 1860 nearly every major religious group was represented in that state.

1850—Beginning of a new surge of nativism, or anti-Catholicism.

—The Republican party becomes a major magnet for evangelicals.

1851—First school for higher education for women west of the Mississippi is founded by Cherokee Indians in Park Hill, Oklahoma.

1852—Plural marriage is openly practiced by the Mormons until 1890, despite federal opposition.

1855—California legislature moves "to prohibit barbarous and noisy amusement on the Christian Sabbath" with fines for violations that could range from fifty dollars to five hundred dollars.

1856—Mormon immigrants travel to Salt Lake City, pushing their belongings in handcarts.

1860—A third of New York City's adult population estimated to belong to at least one of the scores of church-related associations.

1861—The Civil War begins when Confederates fire on Fort Sumter, Charleston, South Carolina.

1863—Lincoln issues the Emancipation Proclamation.

—Olympia Brown becomes the first ordained woman minister in the country.

1865—Reconstruction begins.

—The Salvation Army founded in England.

—The Thirteenth Amendment is passed, outlawing slavery in the United States.

1866—Catholic social activism is promoted by controversial Catholic spokesman Edward McGlynn, who contradicts official church teaching concerning the sanctity of private property by advocating a general rethinking of property distribution.

—The Civil Rights Act grants citizenship to blacks.

1870—The Fifteenth Amendment is adopted, forbidding any state from depriving a citizen of his vote because of race, color, or previous condition of servitude.

—The Sisters of Charity arrive in Mexican Hill, Colorado, from Ohio; establish first parochial school in an adobe building.

1874—The Women's Christian Temperance Union begins campaign against alcohol.

—The commissioner for Indian Affairs named.

—First Chautauqua Assembly meets at Chautauqua Lake, New York, to train church and Sunday school teachers during the summer months.

1875—Mary Baker Eddy founds the Church of Christ, Scientist.

—Archbishop John McClosky becomes the first American Catholic cardinal.

1876—Religious composer Fanny Crosby, author of thousands of hymn texts, leads the emergence of a new class of professionals: gospel song composers.

1886—Eastern Tennessee mountain revival leads to the estab-

A parade float commemorating a mission, 1849

Snowbound chapel and teepee on Thanksgiving morning, St. Michael's Episcopal Mission, Wyoming

lishment of the Pentecostal denomination of the Church of God in Cleveland, Tennessee.

1887—The American Protective Society formed to prevent Catholic parochial schools from receiving public funds.

—The General Allotment Act passed to abolish Indian reservations; divides aboriginal holdings in the United States in half and subdivides reservations into 80- to 160-acre tracts.

1890—Heyday of Pentecostalism; identified by the desire for baptism in the Holy Spirit, faith healing, and speaking in tongues.

1892—The Geary Chinese Exclusion Act effectively excludes Chinese from the United States by calling for registration and, in many cases, deportation.

1893—Federal government offers amnesty to Mormon polygamists who agree to heed antipolygamy laws.

1895—The Anti-Saloon League formed.

—The Federal Council of Churches in America founded.

—Negro Baptist groups decide to merge and form the National Baptist Convention of the United States.

1897—Congregational minister Charles Sheldon publishes *In His Steps,* a collection of sermons instructing young people what they would do in one year if they copied Jesus Christ.

1899—The first Gideon Bible is placed in the Superior Hotel, Iron Mountain, Montana, by the Christian Commercial Men's Association of America.

1900—Temperance advocate Carrie Nation leads a group of women through Kansas, damaging saloons and liquor-selling establishments.

1903—Catholic social movement begins in earnest with the foundation of the American Federation of Catholic Societies.

1908—The Home Missions Council established to direct noncompetitive missionary activity.

1909—W. E. B. Du Bois founds the National Association for the Advancement of Colored People.

1919—Pentecostal Assemblies of the World incorporated in Indianapolis, Indiana.

A noonday meal in the Papago desert

A Franciscan friar shields himself from the sun while enjoying lunch in the Papago desert.

# Bibliography

Allison, W. Glenn. "Education by the Sisters of Loretto in Bernalillo, New Mexico, 1876–1887." University of New Mexico paper. New Mexico State Archives: Woodward Collection, 1939.

Anderson, Charles H. *White Protestant Americans.* University of Umea, Sweden. Englewood Cliffs, New Jersey: Prentice-Hall, 1970.

Armstrong, Maurice W., Lefferts A. Loetscher, and Charles A. Anderson. *The Presbyterian Enterprise: Sources of American Presbyterian History.* Philadelphia: The Westminster Press, 1955.

Armstrong, O. K., and Marjorie Armstrong. *The Baptists in America.* Garden City, New York: Doubleday-Galilee, 1979.

Asbury, Francis. *The Journals and Letters of Francis Asbury.* Vol. 4. Edited by G. Manning Potts. London: Epworth Press, Nashville: Abingdon Press, 1958.

Bailey, H. C. "California in '53." Typed transcript of reminiscences of an early pioneer. Bancroft Library, University of California.

Bakanowski, Adolf. *Polish Circuit Rider: The Texas Memoirs of Adolf Bakanowski, O.R.* Cheshire: Cherry Hill Books, 1971.

Belknap, Keturah. "Keturah Belknap: Chronicle of the Bellfountain Settlement." Edited by Robert Moulton Gatke. *Oregon Historical Quarterly* (September 1937): 38:3, pp. 265–299.

Bellah, Robert N., Richard Madsen, William S. Sullivan, Ann Swidler, and Steven M. Tipton. *Habits of the Heart, Individualism and Commitment in American Life.* Berkeley, Los Angeles, London: University of California Press, 1985.

Bercovitch, Sacvan. *The Puritan Origins of the American Self.* New Haven and London: Yale University Press, 1975.

Bond, Beverly W., Jr. *The Civilization of the Old Northwest.* Freeport, New York: Books for Libraries Press, 1934.

Boyd, Lois A., and R. Douglas Brackenridge. *Presbyterian Women in America: Two Centuries of a Quest for Status.* Westport, New York: Greenwood Press, 1983.

Braver, Jerald C. *Protestantism in America (a Narrative History).* Philadelphia: The Westminster Press, 1955.

Brawley, Edward M., Ed. *The Negro Baptist Pulpit: A Collection of Sermons and Papers by Colored Baptist Ministers.* Freeport, New York: Books for Libraries Press, 1971, reprint of 1870 edition.

Bristol, Rev. Sherlick. *The Pioneer Preacher, Rev. Sherlick Bristol, 1815–1906.* New York: Fleming H. Revell, 1887.

Britton, Davis, Ed. *The Redoubtable John Pack.* Eden Hill: The John Pack Family Association, 1982.

Britton, Davis, Ed. *The Reminiscences and Civil War Letters of Levi Lamoni Wright.* Salt Lake City: University of Utah Press, 1970.

Brown, Benjamin. *Testimonies for the Truth.* Liverpool: S. W. Richards, 1853.

Brown, Earl Kent. *Women of Mr. Wesley's Methodism.* New York and Toronto: The Edwin Mellen Press, 1983.

Carroll, Jackson W., Barbara Hargrove, and Adair P. Lummis, Eds. *Women of the Cloth.* San Francisco: Harper and Row, 1982.

Carroll, Peter N. *Puritanism and the Wilderness.* New York and London: Columbia University Press, 1969.

Cartwright, Peter. *Autobiography of Peter Cartwright, the Backwoods Preacher.* Edited by W. P. Strickland, L. Swormstedf, and A. Poe. Cincinnati: L. Swormstedf and A. Poe, 1856.

Carus, Rev. William, Ed. *Memorials of the Rt. Rev. Charles Pettit McIlvaine.* New York: Thos. Whittaker, 1882.

Church, Peggy Pond. *The Story of Edith Warne and Los Alamos.* Albuquerque: University of New Mexico Press, 1959–1960.

Clark, John G., Ed. *The Frontier Challenge,* Lawrence, Manhattan, Wichita: University Press of Kansas, 1971.

Clark, Malcolm, Jr. *Eden Seekers: The Settlement of Oregon 1818–1862.* Boston: Houghton Mifflin Co., 1981.

Crompton, Arnold. *Apostle of Liberty, Starr King in California.* Boston: The Beacon Press, 1950.

———. *Unitarianism on the Pacific Coast: The First Sixty Years.* Boston: Beacon Press, 1957.

De Smet, Rev. P. J. *Western Missions and Missionaries: A Series of Letters.* New York: T. W. Strong, late Edward Dunigan & Bro., Catholic Publishing House, 1859.

de Toqueville, Alexis. *Democracy in America.* Edited by Richard Heffner. New York: Mentor Books, 1955.

Dick, Everett. *The Sod House Frontier, 1854–1890.* Lincoln and London: University of Nebraska Press, 1937, 1954. Bison Book printing, 1979.

Douglas, Ann. *The Feminization of American Culture.* New York: Avon Books, 1977.

Dow, Lorenzo. *The Dealings of God, Man and the Devil.* St. Louis, 1849.

Drury, Clifford Merrill. "Chronology of Protestant Beginnings in California." *California Historical Society Quarterly* 76 (June 1947): 163–174.

Drury, Clifford Merrill, Ed. *First White Women Over the Rockies: Diaries, Letters and Bibliographical Sketches of the Six White Women Who Made the Overland Journey in 1836 and 1838.* Vols. 1, 2, 3. Glendale, California: Arthur H. Clark Co., 1963.

The Reverend W. W. Van Orsdel, known as "Brother Van," rode the Montana circuit.

————. *Nine Years with the Spokane Indians: The Diary of Elkanah Walker.* Glendale, California: Arthur H. Clark Co., 1976.

Drury, Clifford Merrill. *Presbyterian Panorama.* San Francisco Theological Seminary Board of Christian Education. Philadelphia: Presbyterian Church in the United States of America, 1952.

Duff, Kathryn, Ed. *Pioneer Days ... Two Views, Early Days in W. Texas: Recollections of Miss Tommie Clack.* Abilene, Texas: Reporter Publishing Co., Zachary Associates Inc., 1979.

Ferm, Vergilius. *Pictorial History of Protestantism.* New York: Philosophical Library, 1957.

Fletcher, Christiane, Ed. *Let Them Speak for Themselves: Women in the American West.* New York: Dutton, 1978.

Gailland, Fr. Maurice, S.J. "Diary: Early Years at St. Mary's Pottawatomie Mission." *Kansas Historical Quarterly* (August 1953): 20:7, pp. 501–509.

Galley, James P. *Citizen of No Mean City: Archbishop Patrick Riordan of San Francisco 1841–1914.* Consortium, 1976.

Gaustad, Edwin S. *A Documentary History of Religion in America to the Civil War.* Grand Rapids, Michigan: William B. Eerdmans Publishing Co., 1982.

Gipson, Lawrence H., Ed. *The Moravian Indian Missions on the White River.* Indianapolis, Indiana: Indian History Bureau, 1938.

Godfrey, Kenneth W., Audrey M. Godfrey, and Jill Mulivay Derr, Eds. *Women's Voices: An Untold History of the Latter-Day Saints 1830–1900.* Salt Lake City, Utah: Deseret Book Co., 1982.

Gottlieb, Robert, and Peter Wiley. *America's Saints: The Rise of Mormon Power.* New York: G. P. Putnam & Sons, 1984.

Graves, William W. *The First Protestant Osage Missions 1820–1837.* Oswego, Kansas: The Carpenter Press, 1949.

Hall, Carolyn Foreman. "Charity Hall." *Chronicles of Oklahoma* 11:3: pp. 912–921 (September 1933).

Hall, Mark Heathcote. "Bishop McIlvaine, The Reluctant Frontiersman." *Historical Magazine of the Protestant Episcopal Church* 54:1: pp. 81–90 (March 1975).

Hammond, Sue. "Socioeconomic Reconstruction in the Cherokee Nation 1865–1870." *The Chronicles of Oklahoma* 51:2: pp. 158–170 (Summer 1978).

Handy, Robert T. *A History of the Churches in the United States and Canada.* Oxford, New York, Toronto, Melbourne: Oxford University Press, 1976.

Hansen, Klaus J. *Mormonism and the American Experience.* Chicago and London: University of Chicago Press, 1981.

Heizer, Robert F., and Alan J. Almquist. *The Other Californians: Prejudice and Discrimination Under Spain, Mexico, and the United States.* Berkeley, Los Angeles, London: University of California Press, 1971.

Hennesey, James, S.J. *A History of the Roman Catholic Community in the United States.* New York, Oxford: Oxford University Press, 1981.

Hinckley, Ted C. "American Anti-Catholicism During the Mexican War." *Pacific Historical Review* 31:2: pp. 121–137 (May 1962).

Howe, M. H. De Wolf. *Life and Labors of Bishop Hare.* New York: Sturgis and Walton, 1914.

Jeffrey, Julie Roy. *Frontier Women.* New York: Hill & Wang, 1979.

Johnson, Charles A. *The Frontier Camp Meeting.* Dallas: Southern Methodist University Press, 1956.

Keller, Robert H., Jr. *American Protestantism and United States Indian Policy, 1869–82.* Lincoln: University of Nebraska Press, 1983.

Kenton, Edna, Ed. *The Jesuit Relations and Allied Documents.* Toronto: McClelland and Stewart, 1896.

Kerr, Hugh T., and John M. Mulder, Eds. *Conversions.* Grand Rapids, Michigan: William B. Eerdmans Publishing Co., 1983.

Koren, Elizabeth. *The Diary of Elizabeth Koren, 1853–1855.* Northfield, Minnesota: North Central Publishing Co., 1955.

Levorson, Barbara. "The Quiet Conquest." *Hawley Herald.* Hawley, Minnesota. May 1974.

Lockley, Fred., Ed. *Conversations with Pioneer Women.* Eugene, Oregon: Rainy Day Press, 1981.

Loofbourow, Leon L. *In Search of God's Gold: A Story of Continued Christian Pioneering in California.* San Francisco: The Historical Society of the California-Nevada Annual Conference, 1950.

Losee, Almira. *Life Sketches: Being Narrations of Scenes Occur-*

Methodist women of the Home Mission Society packing supply boxes for Methodist outposts in the Far West

Methodist Home Mission Society relief delivery

ring in the Labours of Almira Losee. New York: Hunt and Eaton, 1890.

Luchetti, Cathy Lee, and Carol Olwell. *Women of the West*. St. George, Utah: Antelope Island Press, 1982.

Luvis, Marvin, Ed. *The Mining Frontier*. Norman, Oklahoma: University of Oklahoma Press, 1967.

Mallon, Sister Catherine. "Sister Catherine Mallon's Journal." Edited by Thomas Richter. *New Mexico Historical Review* 52:2, pp. 135–153 (April 1977).

Marty, Martin E. *Pilgrims in Their Own Land: 500 Years of Religion in America*. New York: Viking Penguin, 1928, 1984.

McClain, Laurene Wu. "Donaldina Cameron: A Reappraisal." *The Pacific Historian* 27:3 (Fall, 1983).

McClure, David. *Diary of David McClure, D.D., 1748–1820*. New York: Knickerbocker Press, 1899.

McDermott, John Francis, Ed. *Travelers on the Western Frontier*. Urbana, Chicago, London: University of Illinois Press, 1970.

McLoughlin, William G. *The American Evangelicals 1800–1900*. New York: Harper Torchbooks, Harper & Row, 1968.

McNemee, A. J. *Brother Mack, The Frontier Preacher*. Edited by Harlan D. Jones. Fairfield, Washington: Ye Galleon Press, 1980.

McWilliams, Mrs. George A. *Women and Missions in Missouri*. Woman's Missionary Union: Missouri Baptist General Association, 1951.

Mills, Edward Laird, *Plains, Peaks and Pioneers: Eighty Years of Methodism in Montana*. Portland, Oregon: Binfords and Mort, 1947.

Moreno, Francisco Garcia Diego y. *The Writings of Francisco Garcia Diego y Moreno Obispo de Ambas Californias*. Translated and edited by Msgr. Francis J. Weber. Los Angeles: Archdiocese, 1960.

Morris, Joan. *Against Nature and God: The History of Women with Clerical Ordination and the Jurisdiction of Bishops*. London, Oxford: Mowbrays, 1973.

Nelson, E. Clifford, and Eugene Ferold. *A History of the Evangelical Lutheran Church*. Minneapolis: Augsburg Publishing House, 1960.

Niehbuhr, H. Richard, and Daniel D. Williams, Eds. *The Ministry in Historical Perspectives*. New York: Harper & Bros., 1956.

Noll, Mark, Nathan Hatch, David Wells, George Mardsen, and John D. Woodbridge, Eds. *Eerdmans' Handbook to Christianity in America*. Grand Rapids, Michigan: William B. Eerdmans Publishing Co., 1983.

Novak, Michael. *Freedom with Justice*. San Francisco: Harper & Row, 1984.

O'Connell, Father E. *Letters to All Hallows College, Dublin, 1851–1859*. Typed transcript, Chancery Archives, San Francisco.

Paris, Arthur E. *Black Pentecostalism: Southern Religion in an Urban World*. Amherst: University of Massachusetts Press, 1982.

Payne, Daniel Alexander. *History of the African Methodist Episcopal Church*. Vol. 1. New York: Arno Press, 1969.

Peacock, Mary Thomas. *The Circuit Rider and Those Who Followed*. Chattanooga, Tennessee: The Hudson Printing and Lithographing Co., 1957.

Peck, John. *Forty Years of Pioneer Life: Memoir of John Peck*. Edited by Rufus Babcock. Philadelphia: American Baptist Publishing Society, 1864.

Penn, William. *No Cross, No Crown*. Edited by Ronald Selleck. Richmond, Indiana: Friends United Press, 1981.

Peterson, Susan. "Holy Women and Housekeepers: Women Teachers on South Dakota Reservations, 1885–1910." *South Dakota History* 13:3, 246–260 (Fall, 1983).

Phelan, Macum. *A History of Early Methodism in Texas, 1817–1866*. Nashville, Dallas, San Francisco, Richmond: Cokesbury Press, 1924.

Pond, William C., D.D. *Gospel Pioneering, 1853–1920*. Oberlin, Ohio: Press of the News Printing Co., 1921.

Pope, Liston. *Millhands and Preachers*. New Haven, London: Yale University Press, 1942.

Powell, Sumner. *Puritan Village*. Middletown, Connecticut: Wesleyan University Press, 1963.

Raboteau, Albert J. *Slave Religion*. Oxford, New York, Toronto, Melbourne: Oxford University Press, 1978.

Reggio, Michael H. "Troubled Times: Homesteading in Shortgrass Country, 1892–1900." *The Chronicles of Oklahoma* 52:2, pp. 196–211 (Summer, 1979).

Reinders, Robert. "Training for a Prophet: The West Coast Missions of John Alexander Dowie 1888–1890." *The Pacific Historian* 30:1: pp. 3–13 (Spring, 1986).

Rideout, Lionel Utley. *Renegade, Outcast and Maverick: Three Pioneer California Clergy 1847 to 1893.* San Diego: University Press, San Diego State University, 1973.

Robinson, William H. *From Log Cabin to the Pulpit, or Fifteen Years in Slavery.* Alabama, Iowa, 1848.

Ross, Nancy. *Westward the Women.* New York: Alfred A. Knopf, 1944.

Rothman, Sheila. *Woman's Proper Place.* New York: Colophon Books, 1978.

Sandmeyer, Elmer. *The Anti-Chinese Movement in California.* Urbana: University of Illinois, 1973.

Serra, Junipero. *Writings of Junipero Serra.* Antonine Ibesas, O.F.M., Ed. Washington, D.C.: Academy of American Franciscan History, 1955.

Simms, Rev. James M. *The First Colored Baptist Church in North America.* New York: Negro University Press, 1969.

Smith, James Ward, and A. Leland Jamison. *The Shaping of American Religion.* Vol. 1, *Religion in American Life.* Princeton, New Jersey: Princeton University Press, 1961.

———. *Religious Perspectives in American Culture.* Vol. 2, *Religion in American Life.* Princeton, New Jersey: Princeton University Press, 1961.

Stapleton, Ernest S., Jr. "The History of Baptist Missions in New Mexico 1849–1866." Master's thesis, University of New Mexico, 1954.

Stegner, Wallace. *The Gathering of Zion: The Story of the Mormon Trail.* New York: McGraw-Hill Book Company, 1964.

Sterling, Dorothy. *We Are Your Sisters, Black Women in the Nineteenth Century.* New York: W. W. Norton & Co., 1984.

Stewart, Eleanor Pruitt. *Letters on an Elk Hunt.* Lincoln, London: University of Nebraska Press, 1943, 1979.

Stratton, Joanna L. *Pioneer Women: Voices from the Kansas Frontier.* New York: Simon & Schuster, 1981.

Sweet, William Warren. *Makers of Christianity.* New York: Henry Holt and Company, 1937.

Tillich, Paul. *The Protestant Era.* Translated by James Luther Adams. Chicago: University of Chicago Press, 1948, 1957.

Tubbs, Stephanie Ambrose. "Montana Women's Clubs." *Montana: The Magazine of Western History* 36:1: pp. 27–35 (Winter, 1986).

Unruh, John D., Jr. *The Plains Across: The Overland Emigrants and the Trans-Mississippi West 1840–60.* Urbana, Chicago, London: University of Illinois Press, 1982.

Warnecke, Gustav. *Outline of a History of Protestant Missions.* Edited by George Robeson, D.D. New York, Chicago: Fleming H. Revell Co., 1901.

Wendte, Charles William. *The Wider Fellowship, 1844–1927.* Vols. 1 and 2. Boston: The Beacon Press, 1927.

Whitson, Robley Edward. *The Shakers, Two Centuries of Spiritual Reflection.* New York: Paulist Press, 1983.

Widtsoe, John A., and Franklin S. Harris, Jr. *Seven Claims of the Book of Mormon.* Independence, Missouri: Press of Zion Printing and Publishing Co. n.d.

Williams, William Henry. *The Garden of American Methodism, The Delmarva Peninsula 1769–1820.* Wilmington: The Peninsula Conference of the United Methodist Church, 1984.

Woodson, Carter G. *History of the Negro Church.* Washington, D.C.: Associated Publishers, 1921.

Young, Brigham. *The Diary of Brigham Young, 1857.* Edited by Everett L. Cooley. Salt Lake City, Utah: University of Utah Library, Tanner Trust Fund, 1980.

*Bibliography*

Ornate interior with family Bible

# Acknowledgments

I am indebted to the following persons and institutions for their generous gifts of time and information, and for making available the manuscripts, documents, and special collections necessary to produce this book: The Bancroft Library in Berkeley, California, for permission to use the writings of Annie Bidwell and for help given in the spirit of scholarly assistance; The Huntington Library in San Marino, California, for granting permission to use excerpts from the journal of Elkanah Walker and for making available its excellent research facilities; The Oregon Historical Society, Portland, Oregon, for granting permission to use excerpts from their Elkanah Walker collection; The Sisters of Notre Dame de Namur for granting permission for the use of Sister Mary Alenie's journal; the South Dakota Historical Society for permission to use segments from the life of Mary Collins; and the United Methodist Church Pacific Northwest Annual Conference Archives for permission to quote from the writings of A. J. McNemee.

The range and scope of this book have been greatly enhanced by the kindly assistance of the following individuals: Sister Anne C. Stark, who reviewed and corrected the chapter on Sister Alenie; Manuscripts Curator John Borst and editor Nancy Koupal of the South Dakota Historical Society; Archivist Susan Miller of the Salvation Army Research Center, New York; Archivist Jeffrey M. Burns of the Chancery Archives; and Lisa Rubins.

Special thanks for research assistance and encouraging advice to Carol Olwell, Rev. Bill Beatty, Tom Phillips, Virginia Turner, Ben Mohamed, and Barbara Quevedo Davis, and to Eldon G. Ernst, professor of American religious history, Graduate Theological Union, Berkeley, California, for his perceptive historical analysis.

I would also like to acknowledge the primary research done by Richmond L. Clow on Mary Collins in his article "Autobiography of Mary C. Collins, Missionary to the Western Sioux," *South Dakota Historical Collections,* vol. 41, 1892; by Dr. Clifford Merrill Drury, on the diary of Elkanah Walker, in *Nine Years with the Spokane Indians: The Diary of Elkanah Walker* (Glendale, California: The Arthur H. Clark Company, 1976); and by Harlan D. Jones in his editing of *Brother Mack, the Frontier Preacher* (Fairfield, Washington: Ye Galleon Press, 1980).

My special gratitude to the following librarians and archivists for their photographic research; for patiently answering queries, forwarding information, and selflessly volunteering their time to make sure I had a comprehensive selection of photographs from each collection. My particular thanks to Assistant Curator of Photographs Carol Roark, Amon Carter Museum, Fort Worth, Texas; Mark G. Thiel, Marquette University; Archivist Elinor S. Hearn, the Archives of the Episcopal Church, Austin, Texas; Peter Palmquist; Curator Bonnie Gardner of the South Dakota Historical Society; and Director David A. Haury, Mennonite Library and Archives. In particular, I would like to commend the directors and librarians of church archives throughout the country for their careful guardianship of so many well-preserved and unexpectedly poignant photographs.

Finally, a genuine thanks to Page Smith and to Professor Robert Bellah and associates, whose landmark work on American community, *Habits of the Heart,* has offered continued inspiration and guidance throughout the making of this book. Editor John Radziewicz has sustained the book's vision throughout—for which I am most grateful. I also appreciate the keen eye of his colleague, Vicki Austin, in the editorial process.

234

*Acknowledgments*

Third grade students (Willie Menard, left, and Frank Brave, right) with rosary beads, St. Francis Mission, Rosebud Sioux Reservation, St. Francis, South Dakota, ca. 1910

# Photographic Sources

Siri Rustebakke (center) with daughters and daughter-in-law and unidentified man as photographed by Lutheran pastor Andrew Dahl in Black Earth, Wisconsin, ca. 1873

Teacher Rose N. Meeham with her class in Montara, California, September 21, 1893

A missionary summer camp in Wyoming

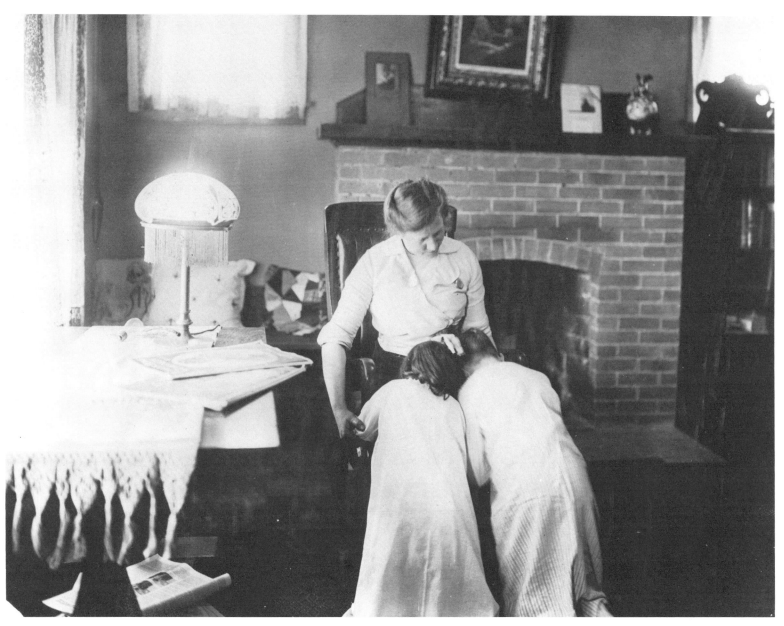

Children with mother at devotions

Two young residents of Clifton, Texas, with a half-built church in the background, ca. 1890

# Text Sources and Permissions

The words of Sister Mary Alenie are reproduced herein by permission of the Sisters of Notre Dame de Namur, Office of the Provisional Archives, College of Notre Dame, Belmont, California, and Copyrighted, 1987, Sisters of Notre Dame de Namur.

Excerpts from the life of David McClure come from *Memoirs of the Reverend Eleazar Wheelock,* D.D., by David McClure and Elijah Parish, published in 1811 and reprinted in 1972 by Arno Press, as part of the Religion in America series.

Materials on Lorenzo Dow are excerpted from *The Dealings of God, Man and the Devil,* by Lorenzo Dow (St. Louis, 1849).

James Scott's *A Journal of a Missionary Tour* was published in 1843 by the author and reprinted by Readex Microprint Corporation in 1966 as part of their Great Americana series.

The life of the Rt. Rev. Charles McIlvaine is drawn from *The Memorials of the Rt. Reverend Charles Petit McIlvaine,* edited by Rev. William Carus, M.A. (New York: Thomas Whittaker, 1882).

Benjamin Brown's book *Testimonies for the Truth: Manifestations of the Power of God, Miraculous and Providential* was published in 1853 by S. W. Richards, London.

Material on the life of A. J. McNemee has been excerpted from *Brother Mack, the Frontier Preacher,* by A. J. McNemee (Port-land, Oregon: T.G. Robison, 1924), and later edited by Harlan D. Jones (Fairfield, Washington: Ye Galleon Press, 1980). Permission to quote from *Brother Mack* has been granted by the United Methodist Church Pacific Northwest Annual Conference, Portland, Oregon.

Mary Collins's autobiography is from a handwritten document, "Autobiography of Mary C. Collins, in Her Handwriting," which is part of a collection of letters, manuscripts, and papers contained in the Mary C. Collins papers at the South Dakota State Historical Society. The original editing is by Richmond L. Clow, whose introduction appeared along with the Collins story in "Autobiography of Mary C. Collins, Missionary to the Western Sioux," *South Dakota Historical Collections,* Vol. 41, 1982, copyright 1983 by the South Dakota Historical Society, which has granted permission to reprint sections.

Permission to publish excerpts from the journal of Elkanah Walker has been granted by the Huntington Library, San Marino, California, and by the Oregon Historical Society, Portland, Oregon.

William Robinson's memoirs, *From Log Cabin to Pulpit,* were published in Albia, Iowa, in 1907.

Evangelist Missy Reade's wagon, worn out in service